JOURNAL FOR THE STUDY OF THE OLD TESTAMENT SUPPLEMENT SERIES
236

Editors
David J.A. Clines
Philip R. Davies

Executive Editor
John Jarick

COPENHAGEN INTERNATIONAL SEMINAR
3

General Editors
Thomas L. Thompson
Niels Peter Lemche

Associate Editors
Frederick H. Cryer
Mogens Müller
Hakan Ulfgard

Sheffield Academic Press

Freedom beyond Forgiveness

The Book of Jonah Re-Examined

Thomas M. Bolin

Journal for the Study of the Old Testament
Supplement Series 236

Copenhagen International Seminar 3

In Memoriam—

William O. Bolin
1923–1975

Published by Sheffield Academic Press Ltd
Mansion House
19 Kingfield Road
Sheffield S11 9AS
England

Printed on acid-free paper in Great Britain
by Bookcraft Ltd
Midsomer Norton, Bath

British Library Cataloguing in Publication Data

A catalogue record for this book is available
from the British Library

ISBN 1-85075-642-2

CONTENTS

PREFACE

This book is a revision of my doctoral dissertation from Marquette University, Milwaukee, WI (1995). It questions the interpretative judgments, assumptions and methodologies of much of the modern exegesis of Jonah. It also critiques as inherently flawed the dominant method in biblical studies which uses Israelite history and the Bible to mutually support and explain each other. It analyzes the book of Jonah by means of a combination of the standard historical tools, lacking in many of the newer literary approaches, with the freedom from the failed attempts of traditional biblical scholarship to assign a date or detect a historical background for the book. An interpretation of Jonah is offered independent of any historical speculation derived from hypothetical reconstructions of Israelite history.

This study is broadly arranged along the lines of a commentary. After an overview of the history of scholarship in Jonah, the analysis follows the outline of the book. Each of the four chapters of Jonah receives a separate treatment. Much space is devoted to textual and grammatical analysis, attention being given in particular to ancient translations. In addition, biblical and extra-biblical traditions, motifs and conventions which also appear in Jonah are examined to provide an interpretative context for the book. Through this latter analysis, an opportunity is gained for renewed study of the distinct theological themes of the Hebrew Bible. The implications of this finding are discussed in a concluding chapter. Translations of Jonah are my own, except where otherwise specified. Block quotations of biblical texts are taken from the RSV. While the bulk of the research and writing was done from 1993–1995, I have tried to supplement the bibliography and notes with more recent publications on the subject. Many readers will doubtless find lacunae.

Sincere thanks go to those who have helped in the writing of this book with their support and critique. First of these is my wife, Megan Wood Bolin. Among others for whose assistance I am grateful are:

Willliam J. Bolin, Robert C. Helmer, Julian V. Hills, Thomas L. Thompson, John J. Schmitt, Philip R. Davies, Sharon Pace Jeansonne, Richard A. Edwards and Deirdre Dempsey. A profound intellectual debt is owed to Jack Sasson's Jonah commentary in the Anchor Bible Series, which is at once a first-rate discussion of the book as well as a delightful read. Special mention must be made of the directors of the Arthur J. Schmitt Foundation, whose dissertation fellowship for the 1994–95 academic year offered me the opportunity to complete the work. Finally, I would like to offer my thanks to the editors of the Copenhagen International Seminar Series for accepting this study for publication.
    This book is dedicated to the memory of my father.

Thomas M. Bolin
San Antonio, TX
April, 1996

ABBREVIATIONS

AB	Anchor Bible
ABD	D.N. Freedman (ed.), *Anchor Bible Dictionary*
AbrN	*Abr-Nahrain*
ABRL	Anchor Bible Reference Library
AJA	*American Journal of Archaeology*
AnOr	Analecta orientalia
AOAT	Alter Orient und Altes Testament
ARW	*Archiv für Religionswissenschaft*
ATAT	Arbeiten zu Text und Sprache im Alten Testament
ATANT	Abhandlungen zur Theologie des Alten und Neuen Testaments
BA	*Biblical Archaeologist*
BASOR	*Bulletin of the American Schools of Oriental Research*
BDB	F. Brown, S.R. Driver and C.A. Briggs, *Hebrew and English Lexicon of the Old Testament*
BHS	*Biblia hebraica stuttgartensia*
Bib	*Biblica*
BibOr	Biblica et orientalia
BibRev	*Bible Review*
BIOSCS	*Bulletin of the International Organization for Septuagint and Cognate Studies*
BJS	Brown Judaic Studies
BK	*Bibel und Kirche*
BSac	*Bibliotheca Sacra*
BWANT	Beiträge zur Wissenschaft vom Alten und Neuen Testament
BZ	*Biblische Zeitschrift*
BZAW	Beihefte zur *ZAW*
CAD	*The Assyrian Dictionary of the Oriental Institute of the University of Chicago*
CAT	Commentaire de l'Ancien Testament
CB	*Cultura bíblica*
CBQ	*Catholic Biblical Quarterly*
ConBOT	Coniectanea biblica, Old Testament
CurTM	*Currents in Theology and Mission*
DACL	*Dictionnaire d'archéologie chrétienne et de liturgie*
DBSup	*Dictionnaire de la Bible, Supplément*

DJD	Discoveries in the Judaean Desert
EncJud	*Encyclopaedia Judaica*
ETR	*Etudes théologiques et religieuses*
EvT	*Evangelische Theologie*
ExpTim	*Expository Times*
FRLANT	Forschungen zur Religion und Literatur des Alten und Neuen Testaments
GKC	*Gesenius' Hebrew Grammar*, ed. E. Kautzsch, trans. A.E. Cowley
GTJ	*Grace Theological Journal*
HAR	*Hebrew Annual Review*
HTR	*Harvard Theological Review*
HUCA	*Hebrew Union College Annual*
ICC	International Critical Commentary
IDB	G.A. Buttrick (ed.), *Interpreter's Dictionary of the Bible*
IDBSup	*IDB*, Supplementary Volume
IEJ	*Israel Exploration Journal*
Int	*Interpretation*
ISBE	G.W. Bromily (ed.), *International Standard Bible Encylopedia*, rev. edn
JAAR	*Journal of the American Academy of Religion*
JB	*Jerusalem Bible*
JBL	*Journal of Biblical Literature*
JBQ	*Jewish Bible Quarterly*
JETS	*Journal of the Evangelical Theological Society*
JJS	*Journal of Jewish Studies*
JPOS	*Journal of the Palestine Oriental Society*
JPSV	*Jewish Publication Society Version*
JQR	*Jewish Quarterly Review*
JR	*Journal of Religion*
JSOT	*Journal for the Study of the Old Testament*
JSOTSup	*Journal for the Study of the Old Testament*, Supplement Series
JSP	*Journal for the Study of the Pseudepigrapha*
Judaica	*Judaica: Beiträge zum Verständnis ...*
KAT	Kommentar zum Alten Testament
KB	L. Koehler and W. Baumgartner (eds.), *Lexicon in Veteris Testamenti libros*
KJV	*King James Version*
NAB	*New American Bible*
NEB	*New English Bible*
NICOT	New International Commentary on the Old Testament
NovT	*Novum Testamentum*
NTS	*New Testament Studies*
OTE	*Old Testament Essays*

OTL	Old Testament Library
OTP	*Old Testament Pseudepigrapha*
OTS	*Oudtestamentische Studiën*
PL	J. Migne (ed.), *Patrologia latina*
PSTJ	*Perkins (School of Theology) Journal*
RB	*Revue biblique*
RGG	*Religion in Geschichte und Gegenwart*
RHPR	*Revue d'histoire et de philosophie religieuses*
RSV	Revised Standard Version
SBL	Society of Biblical Literature
SBLDS	SBL Dissertation Series
SBLSP	SBL Seminar Papers
SBT	Studies in Biblical Theology
SC	Sources chrétiennes
SEÅ	*Svensk exegetisk årsbok*
SJOT	*Scandinavian Journal of the Old Testament*
SJT	*Scottish Journal of Theology*
SNTSMS	Society for New Testament Studies Monograph Series
SSN	Studia Semitica Neerlandiia
TDOT	G.J. Botterweck and H. Ringgren (eds.), *Theological Dictionary of the Old Testament*
TOTC	Tyndale Old Testament Commentaries
TSK	*Theologische Studien und Kritiken*
TTod	*Theology Today*
TynBul	*Tyndale Bulletin*
TZ	*Theologische Zeitschrift*
VT	*Vetus Testamentum*
VTSup	*Vetus Testamentum*, Supplements
WBC	Word Biblical Commentary
WUNT	Wissenschaftliche Untersuchungen zum Neuen Testament
ZAW	*Zeitschrift für die alttestamentliche Wissenschaft*
ZHT	*Zeitschrift für Kirchengeschichte*
ZKG	*Zeitschrift für Kirchengeschichte*

Chapter 1

PLOTTING A COURSE

> What he asks about the resurrection of the dead could be settled... But if
> he thinks to solve all such questions as... those about Jonah... he little
> knows the limitations of human life or of his own.
>
> —Augustine, *Ep.* 102.38[1]

Augustine's response to an inquiry made by a potential Christian
convert bears much merit when looking at the book of Jonah through
the eyes of modern biblical criticism. The book is, in the words of
Julius A. Bewer, 'an occasion for jest to the mocker, a cause of bewil-
derment to the literalist believer but a reason for joy to the critic'.[2]
To undertake a satisfactory survey of the scholarly literature on Jonah
(or any other biblical text) two tasks are required: 1) analysis of the
trajectories in the numerous commentaries and studies so that relationships between the myriad opinions are observable; 2) use of pre-modern
interpretations where appropriate to shed light on puzzling features in
the text. Failure to consider these two components runs the risk of
yielding a vast survey which would obscure, rather than clarify, the
outlines of the debate thus far. To avoid such an outcome, the
predominant categories of biblical scholarship on the book of Jonah
will be supported by evidence from the literature in a representative
fashion. Jewish and Christian interpretations of the book are selected
as examples of how Jonah is treated by past recipients of the tradition.
It is with pre-modern exegesis, therefore, that this work begins.[3]

---

1.   Latin text in M. Pellegrino, T. Alimonti and L. Carrozzi (eds.), *Le Lettere
di Sant' Agostino* (Opere di Sant' Agostino, 21; Rome: Città Nuova, 1969), p. 992;
ET in W. Parsons (ed.), *St Augustine: Letters* (Fathers of the Church, 9; 90 vols.;
Washington, DC: Catholic University of America Press, 1953), p. 176.

2.   J.A. Bewer, *Jonah* (ICC; Edinburgh: T. & T. Clark, 1912), p. 3.

3.   Comparable overviews of pre-modern exegesis and traditions surrounding
Jonah are to be found in F.-M. Abel, 'Le culte de Jonas en Paléstine', *JPOS* 2

Pre-Modern Interpretation of the Book of Jonah

Jonah in Jewish Tradition

What appears to be mention of Jonah occurs in the Qumran Literature. In 4Q541 6.2 is the directive, בקר ובעי ודע מה יונא בכה ('Search, investigate and know how Jonah wept').[4] It is unclear exactly to which tradition (if any) the text refers. The verb בכה ('weep')[5] is not used by the *Tg. Ps.-J.* in translating either the Hebrew פלל or קרא in Jonah. It could perhaps allude to Jonah's misery in 4.8-10. The three imperatives beginning the phrase give the impression that the text is referring to a tradition that may be sought out and investigated.[6] The issue is further complicated by the fact that the Aramaic proper name יונא, and its Hebrew equivalent יונה can also mean 'dove'. Substituting the common noun for the proper name gives the grammatically coherent reading 'Search, investigate and know how a dove wept.'[7] The substitution also makes sense contextually, since the text speaks of suffering,

---

(1922), pp. 175-83; E.J. Bickerman, 'Les deux erreurs du Prophète Jonas', *RHPR* 45 (1965), pp. 232-64; ET in *idem*, *Four Strange Books of the Bible: Jonah, Daniel, Koheleth, Esther* (New York: Schocken Books, 1967), pp. 10-19; Y.-M. Duval, *Le livre de Jonas dans la littérature chrétienne grecque et látine* (2 vols.; Paris: Etudes Augustiniennes, 1973); *EncJud*, X, pp. 173-77; and J. Limburg, *Jonah* (OTL; Louisville, KY: Westminster/John Knox, 1993), pp. 99-123. Limburg's appendix also treats Calvin, Luther and Islamic tradition. Bickerman focuses on classical writers.

4.   R. Eisenman and M. Wise, *The Dead Sea Scrolls Uncovered* (Shaftesbury: Element Books, 1992), pp. 142-45. No date is given for these texts. Eisenman has elsewhere put forward the opinion that the Qumran scrolls are written in the mid- to late-first century CE and deal with events surrounding the two Jewish revolts. This is almost two full centuries later than the dates assigned by mainline Qumran scholarship. A full discussion of Eisenman's position is his *Maccabees, Zadokites, Christians and Qumran* (Leiden: Brill, 1983); cf. F. García Martinez, *The Dead Sea Scrolls Translated: The Qumran Texts in English* (trans. W.G.E. Watson; Leiden: Brill, 1994), pp. 269-70.

5.   M. Jastrow (ed.), *Dictionary of the Targumim, Talmud Babli, Yerushalmi and Midrashic Literature*, I (repr.; New York: Judaica, 1992 [1903]), p. 169.

6.   Even if this is the case, such a tradition may have since been lost, or may never have existed.

7.   This is the translation of García Martinez (*Dead Sea Scrolls Translated*, p. 270). Although a feminine noun, יונא with the meaning 'dove' occasionally takes a masculine verb, as would be the case in 4Q541 (Jastrow, *Dictionary*, I, p. 570).

and similar language about doves as a metaphor for human sorrow is found in the Old Testament (e.g., the image of a moaning dove in Isa. 38.14). The Qumran text goes on to speak of those who suffer, commanding the reader immediately after the Jonah/dove reference, 'Thus, do not destroy the weak...'[8] It is not sufficiently certain that 4Q541 is in fact a reference to Jonah.

Josephus's[9] paraphrase of the Old Testament contains a re-telling of the Jonah story in *Ant.* 9.208-14. Josephus places the story of Jonah immediately after his treatment of the material found in 2 Kings 14 which mentions Jonah as a prophet under Jeroboam. Given Josephus's penchant for minimizing miraculous elements in the biblical tradition, it is no surprise that he introduces the story of Jonah reluctantly:

> But since I have promised to give an exact account of our history, I have thought it necessary to recount what I have found written in the Hebrew books concerning this prophet (9.208).

When he treats Jonah's sojourn in the fish, Josephus uses the qualifying phrase 'the story has it' (τὸν δὲ λόγος, 9.213), and ends the brief account with a reiteration that he has only recounted the story as he found it written.[10] Other noteworthy points in Josephus's account are 1) glaring omission of the Ninevites' repentance; Josephus merely states that, after Jonah proclaimed his message, he left; and 2) agreement with the MT of Jon. 1.9. The LXX reads the MT עברי as the abbreviated form עבד יהוה and consequently has δοῦλος κυρίου. Josephus has Ἑβραῖος εἶναι (9.211).

Jonah is treated extensively in rabbinic traditions.[11] *PRE* 10 has a detailed account of Jonah, including many embellishments. Before being sent to Nineveh Jonah preaches to Jerusalem, and there is a widespread repentance there. When he arrives at Joppa his ship has already been departed two days, but God causes a tempest to drive the

---

8.   ואל תמחי להי (Eisenman and Wise, *Dead Sea Scrolls*, pp. 144-45).

9.   There is no reference to Jonah in the Philonic corpus, although there is a homily on Jonah attributed to Philo.

10.   9.214; διεξῆλθον δὲ τὴν περὶ αὐτοῦ διήγησιν, ὡς εὗρον ἀναγεγραμμένην.

11.   A complete list of references to Jonah in the rabbinic literature is in E. Levine, *The Aramaic Version of Jonah* (New York: Hermon, 1978), pp. 105-106. In the Mishnah, reference is made to the Ninevites' repentance (*m. Ta'an.* 2.1), and Jonah is part of a list of biblical figures recounted in a blessing (*m. Ta'an.* 2.4). The latter citation, and the material in the Zohar, are discussed below, pp. 20, 42.

ship back to Joppa so Jonah can depart. The sailors, after their repentance, fulfill their vow to sacrifice to God (1.16) by returning to Jerusalem and being circumcised. The fish which God appoints has been set aside from the creation specifically to swallow Jonah. Inside the fish, Jonah can stand and walk and see the depths. The fish takes Jonah on a tour of the underworld. After the fish has fulfilled his mission he is to be devoured by Leviathan. Jonah directs him to swim alongside the monster and vows to slay Leviathan and serve him as the feast at the eschatological messianic banquet of the just.

> On thy account I have descended to see thy abode in the sea, for moreover, in the future will I descend and put a rope in thy tongue, and I will bring thee up and prepare thee for the great feast of the righteous.

This is the vow which in 2.9 Jonah swears he will fulfill.[12]

Midr. R. Thazvia 15.1 speaks of only three unlimited winds in history: that experienced by Elijah on the mountain (1 Kgs 19.11), the one that blew down Job's house (Job 1.19) and the one hurled at Jonah's boat (Jon. 1.4). *Midrash Rabbah Bereshith* 20–21 draws two interesting parallels between Jonah and the second creation account. In regard to the curses in Gen. 3.14-19, it is explained that all animals copulate front to back, except three who copulate face to face. They do so because God spoke directly to them: serpents (Gen. 3.14-15), people (Gen. 3.16-19) and fish (Jon. 2.11).[13] Later in the same rabbinic text a parallel is drawn between Jonah and Adam:

> Just as the latter [Adam] fled so the former [Jonah] fled; just as that one's glory did not stay the night with him so too this one's glory did not stay the night with him (21.6).

There is a dispute recorded as to Jonah's tribe in the midrash to Gen. 49.12-13,[14] one opinion (based on Gen. 49.13) being that he is from the tribe of Zebulun, the other (based on Judg. 1.31) that he is of Asher. Relationship to Jonah is made clear in the fact that both supporting texts clearly show Zebulun and Asher dwelling in coastal

---

12.   E.R. Goodenough examines fish iconography in early Judaism and charts the development of the idea of fish as sacred/mystical food (*Jewish Symbols in the Graeco-Roman Period*, V [13 vols.; New York: Pantheon, 1956–68], p. 37). Goodenough argues for a uniquely Jewish tradition of fish iconography, independent of Greco-Roman influence.

13.   *Midr. Ber. R.* 20.3; Jon 2.11: ויאמר יהוה לדג.

14.   *Midr. R. Wayehi* 98.11.

areas and/or engaging in seafaring. This appears to be the criterion for either tribe being Jonah's. In *b. Yeb.* 61a, Jon. 4.11[15] is used to prove that gentiles are not animals, and hence that the graves of idolaters impart uncleanliness. In *b. Sanh.* 89a, six types of false prophets are listed. There are three who are slain by humankind: those who prophesy what they have not heard, prophesy what they have not been told, or prophesy in the name of an idol. Correspondingly, there are three who are slain by heaven: those who suppress a prophecy, disregard a prophet's words, or transgress their own prophetic words. Jonah is held up as an example of a prophet who suppresses his prophecy, and consequently deserving of death at the hands of the heavenly power.

Rabbinic traditions are unanimous in identifying Jonah with the prophet Jonah mentioned in 2 Kgs 14.25. In addition there is a well-attested belief that Jonah is the nameless son of the widow of Zarephath raised by Elijah in 1 Kings 17. This identification is justified by appeal to the etymological contact between the name of Jonah's father (אמתי) and the words of the widow to Elijah upon the raising of her son in 1 Kgs 17.24 (ודבר יהוה בפיך אמת).[16] This identification is puzzling because Jonah is consequently and paradoxically seen by the rabbis as so scrupulous regarding God's/Israel's honor that he will not obey a summons to prophesy to Gentiles and identified as a Gentile himself by virtue of being the son of the widow of Zarephath. That this fact is overlooked by the rabbis in favor of the identification is important, especially given the great thematic contacts between the Elijah cycle and Jonah. Other traditions identify Jonah as the unnamed prophet sent by Elisha to anoint Jehu in 2 Kgs 9.1-10.[17] Indeed, Jonah is the prophet for the entire Jehu dynasty, uttering all its prophecies, anointing all its kings and living to the age of 120.[18]

---

15. Specifically, God's distinction between the witless Ninevites and their cattle.

16. *PRE* 33 and the *Lives of the Prophets* (*OTP*, II, pp. 392-93); further refs. in M. Zlotowitz, *Jonah/Yona: A New Translation with a Commentary Anthologized from Midrashic and Rabbinic Sources* (Brooklyn, NY: Mesorah, 1980), p. xxiv.

17. E.g. *PRE* 10.

18. Zlotowitz (*Yona*, pp. xxxiv-xxxvi); L. Ginzberg (*Legends of the Jews*, IV [7 vols.; Philadelphia: Jewish Publication Society, 1909–1938], pp. 246-53); and O. Komlós ('Jonah Legends', *Etudes orientales à la mémoire de Paul Hirschler* [Budapest: Allamosított Kertész–nymoda, 1950] pp. 41-61) summarize most of the rabbinic legends concerning Jonah. There is a Midrash of Jonah, but it draws mainly on material from the *PRE* (see Komlós, 'Jonah Legends', pp. 47-48).

There is a lengthy sermon on Jonah attributed to Philo which is preserved in a sixth-century CE Armenian MS.[19] It deals not so much with allegorical readings as with the issues of the Ninevites' salvation and God's mercy. This is summarized in a series of statements made to Jonah by God:

> If the piety of these people angers you, then you are unjust. If you are jealous of their salvation, then you are inhuman. But on the other hand if you are troubled by the fact that your preaching has been considered as false, such an accusation concerns me and not you (§ 46).

Jonah's concern that the Ninevites' repentance lead him to be labelled a false prophet is a strong link between this Hellenistic homily and the rabbinic traditions which use that reason for Jonah's flight.

In sum, pre-modern Jewish traditions about Jonah exhibit the same variety that typifies modern exegesis of the book. The book is seen to deal with the nature of prophecy (both true and false), the efficacy of repentance, and the fate of non-Jews.

Jonah in Early Christian Tradition
Certainly the most well-known Christian use of Jonah traditions is the sign of Jonah pericope (Mt. 12.38-42//Lk. 11.29-32).[20] Two substantial differences between these passages are: 1) the typological reading of Jonah's sojourn in the whale with the death and burial of Jesus is found only in Mt. 12.40; 2) Mt. 12.41 first mentions the Ninevites followed by the queen of the South, while Lk. 12.31-32 has the opposite order. Rudolf Bultmann classifies this tradition as a 'minatory saying', and argues that the reference to Jonah is original to the story and subsequently is deleted in Mark 8. Matthew adds the typological reading, drawing it from the preaching of the church. In its original context, the saying made the comparison between Jonah and Jesus as two divine messengers who come from afar on their missions.[21] Krister Stendahl holds that the three-day typology in

19.   Commentary and translation in F. Siegert, *Drei hellenistischen-jüdische Predigten: Ps.-Philon 'Über Jona', 'Über Samson', und 'Über die Gottesbezeichnung "wohltätig verzehrendes Feuer"'* (WUNT, 20; 2 vols.; Tübingen: Mohr [Paul Siebeck], 1980), I, pp. 9-51; II, pp. 92-230; summary and analysis in Duval, *Livre de Jonas*, I, pp. 77-86.

20.   Mk 8.11-12 contains the refusal of Jesus to give a sign. Its parallel in Mt. 16.1-2 refers to the sign of Jonah, but without any further elaboration.

21.   R. Bultmann, *History of the Synoptic Tradition* (repr.; Oxford: Basil

Mt. 12.40 is not original to that Gospel, but added much later. Stendahl argues on the basis of Justin, *Dialogue* 107.2, in which Justin, in an attempt to show that Jesus is destined to rise after three days, cites Mt. 12.39 but does not include v. 40. Because v. 40 is the perfect prooftext for Justin's argument (he formulates the same argument himself by implication from v. 39) Stendahl surmises that Mt. 12.40 must not have been in Justin's text of Matthew.[22]

The most detailed work on the sign of Jonah in the NT is that of Richard A. Edwards. Examining the pericope within the larger context of the redactional theology of the Q community, Edwards first identifies a form created by that community which he calls the 'eschatological correlative'. The form is found in four of the six future-oriented Son of Man sayings in Q, and consists of a protasis in the present or past tense combined with an apodosis in the future tense.[23] This form is present in the sign of Jonah passages:

> For just as Jonah was (ὥσπερ γὰρ ἦν) in the belly of the whale... so will (οὕτως ἔσται) the Son of Man be... (Mt. 12.40)

> For just as Jonah was (καθὼς γὰρ ἐγένετο) a sign... so will (οὕτως ἔσται) the Son of Man be... (Lk. 11.30)

In reconstructing the tradition's history, Edwards argues that it originated as the refusal of a sign by Jesus as is found in Mark. The Q community added the reference to Jonah, the eschatological correlative and the double saying of the Ninevites/queen of the South. Luke preserves a reading more faithful to Q than Matthew, since the latter has added the three-day typology.[24]

Edwards's reconstruction is well-argued and plausible, and the following observations serve to supplement his conclusions.

Blackwell, rev. edn, 1963 [1921]), pp. 112-13, 117-18. Acknowledging a debt to John Kloppenborg, J.D. Crossan maintains Bultmann's view that the reference to Jonah is an original part of the saying later deleted by Mark (*The Historical Jesus: The Life of a Mediterranean Jewish Peasant* [San Francisco: HarperCollins, 1991], pp. 252-53).

22.   K. Stendahl, *The School of St. Matthew and its Use of the Old Testament* (Philadelphia: Fortress Press, first American edn, 1968), pp. 132-33. Stendahl also argues for a later interpolation of v. 40 on the basis of its verbatim citation of the LXX without a characteristic Matthean fulfillment formula.

23.   R.A. Edwards, *The Sign of Jonah in the Theology of the Evangelists and Q* (SBT, 18; Naperville, IL: Allenson, 1971) pp. 49-55.

24.   Edwards, *Sign of Jonah*, pp. 71-89.

Although Edwards has shown that the typological equation between Jonah and Jesus is a late entry into the tradition's history, and Stendahl has argued that the entry may even be much later than the first gospel, it can be argued that Matthew preserves a more original reading in the order Ninevites/queen of the South. Lk. 11.30 predicts that Jesus will be a sign to this generation, as Jonah was to the Ninevites. Verse 31 then mentions the queen of the South and Solomon before returning to the men of Nineveh. A more natural order would be:

> As *Jonah* was *to the Ninevites*, so will Jesus be to *this generation* (Lk. 11.30). The *men of Nineveh* will rise in judgment of *this generation* because they repented at the preaching of *Jonah* (Lk. 11.32).

Into this repeated cluster of Jonah, the Ninevites and the generation of Jesus, the reference to the queen of the South appears an intrusion. Moreover, the order of Jonah followed by Solomon is also preserved in a prayer cited in *m. Ta'an.* 2.4.[25]

Of interest in the analysis of the use of Jonah in Christian literary tradition is the fact that Jonah's mission to the Ninevites is drawn upon by Christian writers at an earlier period than the story of his sojourn in the fish. This latter element of the Jonah story only appears in Christian writings (Matthew) at a point in the late first to early second centuries CE, at least a half-century to a century (the latter following Stendahl) after the earliest reference to Jonah and the Ninevites. This emphasis in the earliest levels of Christian literary tradition on Jonah's mission to Nineveh, rather than his ingestion by the fish, is the opposite of the emphasis that is present in the earliest Christian non-literary traditions which comprise the next area of investigation.

Before further examining the use of Jonah among the literary remains of early Christianity, the prophet's widespread presence in

---

25.   'May God who answered Jonah from the fish's belly, answer you... May God who answered David and Solomon his son in Jerusalem, answer you'. Text and analysis in D. Correns, 'Jona und Salomo', in W. Haubeck (ed.), *Wort in der Zeit* (Leiden: Brill, 1980), pp. 86-94. Correns sees in the juxtaposition of Jonah and Solomon a link between preaching and wisdom (pp. 92-93). This is also the opinion of Burton Mack in regard to Q's double saying of Jonah/Ninevites and Solomon/queen of the South. Mack argues that the sign of Jonah saying originated in the Q^2 level. Jonah and Solomon are chosen as representative figures of judgment and wisdom, and function to highlight the contrast between John the Baptist (judgment) and Jesus (wisdom) (B.L. Mack, *The Lost Gospel: The Book of Q and Christian Origins* [San Francisco: HarperCollins, 1993] p. 159).

early Christian grave art merits a detailed look. Through such an investigation it is clear that not only does artistic representation of Jonah exhibit few, if any, influences from the literary tradition, but rather that the art itself flourishes independently of the literary tradition and even influences it. Concerning Jonah in early Christian art Graydon Snyder observes, 'There can be no doubt that the primary artistic representation of early Christianity was the Jonah cycle'.[26]

Thus, of all known pre-Constantinian Christian[27] frescoes, mosaics, sarcophagi and sarcophagi fragments, Jonah at rest appears 42 times, Jonah cast into the sea 38 times and Jonah vomited from the fish 28 times. By way of contrast, the next frequent figure is that of Noah, who appears in eight instances. The most frequent New Testament scene is the baptism of Jesus with six occurrences.[28] After the Constantinian peace the cycle wanes quickly and disappears. From this data Snyder draws several conclusions:

1.   The cycle does know some version of the biblical account, but it is either different from the canonical version or has been greatly modified (specifically regarding Jonah's nudity and the emphasis on Jonah at rest).

2.   The cycle is clearly not based on a New Testament reading of Jonah as a sign of the resurrection, in spite of the artwork's funereal milieu. The emphasis is on Jonah at rest, not his exit from the fish.

3.   The cycle cannot conclusively be determined to be portraying

---

26.   G. Snyder, *Ante Pacem: Archaeological Evidence of Church Life before Constantine* (Macon, GA: Mercer University Press, 1985) p. 45. The Jonah cycle consists of three scenes: Jonah in the boat/being cast into the sea, Jonah being vomited forth from the monster, Jonah at rest beneath a tree. In all of the scenes the prophet is in the position of the *orans*. H. Rosenau argues for a rare fourth scene, Jonah angry under the withered tree, which was originally in Jewish depictions and dropped by Christian artists ('The Jonah Sarcophagus in the British Museum', *Journal of the British Archaeological Association* 23 [1961] pp. 60-66 [61, 65-66]). For an exhaustive collection of Christian depictions of Jonah see H. Leclercq, 'Jonah', *DACL*, VII/II, pp. 2572-2631. For a summary of variations in the Christian sarcophagi containing the Jonah cycle, see M. Lawrence, 'Ships, Monsters and Jonah', *AJA* 66 (1962) pp. 289-96. Limburg's commentary utilizes descriptions of artistic representations of Jonah throughout history.

27.   Snyder remarks on the difficulty of determining whether ancient Greco-Roman art comes from or is directed towards a specifically Christian milieu (*Ante Pacem*, p. 2).

28.   Table in Snyder, *Ante Pacem*, p. 43.

any cultic rites, as it is uncertain whether cultic practice is reflected in art or influenced by it.

4. It is clear that the most popular scene of the cycle, Jonah at rest, borrows heavily on the Greek tradition (and corresponding artwork) of Endymion, the lover of Selene (the moon), who requests and is granted eternal sleep, thereby never growing old.[29]

5. The frequent appearance of Jonah in the pre-Constantinian period reflects and emphasizes the Christian self-identity as strangers in a hostile environment. As mentioned above, Jonah appears in the cycle always in the posture of an *orans*. Thus, Jonah in the boat/cast into the sea (similar to Noah in the ark or Daniel in the lions' den) represents the believer in a dangerous situation. Jonah being vomited out signifies the escape from death. The final scene, with elements borrowed from myths of Endymion, is Jonah at rest and peace.[30]

Another factor not to be overlooked concerning this artistic represen-tation is the clear lack of influence or even knowledge of the typo-logical Christian interpretation of Jonah=Jesus found in the Synoptics and early Christian literature.[31] A clear distinction can be made

29.   P. Grimal, *The Dictionary of Classical Mythology* (Oxford: Basil Blackwell, 1986), pp. 145-46, esp. plate on 146. Endymion is most often depicted in his sleep, reclining under a tree and surrounded by a scene of pastoral tranquility. While there is widespread agreement on the thematic contact between the two figures, that anything more than a pictorial comparison is being made is denied. So Snyder: 'Surely the artisans who drew Jonah had Endymion as the iconographical model. Yet Endymion can in no way be equivalent to Jonah' (*Ante Pacem*, p. 43); William S. Babcock: 'Jonah—Endymion has subtly but clearly altered the force and focus of the Jonah story itself... in this story the gourd is not a divinely enacted moral lesson for a vexed prophet, but rather a sign of safety and peace' ('Image and Culture: An Approach to the Christianization of the Roman Empire', *PSTJ* 41 [1988], pp. 1-10 [5]); and J. Allenbach ('La figure de Jonas dans les textes préconstantiniens ou l'histoire de l'exégese au secors de l'iconographie', in M. Aubineau (ed.), *La Bible et les Pères* [Paris: Université de France, 1971], p. 110). Goodenough (*Symbols*, V, pp. 29-30, 47-48) posits a Hellenistic–Jewish background for the portrayal of Jonah in Christian grave art, specifically regarding the sea-monster.

30.   Snyder, *Ante Pacem*, p. 48. *3 Macc.* 6.6-8 also groups together the three young men in the furnace, Daniel and Jonah, as faithful Jews in dangerous situations. Daniel and Jonah also appear together in the Hellenistic synagogal prayers (*OTP*, II, p. 685).

31.   The sign of Jonah interpretation does not figure very prominently among early Christian authors. Allenbach has examined 67 early Christian texts with 91 allusions to and/or citations of Jonah. Of these 91, only 26 clearly make reference to

between traditions found in literature and those in material remains. Such a distinction is familiar to anthropologists, following Robert Redfield, as that between the 'Great Tradition' and 'Little Tradition'.[32] Regarding Jonah, rather than an influence of the Great Tradition on the Little, the opposite is apparent in ideas from the artwork making their way into the the the cultural *Geist* and appearing in literary evidence. William S. Babcock charts how the Jonah cycle moves out from its specifically Christian setting to become part of the larger culture, from where it is taken up by the Great Tradition.[33] This trajectory is part of a dialectic where symbols intersect between the sub-culture and dominant culture, moving either from the outside in or from the inside out. Babcock uses as an example of the former, the image of the Good Shepherd, of the latter, Jonah.[34] Thus, when Celsus taunts Origen regarding the inadequacy of Jesus as a hero when there are so many others in the Bible to choose from, he remarks: 'How much more fitting for you is Jonah under the gourd...or others yet still more marvelous' (*Contra Celsum* 7.53). It is no coincidence that Celsus here points out the one aspect of the Jonah story which is also the most common scene of the Jonah cycle: Jonah–Endymion at rest under the gourd, a theme not emphasized by Christian authors. Hence Babcock can write that

> the borrowed iconography may have given Jonah a faintly familiar air to Roman viewers; it will not have altered his identity... Consequently we

the sign of Jonah found in the gospels. Rosenau remarks that Jonah is not closely associated with any New Testament typology, but 'represented for its own sake' until Origen begins the comprehensive typological reading of the Old Testament ('Jonah Sarcophagus', p. 62).

32.   Pointed out by Snyder, *Ante Pacem*, p. 10; Allenbach, 'La figure', p. 110; and W. Wischmeyer, who notes the disinction between 'piety and theological speculation': 'We see eventually monuments in which a significant relationship between theological and pastoral concerns is minimal' ('Das Beispiel Jonas: kirkengeschichtlichen Bedeutung von denkmälern frühechristlicher Grabeskunst zwischen Theologie und Frömmigkeit', *ZKG* 92 [1981], pp. 161-79 [178]). The terms 'Great Tradition' and 'Little Tradition' are first used in R. Redfield, *Peasant Society and Culture* (Chicago: University of Chicago Press, 1956).

33.   Babcock writes of 'the movement of imagery out from a sub-culture and into a dominant culture...thus 'Christianization' is rather the process whereby Christianity emerged as a factor in the public culture of Rome' ('Image and Culture', pp. 1-2).

34.   Babcock, 'Image and Culture', p. 4.

can guess that Celsus came across the image because it was circulating in some realm that intersected with his own, not because he encountered it in texts that may have been uprooted or displaced from their social contexts.[35]

Similar evidence of non-Christians knowing and asking about the Jonah cycle will be seen below in Augustine's response to a potential convert.

There is a lengthy Latin poem known as 'Carmen de Jona et Ninive' (once ascribed to Tertullian) whose authorship is unknown.[36] The poem is a vivid rendition of Jonah 1, culminating with the prophet's entrance into the fish. It begins with a comparison of Nineveh to Sodom and Gomorrah, noting how the Assyrian city is much more worthy of destruction than the latter two: 'After the death of Sodom and Gomorrah... A city, Nineveh, by transgressing the path of justice and equity, has brought down upon her own head more storms of fire'.[37] In a manner similar to the rabbinic traditions, the text attributes Jonah's flight from God to the fact that the prophet knows God will forgive the Ninevites, and thus make Jonah's prophecy false (*PL* 2.1167). The storm and the sailors' encounter with Jonah are told with great drama. As the storm grows 'there are piteous voices at each crash of the boat'; below, Jonah not only sleeps; he is 'snoring, expanding and resonating his nostrils in snores'. Jonah confesses to be not only the cause of the storm but of all misfortune: 'In me is the storm. I am all the madness of the world.' Jonah's entry into the fish is told in harrowing detail: the monster 'sucked with slimy jaws a living feast' and he lives inside the monster 'amid half-eaten fleets and digested corpses dissolved and putrid'. The poet, who has heretofore demurred from any typological interpretation, ends the poem by noting how Jonah's entry into the monster was to make him a sign 'not of destruction but of the glory of heaven'.

Among the genuine works of Tertullian is a lengthy discussion of Jon. 3.1–4.2 in the *Adversus Marcionem* 2.24.[38] Tertullian uses Jonah

35.   Babcock, 'Image and Culture', p 7. Regrettably, Origen's commentary on the minor prophets and the section of his commentary on Matthew dealing with the sign of Jonah have been lost (Duval, *Livre de Jonas*, I, pp. 191-92).

36.   Latin text in *PL* II, col. 1166-72; translation and discussion of authorship in A. Roberts and J. Donaldson (eds.), *Tertullian* (Ante-Nicene Christian Library, 18; Edinburgh: T. & T. Clark, 1870), pp. xviii-xix, 279-83.

37.   Similarities between Genesis 19 and Jonah have been made by many commentators.

38.   Text and translation in E. Evans, *Tertullian: Adversus Marcionem*, I (2 vols;

to respond to the Marcionites' claims that God is capricious and/or capable of evil because he repents. Tertullian responds in two ways: 1) One can repent of good things that have been done and perhaps been responded to ungratefully; 2) In Jonah, God clearly repents of the 'evil' he will do to the Ninevites. For Tertullian this term (malitia) refers merely to calamities that are not the cause of malice. Thus God repented of a well-deserved punishment which he had intended for the Ninevites. But against the Marcionites' counter-claim that the repentance of God from a decree of justice is itself capricious Tertullian finally declares that the repentance of God is different from that of a human being: 'In all cases divine repentance is of a special character...[and] not to be understood as more than a simple reversal of a prior sentence'.[39]

In the sizable correspondence between Augustine and Jerome[40] the two men exchange harsh words over Jerome's translation of Jonah's plant (Jon. 4.6-7, 9-10).[41] Augustine takes offense over Jerome's rendering of the Hebrew קיקיון as *hedera* ('ivy') rather than following the LXX's κολοκύνθη ('gourd'). Augustine seems to have claimed that a reading of Jerome's translation in an African church caused a riot by the congregation who were used to hearing the term 'gourd'. The bishop's authority was in danger and he was forced to call upon the Jews of the town who (falsely, according to Jerome) stated that the Hebrew was more accurately rendered by the LXX's 'gourd' than by Jerome's 'ivy' (*Ep.* 75).[42] Jerome responded by saying that his translation followed the Greek of Aquila, who translated the term κιττόν ('ivy').[43] 'Therefore in explaining this word (קיקיון) if I had chosen to

---

Oxford: Clarendon Press, 1972), pp. 149-55.

39.   *Adversus Marcionem*, I, pp. 154-55. Tertullian will support this definition of repentance with an etymological appeal to the Greek term μετάνοια: 'Also in Greek the word for repentance... is from a compound signifying change of mind'.

40.   Latin text in J. Schmid (ed.), *SS. Eusebii Hieronymi et Aurelii Augustini Epistulæ Mutuæ* (Florilegium Patristicum, 22; Bonn: Hanstein, 1930); ET in C. White, *The Correspondence (394–419) between Jerome and Augustine of Hippo* (Studies in Bible and Early Christianity, 23; Lewiston, NY: Edwin Mellen, 1990).

41.   The Hebrew term קיקיון is a hapax legomenon whose exact meaning has been debated. See below, pp. 154-56.

42.   Enumeration is that of the collection of Augustine's epistles. The letter is dated c. 404 (Schmid, *SS. Eusebii*, p. 9).

43.   Jerome no doubt here means the version of Symmachus, which reads κισσός. Aquila transliterates the term as κικεῶνα.

carry over "ciceion", no one would have understood; if "gourd", that is not what the Hebrew has. I put "ivy" and it agrees with other interpreters' (*Ep.* 75.7.22).

In Augustine's response to Jerome (*Ep.* 82) he clearly upholds the authority of the LXX over any and all Latin translations from the Hebrew, including Jerome's: 'Therefore I do not want your translation from the Hebrew read in the churches, nor anything just as new published which is against the authority of the Septuagint that might upset the people of Christ with great scandal' (*Ep.* 82.5.35). Augustine bases his decision on 1) the great familiarity the faithful have with the LXX; 2) the authority the LXX held with the apostles; 3) the better knowledge of Hebrew the translators of the LXX had than any later translators (Jerome included):

> If the tree in Jonah is in Hebrew neither an ivy nor a gourd, but is something else... I would prefer gourd read in all Latin versions for I think the Seventy were truly not deceived in putting that but because they understood it as something similar.[44]

Augustine takes the opportunity to comment on Jonah again in *Ep.* 102,

---

44.   Such subtle jabs are in addition to the openly hostile remarks the two men exchange. Thus Jerome accuses Augustine of attacking him with a sword, while he defends himself with a pen (*Ep.* 81.27) and claims that Augustine never told Jerome exactly where the mistranslation in Jonah occurred, thus rendering Jerome incapable of defending himself (*Ep.* 75.7.22). For his part, Augustine appeals to his greater authority in the Church: 'Although according to the titles of honor which the Church maintains and uses, a bishop sits higher than a priest, in many things Augustine is Jerome's inferior. It is allowable in any case for an inferior to correct however he pleases; it is not to be repulsed or deemed unworthy' (*Ep.* 82.4.33). This is a remarkable *double entendre*, for the inferior who properly corrects his better could either be Jerome (thereby asserting Augustine's higher rank in the church) or Augustine (who has acknowledged Jerome his better in certain respects and thus justifies his reproof of Jerome). Calvin sums up the actions of all three parties well. Concerning those African Christians who rioted: 'Those men were certainly thoughtless and foolish who were so offended for a matter so trifling.' Augustine 'did not act so very wisely in this affair; for superstition so possessed him', while Jerome 'answered Augustine in a severe and almost angry manner... he knew that Augustine did not understand Hebrew: he therefore trifled with him as with a child, because he was ignorant' (*Commentaries on the Twelve Minor Prophets* [Grand Rapids: Eerdmans, 1847], pp. 135-36). Luther refers to the debate as 'a truly strange, cold controversy' by which 'nothing is gained' as it is 'a matter of no importance' (H.C. Oswald [ed.], *Luther's Works*. XIX. *Lectures on the Minor Prophets: Jonah and Habakkuk* [55 vols . "t. Louis, MO: Concordia, 1974], p. 29).

addressed to an otherwise unknown priest, Deogratias. The priest has come to Augustine with six questions from an anonymous catechumen. In reality, five of the six questions are from Porphyry.[45] The sixth is not; it concerns Jonah and is really two questions concerning Jonah's survival in the fish and the miraculous tree. Augustine argues for the historicity of the fish by recounting the skeleton of a sea-monster he saw on display in Carthage: 'What an immense opening the mouth had, like the gateway of a cave'! (*Ep.* 102.31). He also surmises that Jonah would have fit into the fish as he was in all probability thrown in nude: 'It would be possible to suppose that he entered there naked, if there were need for his clothing to be removed, as a shell from an egg, to facilitate swallowing'.[46] Augustine also interprets the worm who attacks the gourd typologically: the worm is Christ by whom the privileged promises of the Old Covenant were devoured (102.36).[47]

Apparent in both the debate between Augustine and Jerome concerning Jonah and the questions of the catechumen is that they center on facets of Jonah which are emphasized in the Jonah cycle of Christian art. Thus, the African Christians take offense that the plant under which Jonah reposes is now an ivy and not a gourd. It is not coincidental that this text in Jonah is also the single most popular element of the Jonah cycle, and it is feasible to assume that these illiterate faithful[48] notice Jerome's change due to their familiarity with the pictorial (or other non-literary) representation of Jonah rather than with the text of the LXX. Similarly the two questions put to Augustine in *Ep.* 102 concern two of the three elements in the Jonah cycle: the prophet in the fish and under the gourd. Augustine's opinion that Jonah would have been vomited nude from the fish has no basis in the biblical text, but is a common element in the pictorial representations. As in the case of Celsus and the African faithful, the anonymous non-Christian exhibits a popular knowledge of Jonah informed by artwork

45. The questions concern the resurrection, the fate of those who lived before Christ, the different types of sacrifice, Mt. 7.2 and Solomon's denial that God has a son (Prov. 30.4).

46. The medieval Muslim commentator Al-Kisa'ai, remarks that Jonah was vomited onto land 'like a small chicken without feathers' (quoted in Komlós, 'Jonah Legends', p. 61).

47. Augustine uses as a prooftext Ps. 22.7. Another correlation for Augustine between Christ and the worm is that both are born without mating.

48. Called by Augustine the 'plebes Christi'.

and non-literary traditions rather than by the biblical text.

Jerome's commentary on Jonah, written towards the end of 396,[49] exhaustively treats the issues he hints at in his debate with Augustine. Noteworthy is the commentary's use of traditions from rabbinic sources, and its emphasis on Jonah as a type of the failure of the Jews and of their rejection by God. In the preface Jerome cites the rabbinic tradition that Jonah is the widow's son raised by Elijah in 1 Kings 17.[50] The first line of the commentary proper clearly states what is for Jerome the purpose of the biblical book: 'For the condemnation of Israel Jonah is sent to the nations'. Again, following rabbinic tradition Jerome reads Jonah's flight as indicative of the prophet's knowledge that salvation of gentiles denotes rejection of the Jews. In two memorable maxims, Jerome succinctly captures the essence of the futility of Jonah's flight recounted in ch. 1: 'No one whom God opposes is safe... Great is the one who flees, but greater is he who pursues.'[51] Jerome notes that Jonah does not identify himself as a Jew to the sailors, but rather as a Hebrew, a term which Jerome renders with the Greek περάτης.[52] Jerome makes two stylistic remarks concerning Jonah. First he compares the sailors' rapid-fire questioning of the prophet in 1.8 to the admirable terseness of a passage in Virgil (*Aeneid* 8.112-14).[53] Next, in a very early example of a biblical scholar's appreciation of a text's 'narrative artistry', Jerome admires the narrator's (*historicus*) skill in heightening the tension of the storm in 1.11 by use of the phrase 'the sea grew more and more tempestuous'.[54]

For the most part Jerome reads Jonah as a typological text prefiguring Christ's rejection by the Jews and God's subsequent rejection of them. Thus, the storm in Jonah 1 prefigures the stilling of the storm in Mark and Matthew.[55] He contrasts the faith of the sailors to the faithlessness of the Jews who killed Jesus, and Jonah's success with

49.   Y.-M. Duval (ed.), *Jerome: Commentaire sur Jonas* (SC, 323; Paris: Cerf, 1985). A recent English translation of is that of T.M. Hegedus, 'Jerome's Commentary on Jonah: Translation with Introduction and Critical Notes' (M.A. Thesis, Wilfrid Laurier University; Ann Arbor, MI: University Microfilms, 1991).

50.   Duval (ed.), *Jerome: Commentaire*, p. 164.

51.   Duval (ed.), *Jerome: Commentaire*, pp. 188, 202.

52.   Duval (ed.), *Jerome: Commentaire*, pp. 198-200.

53.   Duval (ed.), *Jerome: Commentaire*, p. 198.

54.   Duval (ed.), *Jerome: Commentaire*, p. 206. Jerome captures the sense of the Hebrew in his choice of *eo* and *intumesco* to translate הלך and סער.

55.   Duval (ed.), *Jerome: Commentaire*, p. 208.

the sailors to 'Hosea, Amos, Isaiah and Joel, who prophesied at the same time but were not able to convert the people of Judea'.[56] Jerome interprets the entire gourd pericope of Jonah 4 as a typology of Jewish jealousy and rejection by God in favor of the Gentiles: 'Nineveh the great...prefigures the church'.[57] The ricinus is a proper symbol for Israel since 'it strikes shallow roots and attempts to grow, but does not attain to the divine heights',[58] and the scorching east wind of 4.8 is interpreted as the destruction of Jerusalem by the Romans.[59]

In examining the early Christian interpretations of Jonah several features are discernible. First, Christian art differs from Christian literature in its interpretation of Jonah. No typological understanding in relation to Jesus is found in the non-literary evidence. Secondly, among Christian writings, two recurring ideas about Jonah see in him a type of the resurrection and interpret the book in such a way as to make it a divine rejection of Judaism. Both of these dominant understandings exert a strong influence on exegesis of Jonah to the present day.

Jonah in Medieval and Renaissance Christian Tradition
Preserved in a single thirteenth-century MS is the commentary on Jonah by Andrew of St. Victor, written c. 1161–63.[60] Andrew's style

---

56. Duval (ed.), *Jerome: Commentaire*, p. 218.

57. Duval (ed.), *Jerome: Commentaire*, p. 314.

58. Duval (ed.), *Jerome: Commentaire*, p. 302. Augustine also mentions the propriety of the ricinus plant as a symbol for Israel.

59. Duval (ed.), *Jerome: Commentaire*, p. 306. That the wind in Jonah comes from the east, while the Romans under Vespasian and Titus come from the west does not appear to cause any difficulty for Jerome. Other early Christian exegesis of Jonah for the most part focuses on him as a prophet of repentance. This figures particularly in baptismal texts of Tertullian, Justin and Clement of Rome. Jonah is used in the anti-Ebionite polemic of Irenaeus and Clement of Alexandria, where the prophet is seen as a sign of the resurrection. See Allenbach, 'La figure', pp. 101-109; R.H. Bowers, *The Legend of Jonah* (The Hague: Nijhoff, 1971), pp. 30-31; and the exhaustive treatment of Duval, *Livre de Jonas*.

60. Text and introduction in A. Penna, 'Andrea di S. Vittore: Il Suo Commento a Giona', *Bib* 36 (1955), pp. 305-11. On the pre-eminence of Andrew among medieval exegetes, see B. Smalley, *The Study of the Bible in the Middle Ages* (Notre Dame, IN: University of Notre Dame Press, 1978), pp. 112-95. Andrew is one of the more sober of the medieval commentators. Concerning others' works on Jonah, Bowers remarks that they 'continually evidence a considerable degree of fanciful exegesis that would not have bothered Humpty Dumpty... yet they often build on

is characterized for the most part by little or no ethical, aesthetic or typological reading of texts. Only passing reference is made to the sign in the New Testament.[61] Andrew's exegesis is also marked by a slavish adherence to the commentary of Jerome. For example, on the basis of Jerome's work, Andrew equates Jonah with the widow's son of 1 Kings 17; elsewhere he quotes Jerome's commentary verbatim.[62] Andrew notes that Joppa is the place where Perseus freed Andromeda from the sea-monster, whose remains are still visible. He offers an etymological interpretation of the name Jonah—from the Hebrew יֹנָה ('oppress'): 'Jonah, that is "the one who suffers"'.[63]

There is an old English verse rendering of Jonah in the c. 1380 work, 'Patience',[64] which draws heavily on the Vulgate. The work, essentially a piece of propaganda, pairs the disobedient prophet with the recalcitrant serf. Its lesson is that, just as Jonah patiently had to obey the unreasonable wishes of God, so too ought the serf patiently and unquestioningly to obey his lord.[65] The poet writes in the prologue:

> If I am appointed, a destiny to have
> What does my disdain or other dispute avail me?
> Or if my liege lord desires my life to bid—
> whether to ride or to run or to roam in his errand (ll. 49-52).

decent respect for traditional interpretations' (*Legend of Jonah*, p. 39).

61.   Penna, 'Andrea di S. Vittore', pp. 311-12.

62.   The following phrases from Andrew's commentary are taken directly from Jerome: 'the repentance of the gentiles is the ruin of the Jews'; 'No one whom God opposes is secure'; 'Great is the one who flees, but greater is he who pursues' (Penna, 'Andrea di S. Vittore', pp. 320-21, 323).

63.   'Andrea di S. Vittore', p. 329; this is also the interpretation used in the Zohar.

64.   Introduction and text in I. Gollancz, *Patience: An Alliterative Version of Jonah by the Poet of Pearl* (London: Oxford University Press, 1913). Discussion in P.E. Szarmach, 'Three Versions of the Jonah Story: An Investigation of Narrative Technique in Old English Homilies', in P. Clemoes (ed.), *Anglo Saxon England*, I (Cambridge: Cambridge University Press, 1972), pp. 183-92.

65.   'This preface introduces naturally the Jonah legend as an exemplum of a vassal who did disobey a command from his superior and who conducted himself discourteously, but who only succeeded in outsmarting himself... Thus the poet is deliberately placing himself... in precisely the same kind of situation in which Jonah found himself. And he is implying, of course, that he will try to be an example of obedience and of patience' (Bowers, *Legend of Jonah*, p. 64).

And again, in the epilogue, the admonition to bear in silence sufferings from superiors is reiterated:

> For you, when poverty oppresses and pains you enough
> Very softly, with forbearance it behooves you to become calm.
> For patience and pain make bravery their goal—
> and patience is an essential, noble thing, though it oft displeases
> (ll. 528-31).[66]

Jonah continued to enjoy popularity in Tudor England as authors relished drawing comparisons between wicked Nineveh and London. This is a major theme in the play *A Looking-Glass for London and England* by Robert Greene and Thomas Lodge, performed in 1592.[67] It is a farce designed more to entertain than to teach. Jonah does not appear until the third act. The beginning of the play is spent recounting in lurid detail the sins of the Ninevites, complete with tyrants, usurers, incestuous relationships, demons and murderers. In the midst of this enters the prophet and his message:

> Repent England in time; as Ninive that Citie did.
> For that thy sinnes before the Lorde, are not in secret hid.

The play ends with a direct address to the audience:

> Jonah must go, nor is the charge confin'd
> To Jonah, but to all the World enjoyn'd:
> You Magistrates, arise, and take delight
> In dealing Justice, and maintaining right:
> There lies your Nineveh; Merchants arise,
> And mingle conscience with your merchandise;
> Lawyers arise, make not your righteous laws
> A trick for gain...[68]

William Tyndale translated Jonah c. 1531 and added a lengthy prologue which is nothing short of a Reformation treatise.[69] Tyndale

---

66. Note how the poet exhorts his listeners to bear their poverty in silence and how in this lies true nobility.

67. Bowers, *Legend of Jonah*, pp. 74, 80-84.

68. Bowers, *Legend of Jonah*, pp. 81, 83-84.

69. Text in D. Daniell (ed.), *Tyndale's Old Testament: Being the Pentateuch of 1530, Joshua to 2 Chronicles of 1537 and Jonah* (New Haven, CT: Yale University Press, 1992), pp. 628-43. For a good exposition of how Tyndale's theology and politics affected his translation of Jonah see D. Ginsberg, 'Ploughboys versus Prelates: Tyndale and More and the Politics of Biblical Translation', *Sixteenth*

affirms the historicity of the account, advising the reader to read it 'not as a poet's fable, but as an obligation between God and thy soul'.[70] Jonah flees not because he is afraid of the Ninevites' repentance but because he is shocked that God would hold the ignorant Gentiles accountable and, that in their forgiveness the prophet (and derivatively his God) would be seen as a liar. This in turn would further Assyrian oppression of the Israelites.[71] Of interest also is Tyndale's opinion that the psalm of ch. 2 does not fit the context of the story. This lack of contextual congruence is one of the main criteria for some modern commentators' dismissal of the psalm as secondary. For Tyndale the historicity of the entire book of Jonah is a given, thus while the psalm is not what Jonah prayed in the whale, it nonetheless is the prophet's own composition.[72]

Martin Luther's two sermons on Jonah date from 1525–26.[73] In both, Luther draws out meanings that accord well with circumstances surrounding his dealings with the Church. He compares the sailors fleeing to Jonah for aid to the people running to monks for their salvation; the Ninevites clad in sackcloth are 'knaves in skin...as the monks in their cowls are'.[74] Luther even makes an oblique reference to himself when, speaking of Jonah's courage to preach to the king of Nineveh, he remarks, 'How absurd did it often seem when someone ventured to raise his voice against the pope'![75] As Tyndale after him, Luther holds that the psalm in ch. 2 is the prophet's thanksgiving written subsequent to his escape. Luther goes to great pains to show that the Ninevites' fasting and repentance are not the reason for God's forbearance in 3.10 from his announced destruction, emphasizing that

Century Journal 19 (1988), pp. 45-61. Jonah is, not surprisingly, a favorite text among the reformers.

70.   Daniell (ed.), *Tyndale's Pentateuch*, p. 631.

71.   Daniell (ed.), *Tyndale's Pentateuch*, p. 632

'How then should God take so cruel a vengeance on so great a multitude of them to whom his name was never preached... If I shall therefore go preach so shall I lie and shame myself and God thereto and make them more to despise God and set the less by him and to be the more cruel unto his people'.

72.   Daniell (ed.), *Tyndale's Pentateuch*, p. 635. On this question, see further below, Chapter 3.

73.   Both in Oswald (ed.) *Lectures* , pp. 3-104.

74.   Oswald (ed.), *Lectures*, pp. 86-88.

75.   Oswald (ed.), *Lectures*, pp. 42-43.

the Ninevites first believed in God (3.5) before their outward signs of contrition. This belief stems from their fear, which is faith in the power of God.[76] Accepting the historicity of the account, Luther characterizes Jonah as the evangelist extraordinaire:

> I am tempted to say that no apostle or prophet, not even Christ himself performed and accomplished with a single sermon the great things Jonah did.[77]

In the hands of the reformers, Jonah receives kinder treatment than that given him by Jerome and Augustine. Whereas the latter two men portray Jonah as the personification of Judaism now seen as petty and rejected by God, Tyndale and Luther understand Jonah sympathetically. Luther sees in Jonah a type of his struggles with Roman Catholicism: the lone figure sent from God to preach reform/doom to the sinful city and their king. This use of the wicked Ninevites and the story of their salvation as transparent social criticism is also popular among Elizabethan authors. In moving into exegesis of the modern period, it is clear that the older view of Jerome and Augustine is revived, and becomes the dominant understanding of Jonah among both Catholic and Protestant scholars.

Modern Exegesis of Jonah

In an attempt to arrange the vast amount of written material concerning Jonah, modern exegesis is here subsumed under a number of categories. These in turn are arranged under the broad questions of identification and meaning.

Identification: Genre and Date of the Book of Jonah
The question of historicity. Jonah still commands a number of interpreters who argue for the historicity of the book.[78] Older

---

76.   Oswald (ed.), *Lectures*, pp. 23, 90. Luther attributes to Jonah a Law-free preaching, due to his extension of God's grace to Gentiles, and compares the Ninevites to the workers of the last hour in the parable of the vineyard (Mt. 20) who reap the same recompense as those who toiled the entire day (pp. 93-94).

77.   Oswald (ed.), *Lectures*, p. 37. Luther later contradicts this statement when he holds that the book only summarizes what must have been a more detailed oracle: 'Undoubtedly he did not confine himself to these words, but he must have enlarged on the themes' (p. 85).

78.   Most notably D. Stuart (*Hosea–Jonah* [WBC, 31; Waco: Word Books,

arguments appeal to the witness of Jesus (assumed to be an authority on history by virtue of his divinity) in addition to anecdotes of the miraculous survival of sailors who have been swallowed by fish.[79]

More sophisticated arguments use Assyrian history in an attempt to demonstrate and/or reconstruct a mid-eighth century BCE crisis of natural[80] or political sorts.[81] Such a crisis functions either as a miti-

---

1987]); T.D. Alexander (T.D. Alexander, D. Baker and B. Waltke, *Obadiah, Jonah, Micah* [TOTC; Leicester: Inter Varsity, 1988]); G.C. Aalders (*The Problem of the Book of Jonah* [London: Tyndale House, 1948]) and B. Trepanier ('The Story of Jonas', *CBQ* 13 [1951], pp. 8-16).

79.   Against the argument from the authority of Jesus, Paul Haupt writes: 'We may illustrate a point by referring to King Lear without committing ourselves as to the historical accuracy of the Shakespearean tragedy. An astronomer who speaks of a beautiful sunset does not contest the Copernican system' ('Jonah's Whale', *Proceedings of the American Philosophical Society* 46 [1907], pp. 151-64 [153]). Concerning stories of swallowed sailors, one particular version which appears in several commentaries recounts how, in 1758, a man fell overboard from a frigate in the Mediterranean and disappeared into a shark's mouth. A gun was discharged at the shark, which promptly returned the man, shaken but unharmed. The shark was killed and preserved and the man toured Europe with it on exhibition (cited in Haupt, 'Jonah's Whale', p. 154; K.F. Keil and F. Delitzsch, *The Twelve Minor Prophets*, I [2 vols.; Edinburgh: T. & T. Clark, 1900], p. 398 n. 1; and T.T. Perowne, *Obadiah and Jonah* [Cambridge: Cambridge University Press, 1905], pp. 92-93). The standard arguments against the book's historicity are conveniently listed in S.R. Driver, *An Introduction to the Literature of the Old Testament* (repr.; Gloucester, MA: Smith, 1972 [1907]), p. 322. These are: 1) Aramaisms; 2) the secondary nature of the Psalm in ch. 2; 3) the book's use of the teaching of the Latter Prophets; 4) lack of historical accuracy surrounding the book's reference to Nineveh, specifically the non-mention of the king's name and use of the title 'king of Nineveh', one never used by the Assyrians. Stuart responds to the last critique by an appeal to the presence of שמרון מלך in 1 Kings 21 (*Hosea–Jonah*, pp. 440-42). Stanislav Segert argues against the historicity of Jonah on the grounds of the low incidence of personal names in Jonah combined with a high incidence of toponyms. This relationship reflects 'a difference between a fictitious narrative and a narrative based on historical tradition' (S. Segert, 'Syntax and Style in the Book of Jonah: Six Simple Approaches to their Analysis', in J.A. Emerton (ed.), *Prophecy: Essays Presented to Georg Fohrer* [BZAW, 150; Berlin: de Gruyter, 1980], pp. 127-28). Chapter 83 of Herman Melville's *Moby Dick* is entitled 'Jonah Historically Regarded'. In it, arguments are put forward in support of the historicity of Jonah against a skeptic who denies it. However, by listing several contradictory and farcical arguments in rapid succession, it is clear that Melville is in reality satirizing those who would hold for Jonah's historicity.

80.   Donald Wiseman offers a choice of disasters (eclipse, earthquake or

gating circumstance that renders the Ninevites open to the pronouncement of doom/call to repentance of a foreign prophet, or tacit historical proof of Jonah's successful mission to the city. Others attempt to validate the size of Nineveh as depicted in Jonah with reference to the so-called 'Greater Nineveh' or 'Assyrian Triangle' hypothesis, which posits that 'Nineveh' in the book of Jonah is meant to include the area surrounding the city, including Dur Sharrakin (Khorsabad) and Calah (Nimrud).[82] An area this large would warrant the three-day journey mentioned in Jon. 3.3. This theory meets with two grave obstacles: 1) Dur Sharrakin was built from scratch by Sargon II (722–705 BCE) at least a quarter of a century after the supposed lifetime of Jonah;[83] 2) Nineveh itself was not made the capital of Assyria until the reign of Sennacherib (704–681 BCE).[84] Needless to say, arguments for the historical veracity of Jonah have

famine) which may have coincided with Jonah's visit to Nineveh and precipitated widespread religious fervor ('Jonah's Nineveh', *TynBul* 30 [1979], pp. 29-51 [47-50]). Wiseman adduces an Assyrian rite of royal subsistution after an eclipse (the *sar puhi* ritual) to explain why the king of Nineveh remains unnamed in Jonah. This is also the view of P.A. Vaccari, 'Il genere letterario del libro di Giona in recenti publicazione', *Divinitas* 6 (1962), pp. 231-52 (248-49).

81.   So Jay Lemanski uses the Eponym Chronicle to demonstrate this period to be one of Assyrian weakness and therefore vulnerability and openness to repentance ('Jonah's Nineveh', *Concordia Journal* 18 [1992], pp. 40-49). Paul J.N. Lawrence constructs a mid-eighth century period dominated by three named regional governors as historical background for both the weakness of the Assyrian monarchy and the mention of nobles in Jon. 3.7 (P.N. Lawrence, 'Assyrian Nobles and the Book of Jonah', *TynBul* 17 [1986], pp. 121-32 [130-31]). Further such attempts at historical reconstruction are made by: F.W. Mozley, 'Proof of the Historical Truth of the Book of Jonah', *BSac* 81 (1924), pp. 170-200 (196-97) and D.E. Hart-Davies, 'The Book of Jonah in the Light of Assyrian Archaeology', *Journal for the Transactions of the Victoria Institute* 69 (1937), pp. 230-49. Hart-Davies concludes, on the basis of Assyrian reliefs depicting human figures in fish costumes, that Jonah would have been viewed by the Ninevites as the fish god Dagon, and so obeyed.

82.   Proponents listed in Bewer (*Jonah*, p. 52). This argument is recently revived by Alexander (*Jonah*, pp. 57-58) on the basis of the appelative העיר הגדולה in the table of nations in Gen. 10.11-12.

83.   Noted in C.H. Wright ('The Book of Jonah', in *idem*, *Biblical Essays* [Edinburgh: T. & T. Clark, 1886], p. 39).

84.   More recently Wiseman ('Jonah's Nineveh', p. 38) interprets the three days to denote a diplomatic process, a day for arrival, a day for the visit and a day for departure. Other views concerning the role of Nineveh in Jonah are treated below in Chapter 4.

been subjected to increasing criticism and/or simple dismissal. Although the historicity position still has its proponents, more recent arguments for this interpretation show the influence of an exegesis done from more nuanced assumptions.[85]

Linguistic issues and the date of Jonah. Closely tied to the debate over the historicity of Jonah is the issue of so-called Aramaisms or Late Biblical Hebraisms in the book, which has been used by those who would deny it any historical validity.[86] The response to this line of argumentation is the attempt by some scholars to show that such Aramaisms really have their explanations in early Canaanite, Phoenician or even Akkadian words.[87] George M. Landes offers the most comprehensive analysis of the book with regards to language and date and offers only four certain indicators of a post-Exilic dating: the

85.   For example, in light of the supposed large amount of usage of/reference to pre-exisiting biblical material in Jonah, Stuart concedes that the book is patterned after material in 1 Kings 17–19 and 2 Kings 2–9 while still arguing for a basis of raw historical facts (*Hosea–Jonah*, p. 443). Similarly, J.H. Stek joins the highly literary character of Jonah with a historical background through use of the term 'interpreted history' ('The Message of the Book of Jonah', *Calvin Theological Journal* 4 [1969], pp. 23-50 [34]). Alexander argues against Jonah as fiction by appealing to the possibility that, while the events recounted in Jonah may have no historicity, they may have been thought so by the author (*Jonah*, pp. 71-72; *idem*, 'Jonah and Genre', *TynBul* 36 [1985], pp. 35-59 [46]).

86.   Driver lists seven (*Introduction*, p. 322) and Bewer ten, two of which he denies (*Jonah*, p. 12). A more recent articulation of this argument is A. Rofé (*The Prophetical Stories: The Narratives about the Prophets in the Hebrew Bible* [Jerusalem: Magnes, 1988], pp. 152-57). Karin Almbladh deems foreign elements poor indicators of date, and instead analyzes Jonah on the basis of its Hebrew constructions alone (*Studies in the Book of Jonah* [Studia Semitica Uppsaliensis, 7; Stockholm: Almqvist & Wiksell, 1986], pp. 44-46).

87.   So already the lengthy analyses of R.D. Wilson, 'The Authenticity of Jonah', *Princeton Theological Reveiw* 16 (1918), pp. 280-98, 430-56; and O. Loretz, 'Herkunft und Sinn der Jona Erzählung', *BZ* 5 (1961), pp. 18-29; cf. J.J. Glück, 'A Linguistic Criterion for the Book of Jonah', *Die Outestamentiese Werkgemeenskap in Suid-Afrika* 10 (1967), pp. 34-41. A. Brenner sees in the language of Jonah indication of the transition from classical to late Biblical Hebrew which occurs during the Exile ('The Language of Jonah as an Index of its Date [in Hebrew]', *Beth Mikra* 24 [1979], pp. 396-405). See the response to Brenner in E. Qimron 'The Language of Jonah as an Index of the Date of its Composition [in Hebrew]', *Beth Mikra* 25 (1980), pp. 181-82.

use of the verb יתעשׁת ('think, consider'); the presence of 'diachronic chiasmus'; the attachment of the pronominal direct object suffix to a verb; the use of the plural where earlier texts normally used the singular (e.g., גורלות, 'lots'). For Landes there are only three clear instances in Jonah of Aramaic elements coming into Hebrew: the verb יתעשׁת, the noun טעם ('decree') and the use of ל as an accusative marker.[88] Against Landes and the corresponding arguments of Oswald Loretz, John Day argues that

> Aramaic influence on post-exilic Hebrew did not always involve the adaptation of completely new words in Hebrew, but also the greater or exclusive use of words which had hitherto existed but which were rare.[89]

In many respects this linguistic debate and the fluidity of evidence on both sides is indicative of the problems which beset biblical exegesis as a whole when faced with the issue of the history of the Hebrew language. When there are few external criteria by which to date texts it becomes almost impossible to detect changes in the language, or to determine in what direction any given changes occurred. Often what for one scholar is a certain indication of a later linguistic phenomenon is for another proof of great antiquity[90] Jack M. Sasson's observations

---

88.   G.M. Landes, 'Linguistic Criteria and the Date of the Book of Jonah', *Eretz Israel* 16 (1982), pp. 147-70 (155-57, 163).

89.   J. Day, 'Problems in the Interpretation of the Book of Jonah', in A.S. van der Woude (ed.), *In Quest of the Past* (*OTS*, 26; Leiden: Brill, 1990), p. 35. Evidence of the lack of firm data concerning the history of Hebrew is the fact that Day critiques those who argue that there is a paucity of late references in Jonah for their slavish adherence in allowing only those words which make new appearances in Hebrew. This is the same standpoint from which Wilson argues the opposite postion, against those who would hold for a late dating

> 'Let us get rid of the absolutely unscientific view of the Hebrew language and literature which would lead us to believe that new words were invented by the writers in whose works they first appear... and that the boundaries of the literary horizon of the Old Testament writers must be limited to the narrow circle of the canonical books' ('Authenticity', pp. 444-45).

90.   By way of example, presence of the relative pronoun שׁ in Jonah has been seen as indication of a late date, replacing the older אשׁר. Yet S.D. Goitien will argue for the later interpolation of the superscription in the Song of Songs on the basis of the presence of אשׁר in place of שׁ ('The Song of Songs: A Female Composition', in A. Brenner [ed.], *A Feminist Companion to the Song of Songs* [repr.; Sheffield: JSOT, 1993], p. 64). Similarly, Bezalel Porten will argue for a pre-exilic date because of the presence of the title 'god of heaven' in Jon. 1.9 (B. Porten, 'Baalshamem and

Freedom beyond Forgiveness

and implicit caveat serve all involved in this debate:

> Hebrew and Aramaic had the potential to influence each other's *vocabulary* at practically all periods... We are also now more aware how difficult it is to filter aramaisms from pristine Hebrew constructions. Furthermore, we are careful not to depend automatically on the presence (or absence) of aramaisms when dating the *creation* of a text: first because any biblical text remained potentially revisable right through the second Temple period... second, because antiquarians of that late period were always capable of emulating archaic, relatively Aramaic-free diction.[91]

Given the great variety in linguistic interpretations it is not surprising that dates for Jonah range over a span of six centuries.[92] The vast majority of scholars place the book in the relatively little-known post-exilic period, in which Israel is variously and arbitrarily categorized as nationalistic, particularistic, depressed, and experiencing crisis over unfulfilled prophecies.[93] In order to lend credibility to these dates,

the Date of the Book of Jonah', in M. Carrez, J. Doré and P. Grelot [eds.], *De la Tôrah au Messie* [Paris: Desclée, 1981], pp. 237-41).

91. J. Sasson, *Jonah* (AB, 24B; Garden City, NY: Doubleday, 1990), p. 204.

92. Stuart has the highest date at c. 760 (*Hosea–Jonah*, p. xliii) while Haupt, 'Jonah's Whale', p. 159, gives the lowest date of c. 100, specifically during the reign of Alexander Jannaeus. Ferdinand Hitzig comes in just behind Haupt with a Maccabean dating (*Der Propheten Jonas Orakel über Moab* [Heidelberg: Mohr–Siebeck, 1831]). Sasson opts not to assign a date, given the uncertain methodological grounds on which such attempts stand, and the lack of use a given date has for understanding the book (*Jonah*, pp. 26-28).

93. So typically Larry Lee Eubanks: 'Post-exilic Israel was most characterized by a rigid isolationism and exclusivism brought about by a hatred of the nations and confusion over the failure of prophecies concerning the destruction of Israel's enemies' (L.L. Eubanks, 'The Cathartic Effects of Irony in Jonah' [Ph.D. diss., Southern Baptist Theological Seminary; Ann Arbor, MI: University Microfilms, 1988], pp. 105-109). So also André and Pierre-Emmanuel Lacocque's reconstruction of what would have obtained in Israel at this period: 'No doubt the most vexing question was the apparent nonfulfillment of exilic prophecies. Specific promises... could not be reconciled with the dire reality' (*Jonah: A Psycho-Religious Approach to the Prophet* [Columbia, SC: University of South Carolina Press, 1990], p. 20). Similarly Edwin M. Good speaks of the 'arrogant isolationism' representative of Israel which would have obtained in this period (*Irony in the Old Testament* [Sheffield: Almond Press, 2nd edn, 1981], pp. 53-54). Among the many others who date Jonah to this period are Loretz, 'Herkunft und Sinn', p. 28; P. Trible, 'Studies in the Book of Jonah' (Ph.D. diss., Columbia University; Ann Arbor, MI: University

some construct elaborate trajectories, parties and schools of thought
which form complexes of action and reaction and in which Jonah has a
comfortable place.[94] Bruce Vawter's characterization of an exclusive
post-exilic Israel engaged in 'creating—for that must be the word—a
largely fictitious ethnicity'[95] serves as an ironic description of the
creative fiction of biblical scholarship concerning post-exilic Israel.
As with the issue of language, here one confronts a manifestation of the

Microfilms, 1963), pp. 107-110; E.G.H. Kraeling, 'The Evolution of the Story of
Jonah', in *Hommages à A. Dupont-Sommer* (Paris: Maisonneuve, 1971), p. 306; T.
E. Fretheim, *The Message of Jonah: A Theological Commentary* (Minneapolis:
Augsburg, 1977), pp. 29-38; J.S. Ackerman, 'Satire and Symbolism in the Song of
Jonah', in B. Halpern and J. Levenson (eds.), *Traditions and Transformation*
(Winona Lake, IN: Eisenbrauns, 1981), pp. 245-46; Rofé, *The Prophetical Stories*,
p. 158; S. Schumann, 'Jona und die Weisheit: Das prophetische Wort in einer
zweideutigen Wirklichkeit', *TZ* 45 (1989), p. 73-80 (73). Hans Walter Wolff places
Jonah in the early Hellenistic period (*Obadiah and Jonah* [Minneapolis: Augsburg,
1986], pp. 76-78) as does James Nogalski (*Redactional Processes in the Book of the
Twelve* [BZAW, 218; Berlin: de Gruyter, 1993], p. 272). Ronald E. Clements argues
for a date at the end of the exile ('The Purpose of the Book of Jonah', in J.A. Emerton
[ed.], *Congress Volume* [VTSup, 28; Leiden: Brill, 1975], pp. 16-28 [26-28]).

   94.   So, for example, Lacocque and Lacocque have an elaborate 'universalism
trajectory' with five distinct schools/stages, each represented by biblical texts. Within
this schema, Jonah illustrates a 'decentralized universalism' (*Jonah*, pp. 19, 22-23).
Michael Orth argues that the book is half of a two-party debate present in the Old
Testament ('Genre in Jonah: The Effects of Parody in the Book of Jonah', in
W. Hallo [ed.], *The Bible in the Light of Cuneiform Literature* [Ancient Near Eastern
Texts and Studies, 8; Lewiston, NY: Edwin Mellen, 1990], p. 277). David Payne
fits Jonah in the developing trajectory of prophecy–apocalyptic as a reaction to the
latter (D.F. Payne, 'Jonah from the Perspective of its Audience', *JSOT* 13 [1979],
pp. 3-12). This is similar to the view of Lacocque and Lacocque, which identifies
Jonah as the 'hinge in the ideological and literary history of Israel' between prophecy
and apocalyptic (*Jonah*, p. 228). As with the debate surrounding use of linguistic
criteria, what is for one exegete a sign of lateness is for another evidence of antiquity.
Thus the universalism of Jonah, which is for so many the beacon indicator of its
production in the exclusivist post-exilic era, is for K. Kohler a sure indication of its
pre-exilic date. Kohler reasonably argues that if post-exilic Israel is as narrow and
particularistic as claimed, no one could have written such a broad-minded work ('The
Original Form of the Book of Jonah', *Theological Review* 16 [1879], pp. 139-44
[139-40]). Issues of such reconstructions relative to dating bear on the question of the
purpose of Jonah, and are treated below in the section concerning the book's meaning.

   95.   B. Vawter, *Job and Jonah: Questioning the Hidden God* (Ramsey, NJ:
Paulist, 1983), p. 115.

larger difficulty of the dating of most, if not all, of the Old Testament. After analysis of Jonah's use of biblical and extra-biblical traditions, a relative date for the book can be proffered, founded free of the assumption that authors of whatever types of literature represent great social movements or parties of their day. A crisis observable in a text need only be as big as the individual who wrote it.[96] The most that can be said prior to this type of analysis is that a tentative *terminus ante quem* date for Jonah may be assigned on the basis of reference to the prophet in Tob. 14.4 and a reference to the Twelve Minor Prophets in Sir. 49.10—although it must be granted that Sirach is perhaps referring to a different collection of twelve.[97]

Jonah and folklore. Since the rise of exegesis based on folklore studies, Jonah has been a prime candidate for such analysis. Hermann Gunkel treats the book under the motifs of helpful animals, people swallowed by animals and preserved, and rescue by a sea creature.[98] Gunkel's pupil, Hans Schmidt, undertakes the most extensive folklore/*religionsgeschichtliche* analysis to date, comparing Jonah 1–2 with myths and folktales from Greece and India.[99] A similar analysis

96.   I am referring to what Peter Brown so eloquently calls 'the bitter precision of life's small heartbreaks' (*The Making of Late Antiquity* [Cambridge, MA: Harvard University Press, 1978], pp. 5-6). So Alfred Jepsen: 'When, then, is "Jonah" written? (Or ought one perhaps better ask "Against whom?"). Then one can easily come to the positing of groups...whose existence is highly unlikely' ('Anmerkungen zum Buche Jona: Beiträge zur Theologie des Alten Testaments', in H. Stoebe [ed.], *Wort–Gebot–Glaube: Theologie des Alten Testaments* [ATANT, 59; Zürich: Zwingli-Verlag, 1970], p. 304); Schumann: 'A murmur or a question is not to be found in a group or people, but in the solitude of an individual' ('Jona und die Weisheit', p. 80).

97.   The reference to Jonah in Tobit occurs in B, A, V, the majority of the miniscules, and versions. In ℵ, reference is made to Nahum at Tob 14.4. The Jonah reading occurs in those MSS judged by the editor of the critical edition of Tobit as the best witnesses (R. Hanhart [ed.], *Tobit* [*Septuaginta Gottingensis*, 8.5; Göttingen: Vandenhoeck & Ruprecht, 1983], pp. 176-77). Jonah is also listed with the twelve minor prophets in *4 Ezra* 1.39-40 and *Mart. Isa.* 4.22 (*OTP*, I, p. 526; II, p. 163).

98.   H. Gunkel, *The Folktale in the Old Testament* (repr.; Sheffield: Almond Press, 1987 [1917]), pp. 54, 146. For Gunkel the book was written in 'a childlish, cheerful, folkloristic form' ('Jonabuch', *RGG*², pp. 366-69).

99.   H. Schmidt, *Jona: Eine Untersuchung zur vergleichenden Religions-geschichte* (FRLANT, 9; Göttingen: Vandenhoeck & Ruprecht, 1907). Other folkloristic analyses of Jonah are those of L. Radermacher, 'Walfischmythen', *ARW*

had been done by W. Simpson, who sees in Jonah the traces of an ancient initiatory rite into the cult of the fish god, replete with death–rebirth imagery.[100] Beginning with Ferdinand Christian Baur in 1837 connection has been made between Jonah and the traditions preserved in Berossus concerning Ὀάννης, the god who comes out of the sea and gives technology to humankind.[101] More recently, folktale motifs in the book are not as strongly emphasized. Phyllis Trible lists fifteen folkloristic elements in Jonah but concludes that, because of the book's historical character (based as it is on 2 Kgs 14.25), its portrayal of the transcendent power of Yahweh, and its didactic intent, it is not a folktale.[102] With the growing awareness of the highly contrived literary structure in Jonah and its borrowing of other literary traditions of the Old Testament, the appeal to folklore is made less and less.[103]

9 (1906), pp. 248-52; T. Gaster, *Myth, Legend and Custom in the Old Testament*, II (2 vols.; New York: Harper & Row, 1975), pp. 652-56 and I.A. Ben-Yosef, 'Jonah and the Fish as a Folk Motif', *Semitics* 7 (1980), pp. 102-17. The analysis of Ben-Yosef overlooks key variants in the Egyptian 'Tale of the Shipwrecked Sailor' and the Greek myth of Arion.

100. W. Simpson, *The Jonah Legend* (London: Richards, 1899). Jonah has been compared to the myths of Perseus and Andromeda (and the parallel version of Heracles and Hesione), Cassandra, Oannes, Arion and Mittavindaka (Komlós, 'Jonah Legends', pp. 44-45).

101. F.C. Baur, 'Der Prophet Jonas: Ein assyrisch–babylonischen Symbol', *ZHT* 1 (1837), pp. 88-114. H. Clay Trumbull put forward the same equation in 'Jonah in Nineveh', *JBL* 11 (1892), pp. 53-60 (53-58). The most recent treatment of Berossus is in J. Van Seters, *In Search of History: The Yahwist as Historian in Genesis* (Louisville, MO: Westminster/John Knox, 1992), pp. 67-70. The etymological and grammatical leap from Ὀάννης to Jonah is not easily made. E.H. Merrill cites arguments against this equation in 'The Sign of Jonah', *JETS* 23 (1980), pp. 23-30 (27).

102. 'Studies', pp. 146, 148-49, 151-52. Trible's arguments against folktale are based on unfounded theological assumptions, that the book's Yahwistic character emphasizes how 'in Him magic is transformed into miracle' (pp. 151-52) in addition to artificial distinctions between Jonah and folktales. A random sampling of the Grimm brothers' collection will reveal tales replete with historical figures (St. Peter, Jesus), miracles performed by the Christian god and a prominent didactic thrust.

103. Among those who deny any folkloristic elements are A. Feuillet, 'Les sources du livre de Jonas', *RB* 54 (1947), pp. 161-86 (167); M. Burrows, 'The Literary Category of the Book of Jonah', in T.H. Frank and W.L. Reed (eds.), *Translating and Understanding the Old Testament* (Nashville: Abingdon, Press 1970), p. 88 and F. Golka, *The Song of Songs and Jonah* (International Theological Commentaries; Grand Rapids: Eerdmans, 1988), p. 89.

Jonah as Allegory. The Zohar remarks: 'In the story of Jonah we have a representation of the whole of a man's career in this world', and follows with a detailed allegorical reading.[104] Some biblical scholars read the book in the same way,[105] the fullest treatment being that of Charles H. Wright, who identifies Jonah with Israel, the fish with Babylon/the Exile (by appeal to Jer. 51.34), the booth with restored Jerusalem, Nineveh with Babylon and the plant with Zerubbabel.[106] Much like the folkloristic approach, allegorical interpretation has waned with the passage of time, although elements of it still appear in the literature.[107] The enduring legacy of the allegorical approach is found in those exegeses which interpret Jonah as a symbol of everyone, the prophets, post-exilic Israel or some hypothetical party or school.

The unity of Jonah. Johannes G.A. Müller in 1794 appears to be the first to have questioned the single authorship of Jonah. In 1799 J.C.K. Nachtigal divided the book into 1) the psalm, composed by Jonah after his departure from Assyria; 2) chs. 3–4, written in the exile as a corrective against Jewish particularism; 3) ch. 1, written and brought together with the psalm during the time of Ezra–Nehemiah.[108] Otto

104. Aryeh Wineman investigates the Zohar's use of earlier interpretations in its treatment of Jonah, and argues that the Zohar revives older rabbinic views which understand the book as referring to resurrection ('The Zohar on Jonah: Radical Retelling or Tradition?' *Hebrew Studies* 31 [1990], pp. 161-79).

105. Ernst Bloch, Paul Kleinert, Thomas K. Cheyne and George A. Smith, cited in Bewer, *Jonah*, p. 10.

106. Wright, 'Book of Jonah', pp. 34-98.

107. Trible's dismissal of the approach is representative ('Studies', pp. 153-58). For the continuing presence of allegorical interpretation, see the equation of the booth with the first temple and the plant with Hezekiah in D.L. Christensen, 'Andrzej Panufnik and the Structure of the Book of Jonah, Icons, Music and Literary Art', *JETS* 28 (1985), pp. 133-40 (138); the equation of Jonah in the whale with Israel in exile in J.D.W. Watts, *The Books of Joel, Obadiah, Jonah, Nahum, Habbakuk and Zephaniah* (CBC; Cambridge: Cambridge University Press, 1975), p. 85 and Nogalski, *Redactional Processes*, p. 267; and the reading of the worm's destruction of the plant in Jonah 4 as a reference to the destruction of Israel by the Assyrians in Alexander, *Jonah*, p. 129. In a reversal of the view which equates Jonah's sojourn in the fish with the exile, Paul Kahn interprets the fish as the promised land, and Jonah's ejection as the exile; as Jonah is vomited forth from the fish, so is Israel from their land ('An Analysis of the *Book of Jonah*', *Judaism* 43 [1994], pp. 87-100 [91-92]).

108. J.G.A. Müller, 'Jona: Eine moralische Erzählung', in *Memorabilien*, VI

Eissfeldt designates two legends, the first of a prophet commanded to go to Nineveh and the second a debate between Jonah and God.[109] Frank Zimmerman similarly sees two stories brought together in Jonah but placed in the wrong order by a compiler, hence the book's abrupt ending at 4.11.[110] The most elaborate source-critical hypothesis is that which begins with the work of K. Kohler, and is given its fullest expression by Wilhelm Böhme and taken up by Hans Schmidt.[111] Böhme distinguishes a Yahwistic source, followed by an Elohistic author, in turn followed by Elohistic and Yahwistic redactors respectively and finally redactors constituting several minor glosses. More recently, those who hold for literary strata in Jonah have reduced the number of editorial stages to three.[112]

All of these elaborate reconstructions utilize a suspect methodology based in part upon an unrealistically rigorous criterion of logic concerning plot and vocabulary. Several examples will illustrate the overly speculative nature of such exegesis. Kohler argues 3.6-8a to be an insertion because it makes little sense for the king's edict to follow upon the actions already instigated by the populace. He also deletes 4.1-4 because these verses 'interrupt the context of the narrative and

(Leipzig: Cruisius, 1794), p. 142; J.C.K. Nachtigal, 'Über das Buch des Alten Testaments mit der Aufschrift: Jonas', in J. Eichorn (ed.), *Allgemeine Bibliothek der biblischen Litteratur*, IX (Leipzig: Weidmannschen Buchhandlung, 1799), pp. 221-73. The issue of the secondary character of the psalm in Jonah 2 receives separate treatment in Chapter 3 below.

109. O. Eissfeldt, *The Old Testament: An Introduction* (New York: Harper & Row, 1966), p. 405.

110. F. Zimmerman, 'Problems and Solutions in the Book of Jonah', *Judaism* 40 (1991), pp. 580-89 (583-85). W.B. Crouch interprets Jonah's allegedly abrupt ending as a literary device used to engage the reader ('To Question an End, to End a Question: Opening the Closure of the Book of Jonah', *JSOT* 62 [1994], pp. 101-12).

111. Kohler, 'Original Form', pp. 139-44; W. Böhme, 'Die Composition des Buches Jona', *ZAW* 7 (1887), pp. 224-84 and H. Schmidt, 'Die Komposition des Buches Jona', *ZAW* 25 (1905), pp. 285-310.

112. E.g., Kraeling, 'Evolution', pp. 305-18; L. Schmidt, *'De Deo' Studien zur Literakritik und Theologie des Buches Jona, des Gëspraches zwischen Abraham und Jahve in Gen 18.22ff und von Hiob 1* (BZAW, 143; Berlin: de Gruyter, 1976), pp. 48-123; P. Weimar, 'Jon 4.5: Beobachtungen zur Entstehung der Jonaerzählung', *Biblische Notizen* 18 (1982), pp. 86-109; idem, 'Jon 2.1-11: Jonapsalm und Jonaerzählung', *BZ* 28 (1984), pp. 43-68 (62-68) and Nogalski, *Redactional Processes*, pp. 261-62.

spoil its harmony'.[113] Böhme maintains to have discovered the presence of redactional activity in the use of two separate terms for 'ship' in Jonah 1 (ספינה, אניה). The first belongs to Jonah's original Yahwistic kernel; the second is part of a larger editorial activity which recasts two pre-existing sources and an earlier redaction. This editing is itself the fourth phase of a five-step process by which Jonah arrives at its present form.[114] Schmidt deletes the sailors' appeal to Yahweh in 1.13-14 on the grounds that it makes their offerings and vows in 1.16 redundant.[115] Emil G.H. Kraeling designates the entirety of Jonah 1–2 as a separate narrative affixed to the earlier account which begins in 3.1. This is because the present reference in 3.1 to the reiteration of Yahweh's call of Jonah demonstrates what is for Kraeling 'a finesse...improbable to an ancient story'.[116] Similar to Schmidt and Kraeling, James Nogalski holds for the priority of Jonah 3–4, since Jon. 1.1–2.10 (minus the psalm in 2.2-9) is a discrete literary unity which 'presupposes a continuation' a nd hence could not have existed independently. Consequently, it is specifically composed for its inclusion before Jon. 3.1.[117]

Apparent from these examples is the fact that key assumptions concerning how authors and redactors go about their tasks inform this kind of source-critical analysis. Equally apparent is that these assumptions are uncritical in their rigid application of certain characteristics to authors, and others to redactors. Thus, in light of the examples mentioned above, authors are viewed as individuals who adhere to the strictest narrative logic. They are incapable of repetition, digression or any other sophistication, and completely unaware of the availability of synonyms in their native language. Redactors, on the other hand, are imprecise in their work, a Godsend for biblical scholars who otherwise would be unable to detect editorial activity. The work of these later scribes is implicitly characterized by a lack of attention to the vocabulary and narrative logic of the original authors. Such distinctions are unprovable. Why should a redactor have chosen a different word for 'ship' in Jonah 1 when a term was already provided in the text? On what grounds are ancient narratives judged to be con-

113. Kohler, 'Original Form', pp. 140-41.
114. Böhme, 'Die Composition', pp. 283-84.
115. Böhme, 'Die Composition', p. 289.
116. 'Evolution', p. 307.
117. Nogalski, *Redactional Processes*, pp. 261-62.

stituted solely of simple plot lines free from so-called extraneous detail? Why should the fact that a prior episode in a text comes to a close and presupposes what follows be sign of later addition rather than the ubiquitous feature of narrative prose?

In spite of the paucity of commentators who hold for earlier sources in Jonah, the use of divine names in the book continues to pose interpretative problems. The crux of the matter is in ch. 4, where the heretofore clear distinction (with the exception of 1.14) between the use of יהוה by Jonah and אלהים by the sailors and Ninevites breaks down completely. Here, both terms occur in relation to Jonah, along with the composite יהוה אלהים.[118] Some see a reference to the creation accounts of Genesis 1–3 in the varied and composite use of divine names in Jonah 4.[119] Others make the traditional Jewish distinction between the Tetragrammaton as a designation of God's merciful character and the more generic אלהים as an emphasis on divine justice.[120] Still others view אלהים as a remnant of originally foreign material incorporated into the book,[121] or simply attribute the variation to aesthetic reasons and the author's desire to equate the two terms for theological purposes.[122]

118. See the chart in Sasson (*Jonah*, p. 18) and appendix in Bewer (*Jonah*, pp. 64-65). Bewer attributes the anomalies to copyists, and is followed by Day ('Problems', pp. 43-44).

119. Most fully in G. Elata-Alster and R. Salmon, 'The Deconstruction of Genre in the Book of Jonah: Towards a Theological Discourse', *Literature and Theology* 3 (1989), pp. 40-60 (53) but also Golka, *Song of Songs and Jonah*, pp. 121-22. Wilhelm Rudolph attributes the combination of divine names in Jonah 4 to a glossator attempting to draw parallels to similar shifts in Genesis 2–3, 22 (W. Rudolph, 'Jona', in A. Kuschke [ed.], *Archäologie und Altes Testament* [Tübingen: Mohr [Paul Siebeck], 1970], p. 239).

120. J.D. Magonet, *Form and Meaning: Studies in Literary Techniques in the Book of Jonah* (Bible and Literature Series, 8; Sheffield: Almond Press, 2nd rev. edn, 1983), pp. 35-38.

121. G. Fohrer, *Introduction to the Old Testament* (Nashville: Abindgon Press, 1965), p. 442.

122. F.D. Kidner, 'The Distribution of Divine Names in Jonah', *TynBul* 21 (1970), pp. 126-28 (128) and H. Witzenrath, *Das Buch Jona* (ATAT, 6; St. Ottilien: Eos, 1978), pp. 55-56. Critiques of any attempt at analysis of the divine names in Jonah are in Bewer, *Jonah*, p. 21; Trible, 'Studies', pp. 84, 103; Eissfeldt, *Introduction*, p. 406; Wolff, *Obadiah and Jonah*, pp. 78-80; 164 and Sasson, *Jonah*, p. 18.

The genre of Jonah. Jonah has defied definitive classification. Among its many labels are: story about a prophet,[123] parable,[124] legend,[125] didactic history,[126] 'narrative dogmatics',[127] philosophical treatise,[128] tragedy,[129] ironic short story,[130] novella,[131] comedy,[132] parody[133] and

123. Gerhard von Rad calls it 'the last and strangest flowering of this old and almost extinct literary form' (*Theology of the Old Testament*, II [2 vols.; San Francisco: HarperCollins, 1962], p. 291); so also K.M. Craig, 'The Poetics of Jonah: Toward an Understanding of Narrative Strategy' (Ph.D. diss., Southern Baptist Theological Seminary; Ann Arbor, MI: University Microfilms, 1989), p. 33; A. Berlin, 'Rejoinder to John A. Miles, Jr. with Some Observations on the Nature of Prophecy', *JQR* 66 (1976), pp. 227-35; C.A. Keller, 'Jonas, le portrait d'un prophète', *TZ* 21 (1965), pp. 329-40.

124. R.B.Y. Scott sees Jonah as a parable with an allegory based on Jeremiah 51 ('The Sign of Jonah', *Int* 19 [1965], pp. 16-25 [16]). Landes does not identify the book of Jonah as a parable, but sees the prophet functioning as a parable or, in Landes's terminology, a *mashal* ('Jonah: A *Mashal*?' in J. Gammie [ed.], *Israelite Wisdom* [Missoula, MT: Scholars Press, 1978], pp. 137-58). The most detailed elaboration of Jonah as parable is that of A. Rofé, 'Classes in the Prophetical Stories: Didactic Legend and Parable', in J.A. Emerton (ed.), *Congress Volume* (VTSup, 26; Leiden: Brill, 1974), pp. 143-53; *idem*, *The Prophetical Stories*, pp. 152-70. Other works that hold Jonah to be a parable are B.S. Childs, 'The Canonical Shape of the Book of Jonah', in G.A. Tuttle (ed.) *Biblical and Near Eastern Studies* (Grand Rapids: Eerdmans, 1978), p. 124; and most recently E. Eynikel, 'The Genre of the Book of Jonah' (Paper presented at the annual meeting of the Society of Biblical Literature, Chicago, IL: November, 1994). This view is criticized already by Aalders who points out that all parables in the Old Testament are immediately followed by their explanation, which is not true of Jonah (*Problem*, pp. 15-19).

125. Jepsen, 'Anmerkungen zum Buche Jona', p. 299. R. Couffignal relates Jonah to legend by calling it an 'anti–legend' ('Le psaume de Jonas (Jonas 2.2-10): Une catabase biblique, sa structure et sa fonction', *Bib* 71 [1990], pp. 542-52 [542]).

126. Alexander, 'Jonah and Genre', pp. 35-59. Although Craig refutes the idea that Jonah is didactic, he does so on the basis of a caricature of didactic literature as 'militaristic' writing which 'subverts [all] to the exigencies of doctrine'. For Craig Jonah is too 'polyphonic' to be didactic (*A Poetics of Jonah: Art in the Service of Ideology* [Columbia, SC: University of South Carolina Press, 1993], pp. 159-60).

127. Schmidt, '*De Deo*', p. 130.

128. E. Levine, 'Jonah as a Philosophical Book', *ZAW* 96 (1984), pp. 235-45 (236). Levine's own categorization of scholarship is problematic (pp. 235-37).

129. B. Woodard, 'Death in Life: The Book of Jonah and Biblical Tragedy', *GTJ* 11 (1991), pp. 3-16 (11-13).

130. M. West, 'Irony in the Book of Jonah: Audience Identification with the Hero', *Perspectives in Religious Studies* 11 (1984), pp. 233-42 (235-37).

131. Wolff, *Obadiah and Jonah*, p. 85; M.E. Andrew, 'Gattung and Intention of

farce.[134] The problem with most of these classifications is the uncertainty that these genres were known as such in the ancient world. Two genres which do yield ancient examples and which bear closer examination are those of satire and midrash.

In his 1795 deist critique of the Bible, Thomas Paine asserts that Jonah was written to satirize the biblical prophets.[135] Among modern biblical scholars, identification of Jonah as satire has many adherents.[136] Millar Burrows points to the satiric elements of fantastic situations and the ridicule of the main character, to which John C. Holbert adds the presence of a subtle attack on a definite, familiar target, the

the Book of Jonah', *Orita* 1 (1967), pp. 13-18, 78-85 (78-79). For Andrew only Jonah 1–3 is a novella; ch. 4 he classifies as a sermon. Roger Syrén extrapolates the genre of diaspora novella from Tobit and Esther, which contain the following elements: setting in a foreign court, a clear clash between good and evil, and an emphasis on threat to Jews. The presence of opposite characteristics in Jonah ('a mirror reading') leads Syrén to classify it as a reversed diaspora novella ('The Book of Jonah—A Reversed *Diasporanovella*?' *SEÅ* 58 [1993], pp. 7-14).

132. J. Mather, 'The Comic Art of the Book of Jonah', *Soundings* 65 (1982), pp. 280-91; T. Thorardson, 'Notes on the Semiotic Context of the Verb *Niham* in the Book of Jonah', *SEÅ* 54 (1989), pp. 226-35 (230). Mather argues for the presence of burlesque, parody and farce in the book (p. 281).

133. A.J. Band, 'Swallowing Jonah: The Eclipse of Parody', *Prooftexts* 10 (1990), pp. 177-95; Orth, 'Genre in Jonah', pp. 257-81; and B. Peckham, *History and Prophecy: The Development of Late Judean Literary Traditions* (ABRL; Garden City, NY: Doubleday, 1993), p. 690.

134. More specifically 'surrealist farce' (T. Eagleton, 'J.L. Austin and the Book of Jonah', in R. Schwartz [ed.], *The Book and the Text: The Bible and Literary Theory* [Oxford: Basil Blackwell, 1990], p. 231). Compare this list of proposed genres for Jonah with that of Alexander (with accompanying bibliography): history, allegory, midrash, parable, prophetic parable, legend, prophetic legend, novella, satire, didactic fiction and satirical, didactic short story ('Jonah and Genre', pp. 36-37).

135. T. Paine, *The Age of Reason* (repr.; Exton, PA: Wet Water, 1992 [1795]), pp. 113-16.

136. Good, *Irony*, pp. 40-41; Burrows, 'Literary Category', pp. 94-96; Ackerman, 'Satire and Symbolism', pp. 216-17; J.C. Holbert, '"Deliverance Belongs to Yahweh!" Satire in the Book of Jonah', *JSOT* 21 (1981), pp. 59-81 and J.A. Miles, Jr, 'Laughing at the Bible: Jonah as Parody', *JQR* 65 (1974-75), pp. 168-81. Because of the numerous studies of the satiric nature of Jonah already available, Thomas Jemielty omits the book completely in his discussion of satire in the prophets (*Satire and the Hebrew Prophets* [Louisville, KY: Westminster/John Knox, 1992], pp. 15-16).

mockery of inferiority/weakness, and an external viewpoint.[137] John A. Miles categorizes satire as literary parody and identifies five biblical genres being parodied in Jonah: the prophetic call, the mockery of idolatry, the psalm, the rejection of prophet by a king and the prophetic lament.[138]

André and Pierre-Emmanuel Lacocque are the only authors to hold that Jonah is a satire of a variety known to have existed in the ancient world.[139] Their identification of the book as a Menippean satire utilizes Mikhail Bakhtin's list of that genre's characteristics along with an inferred Palestinian milieu for the genre based on Menippus's origins in Gadara.[140] However, classical scholarship has found short-comings in Bakhtin's analysis of the Menippean satire, mainly in its disregard of historical change and context.[141] The term 'Menippean satire' is not used as a genre designation until the sixteenth century. Among the characteristics of Menippean satire observed by Joel C. Relihan, those which do not obtain in Jonah are: journeys to fantastic places (e.g., heaven, the moon), jokes made at the expense of learning, the use and subversion of three standard subtexts (Old Greek Comedy,

---

137. Burrows, 'Literary Category', pp. 94-96; Holbert, '"Deliverance"', p. 62. The logical problem of how one can infer the definite target of a subtle attack is not treated by Holbert. Burrows's use of the term 'literary category' is an attempt to escape the narrow, formal confines of genre. Thus when he calls Jonah a satire he intends 'first of all the dominant spirit and intention... and only secondarily the form which expresses that intention' (p. 96).

138. 'Laughing', pp. 168-77. Berlin, in her response to Miles points out that satire is not a genre known to have existed among the biblical authors. For Berlin the only certain genre designation is the traditional threefold division of law, prophets and writings ('Rejoinder', p. 229). To Berlin's critque it can be added that Miles's 'genres' of the prophetic call, the rejection of prophet by a king, the mockery of idolatry and the prophetic lament are form-critical designations or motif categories, modern scholarly nomenclature applied to the biblical material. These literary conventions are likewise unknown in antiquity. How then, can they be satirized in Jonah?

139. Ackerman also maintains that Jonah most closely resembles Menippean satire ('Satire and Symbolism', p. 228).

140. Lacocque and Lacocque, *Jonah*, pp. 26-48; they list Bakhtin's characteristics of Menippean satire (pp. 39-41).

141. The most recent attempt by a classicist to identify the features of Menippean satire is that of J.C. Relihan, *Ancient Menippean Satire* (Baltimore: The Johns Hopkins University Press, 1993). Relihan critiques Bakhtin's characteristics for being founded upon a static notion of Hellenistic society 'which asserts the essential unity of over six hundred years of history' (pp. 6-8).

the Odyssey and Platonic myths), a prologue which questions the author's intelligence and ability to write the piece, and an epilogue which negates any lessons put forth in the preceding text.[142] These final two formal elements also relate to the most distinct features of the satire, which clearly do not appear in Jonah: the portrayal of the author/narrator as unreliable and the self-parody of the author.[143] In light of this analysis the Lacocques' thesis cannot bear scrutiny.

In her 1962 dissertation, Phyllis Trible revives the view originated by Karl Budde and taken up by Hugo Winckler, that Jonah is a midrash on another biblical text.[144] Trible identifies six characteristics of midrash: its point of departure is always a scriptural text; it is based on 'attentive study' of that text; it expounds in a homiletic/didactic manner; it adapts the meaning of the text to the current situation of the midrash; it may contain halakic elements, but is mainly composed of the haggadic; 'above all' it proclaims the miraculous power of God.[145] Trible finds the scriptural *Urtext* for Jonah to be what she designates a credal formula in Jon. 4.2, also found in Exod. 34.7 and numerous other places within the Old Testament.[146]

In a critique of this methodology, G. Addison Wright observes that biblical scholars often confuse a meaning of the term 'midrash' which denotes an exegetical technique with another sense used to define a literary genre.[147] Wright characterizes the genre midrash as 'literature about literature', an attempt to make past texts relevant to

142. Relihan, *Ancient Menippean Satire*, pp. 12-36. Another distinguishing formal feature for Greek and Latin literature is the mixture of prose and verse. This criterion cannot apply to the biblical material, as such a mixture is evident in every book of the Hebrew Bible.

143. Relihan, *Ancient Menippean Satire*, p. 10.

144. K. Budde, 'Vermutungen zum "Midrasch des Büches der Könige"', *ZAW* 12 (1892), pp. 37-51; H. Winckler, 'Zum Buch Jona', *Altorientalische Forschung* 2 (1900), pp. 260-65. Others who classify Jonah as a midrash are A. Thoma, 'Die Entstehung des Büchleins Jona', *TSK* 84 (1911), pp. 479-502 (498-99); Loretz, 'Herkunft und Sinn', pp. 27-28; R. Coote, *Amos among the Prophets* (Philadelphia: Fortress Press, 1981), p. 129 and Christensen, 'Andrzej Panufnik', p. 137.

145. 'Studies', pp. 162-63.

146. 'Studies', pp. 167-68.

147. G.A. Wright, 'The Literary Genre Midrash', *CBQ* 28 (1966), pp. 105-38, 417-57 (120-21). Although critiquing the method she uses, Wright does not cite Trible's dissertation in his study.

present circumstances. As such, midrash always functions in service to the biblical text cited, and never vice versa.[148] Jonah is not a midrash but free biblical fiction, and Wright argues for classifying such texts as haggadah.[149] In addition to these observations, another substantial problem with identifying Jonah as a midrash is that there is no identifiable scriptural text on which it is based. In the midrashim of the rabbinic period and later, the scriptural text is clearly designated with a formulaic 'as it is written' or its equivalent. That a clear indication is not present in Jonah is evidenced by the fact that Budde, Winckler and Trible adduce different biblical texts on which Jonah is a midrash.[150] Moreover, while Trible explicitly defines Jonah as a midrash in a formal sense, she is forced to admit that the *Gattung* of midrash may contain other *Gattungen*, such as parable, allegory, legend.[151] This admission empties the genre midrash of any explanatory power it may have for Jonah and becomes merely a bin in which to place the book's constituent elements.

Given the lack of information about specific genres which obtained in antiquity, another way of classifying literature centers around the issue of imitation. In this analysis, one determines what kind of prior or contemporaneous writing a text resembles and from there attempts to discover an active process of imitation at work. This kind of approach has yielded fruitful results in New Testament studies on the issue of the genre of the Gospels. Through stylistic comparisons analyzed statistically, Richard A. Burridge has demonstrated that the

---

148. 'Literary Genre', pp. 133-34.

149. 'Literary Genre', pp. 431-32.

150. For Budde ('Vermutungen', pp. 40-43), Jonah is part of the 'Midrash of the Book of Kings' mentioned in 2 Chron 24.27 and is a midrash on 2 Kgs 14.25; for Winckler ('Buch Jona', p. 261) it is part of the lost 'Words of the Seers' mentioned in 2 Chron 33.19. Wolff points this out and adds other texts for which Jonah could serve as a midrash (*Obadiah and Jonah*, p. 81). While Trible argues that כי ידעתי in Jon. 4.2 is a formulaic introduction to the midrashic source text ('Studies', p. 231), there are no other instances in the Old Testament where this phrase is used to introduce quotations.

151. 'Studies', p. 165. The older views of Budde and Winckler are critiqued by Mozley ('Proof', p. 175) for whom Jonah does not exhibit the picturesque detail characteristic of midrash. Burrows argues against Trible on the grounds that the notion of midrash as a specific genre is either insufficiently precise, or insufficiently understood to apply ('Literary Category', p. 89).

canonical gospels most closely resemble Graeco-Roman βίοι.[152] Burridge's conclusion, along with that of Helmut Koester that the term 'gospel' is only first used as a designation of a specific type of writing by Marcion in the second century CE,[153] shows that the Gospels are not to be thought of as a *sui generis* literary genre. Unfortunately, two factors crucial to the success in the case of the Gospels of determining their genre by comparison, but unavailable in regards to Jonah, are: a large database of literature written in the same language (the amount of material preserved in the Old Testament is miniscule in relation to the vast corpus of extant Greek writing) and knowledge of the date for both the writing in question and others to which it is compared. While Jonah may resemble Ruth in length and tone, 1 Kings 17–19 in plot, or Jeremiah in theology, the profound lack of knowledge concerning the date, provenance, means of production and identity of the authors of any of the biblical books makes the attempt at discovering the genre of Jonah too speculative an undertaking.

As we have seen with other issues, the problem of finding a genre for Jonah is but an indication of the larger problem of genre in biblical studies. Genre is a series of common literary conventions, encoded into a text by an author, which limits and focuses the author's intended meaning.[154] Strictly speaking, a genre is a choice by the author of the best set of literary conventions by which to convey meaning and intent.[155] As such, genres assigned to works which date from periods or areas where such genres are not known to have existed cannot apply. Too often in the discussion of genre in Jonah, the particular label chosen is used more as a vehicle to expound the

152. R.A. Burridge, *What Are the Gospels? A Comparison with Graeco-Roman Biography* (SNTSMS, 70; Cambridge: Cambridge University Press, 1992).

153. H. Koester, 'From the Kerygma-Gospel to Written Gospels', *NTS* 36 (1989), pp. 375-81. Discussed more fully in *idem*, *Ancient Christian Gospels: Their History and Development* (Philadelphia: Trinity International, 1990), pp. 1-48.

154. This discussion follows E.D. Hirsch, *Validity in Interpretation* (New Haven, CT: Yale University Press, 1967), pp. 68-126. Craig points out the difficulty of interpreting conventions if one does not know the genre ('Poetics', pp. 30-32). Mary Gerhart treats the problems of genre analysis in the field of religion in 'Generic Studies: Their Renewed Importance in Religious and Literary Interpretation', *JAAR* 45 (1977), pp. 309-25.

155. Such a choice may be a conscious one by the author (e.g., to write a satire), or an implicit decision based on imitation of earlier writings (e.g., to write a story that is like *Gulliver's Travels*).

commentator's views on the book and its meaning than an attempt to discover the author's intent.[156] This lack of attention to authorial intent leads to classifications of such breadth and bulk as to be of little or no use in interpretation.[157] That this unchecked proliferation of appellatives has gone beyond the point of reason is clearly seen in the absurdity of the following:

156. John W. Roffey rightly stresses that the genre of Jonah (whatever it may be) is chosen by its author and therefore 'rather than a means of taxonomy or classification [genre] is a means of *production*' ('God's Truth, Jonah's Fish: Structure and Existence in the Book of Jonah', *Australian Biblical Review* 36 [1988], pp. 1-18 [6, 10-13]; emphasis added). Sasson comments on those who see Jonah as satire or comedy and their adoption of 'a contemptuous diction, a jocose style, or a burlesque tone when assessing specific episodes, investing Jonah with more humor and levity than the text supports' (*Jonah*, p. 331). However, Sasson himself characterizes Jonah as a comic-dupe/comic-hero (pp. 346-47). Craig also critiques those who see humor in the text ('Poetics', p. 173). Similarly Herbert C. Brichto negatively characterizes contemporary genre ananlysis as being founded upon 'metaliterary conventions' of the critic's prior assumptions (*Toward a Grammar of Biblical Poetics: Tales of the Prophets* [Oxford: Oxford University Press, 1992], p. 28). Brichto includes a list of standard metaliterary conventions at work in analysis of ancient texts (p. 34).

157. By way of random sampling: 'a historical midrash...a didactic–religious narrative' (K. Marti, *Das Dodekapropheten* [Tübingen: Mohr (Paul Siebeck), 1904], p. 245); 'a straightforward folk novella with didactic features' (E. Sellin, *Das Zwölfprophetenbuch* [KAT, 12; Leipzig: Scholl, 1922], p. 240); 'prose poem...story with a moral...parable' (Bewer, *Jonah*, p. 4); 'a midrashic and didactic tract in schematic and repetitive style, influenced by wisdom literature' (Fohrer, *Introduction*, p. 442); 'satirical, didactic (or theological) short story' (Fretheim, *Message of Jonah*, p. 72); 'a prophetic narrative...loose designation of a parable' whose 'literary tone [is] parody or satire' (Allen, *Jonah*, pp. 175-78). Even those who come to a decision as to the genre of Jonah seem unable to resist attaching other labels. Thus Trible calls it midrash, didactic story and satire ('Studies', pp. 165-66; 255-56); for Wolff it is both novella and 'ironic protest literature' (*Obadiah and Jonah*, p. 109); so also Good (*Irony*, pp. 40-41); Landes calls it a parable and a didactic novella ('Jonah: A *Mashal*?' pp. 137-58; *idem*, 'Jonah', *IDBSup*, p. 489). After spending an entire chapter in an attempt to show that Jonah is a Menippean satire, Lacocque and Lacocque refer to the book as a parable (*Jonah*, p. 215) and an aretalogy (p. 42). Concerning the classification of Jonah as an aretalogy, R. Reitzenstein deems it as such and places the book in the early portion of the growth of prophetic and missionary aretalogies (*Hellenistische Wundererzählungen* [Stuttgart: Teubner, 2nd edn, 1963], p. 35).

> The book of Jonah is... a short story. It is fiction... Indeed it is fantastic
> fiction... The story is parabolic... It is a didactic story... and it is comic,
> full of irony and satire.[158]

Rather than add to the plethora of terms, this study approaches the author's intended meaning of the book via other avenues. To this end investigation into what type of literature Jonah is furnishes the attempt to discover the kind(s) of writing Jonah may be imitating. It will be seen below that the book utilizes other well-known biblical (e.g., language of distress in the Psalter) and extra-biblical (e.g., sea-storm accounts) narrative traditions in an imitative manner. While this is true of some of the constitutive elements of Jonah, until more is learned about literary activity in the ancient world—apart from that of Greece and Rome, that is—the question of the genre of the work as a whole remains insoluble.[159]

Jonah and literary criticism. Because of its relatively manageable size in comparison with other biblical books, its contrived structure and fictional elements, Jonah is a favorite text for the newer literary approaches in biblical studies. One of the first of such approaches is that of Jonathan Magonet who, through distinguishing the 'overt narrative text' from its 'subliminal' level, reads subtle allusions out of the text and discusses the *Leitwörter*, the repetition of phrases, and rising/falling action.[160] Reminiscent of structuralist exegesis,[161] Magonet's analysis identifies the polarities present in and underneath the text, and emphasizes that, through the ambiguous portrayal of

158. J.M. Ward, *Thus Says the Lord: The Message of the Prophets* (Nashville: Abingdon Press, 1991), p. 246. Craig's observation is appropriate here: 'With the many interpreters combining two, three or even four terms to express their understanding of the literary category of the book, one can only conclude that these taxonomies themselves can no longer be classified' ('Poetics', p. 25).

159. So also Brichto: 'Unless we can come to an agreement as to what are the sine qua non feaures of a genre... we are better off abandoning genre altogether as a tool' (*Grammar*, p. 26).

160. *Form and Meaning*, p. 90. Among the most recent examples of literary analyses of Jonah are those of Crouch, 'To Question an End'; D. Lillegard, 'Narrative and Paradox in Jonah', *Kerux* 8 (1993), pp. 19-30 and M. Peli, 'Jonah as an Artistic Story [in Hebrew]', *Beth Mikra* 39 (1994), pp. 210-13.

161. A method applied to Jonah in 'An Approach to the Book of Jonah: Suggestions and Questions by a Group of Rennes, France', *Semeia* 15 (1979), pp. 85-96.

Jonah, the reader is forced to switch back and forth between identification and rejection.[162] Two dissertations from the Southern Baptist Theological Seminary examine Jonah from the perspectives of audience and reader. Larry Lee Eubanks attempts to discover and analyze the cathartic effects of irony in the book. Working from the standpoint of the necessity of an unaware victim for irony, Eubanks speaks of the catharsis produced when the audience, having identified with the prophet as a figure to be emulated at the outset of the book, quickly (in 48 verses) passes through the conflict of emotions sparked by Jonah's unfavorable behavior, all of which leads to resolution and new insight at the book's conclusion.[163] Kenneth M. Craig subjects the book to a poetical analysis based on the theory of Meir Sternberg. Craig maintains that the author, through the use of gaps, inside/omniscient viewpoints and strategically placed prayers, succeeds in conveying an ideological message in the most efficient and aesthetically pleasing way.[164] Similarly Herbert Chanan Brichto uses on Jonah ˙ the method formulated by Sternberg. Brichto points to the presence of the 'synoptic-resumptive technique', the repetition of an episode in which the second acccont is longer, but dependent on the first.[165]

In examining the foregoing literary analyses, problems of method and assumption become apparent. First there is the presupposition many interpreters make as to the radical difference of Jonah from other literary works, conventions and viewpoints of its day. Hans Robert Jauss characterizes this assumption as 'an aesthetics of negativity'. And so Eubanks will speak of literature's goal as 'correcting a reader's mistaken view of the world', and of irony's task of providing 'a corrective for the faulty world-view of its audience by negating the

162. Magonet, *Form and Meaning*, pp. 87-90; Stuart characterizes Magonet's approach as 'overinterpretation' which turns a simple narrative into a 'complex vocabulary puzzle whose solution or even existence would never have occurred to any reader or hearer' (*Jonah*, pp. 456-57).

163. 'Cathartic Effects', pp. 14-29; 173-85. Fretheim analyzes the ironic elements in Jonah (*Message*, pp. 53-55); similarly, R.I. Gregory discusses the use of irony in the Elijah cycles ('Elijah's Story under Scrutiny: A Literary-Critical Analysis of 1 Kings 17-19' [Ph.D. diss., Vanderbilt University; Ann Arbor, MI: University Microfilms, 1983], pp. 93-104).

164. Craig's dissertation ('Poetics') was published (*Poetics*); his approach is also set forth in 'Jonah and the Reading Process', *JSOT* 47 (1990), pp. 103-14.

165. *Grammar*, p. 13.

old norms'.[166] Lacocque and Lacocque, drawing on John Dominic Crossan's notion of parable as 'story subverting the world', refer to satire (Jonah included) as

> the effective weapon of the dispossessed, the biting retort of the *sans-culotte* to the authoritarian well-to-do.[167]

The consequence of an interpretative stance in which every literary work is seen as different from and challenging to the literature and *Geist* of its day is a homogeneity of all texts in their shared subversion which precludes the existence of established writing or norms which may be challenged.[168]

Second, these literary approaches exile the author from his or her work.[169] Thus, Eubanks's theory of irony is completely divorced from the intentions of the author; interaction occurs between reader and

166. 'Cathartic Effects', pp. 62, 91-92. Eubanks further discusses how a text calls dominant societal systems into question (pp. 94-95), and notes his dependence on Wolfgang Iser's model of a textual strategy known as 'defamiliarization of the familiar' (pp. 8-10). Glenda Abramson's remark demonstrates the fundamentally subjective nature of analysis of irony: 'The fact is that any ambiguity has come to be regarded as ironic. And since all great literature says more than it appears to be saying, because it contains the universal in the particular... practically all great literature or drama can be called ironic' (G. Abramson, 'The Book of Jonah as a Literary and Dramatic Work', *Semitics* 5 [1977], pp. 36-47 [39]). Jauss offers a reading of Jonah based mainly on the work of Wolff and von Rad ('Das Buch Jona—Ein Paradigma der "Hermeneutik der Fremde"', in H.F. Geisser [ed.], *Wahrheit der Schrift—Wahrheit der Auslegung* [Zürich: Theologischer Verlag, 1993], pp. 260-83).

167. Lacocque and Lacocque, *Jonah*, pp. 24-27; 30, drawing on John Dominic Crossan's analysis of Jonah as parable in *The Dark Interval* (Niles, IL: Argus, 1975).

168. Although prevalent in literary analyses, standard historical-critical methodology is not free from the assumption of an aesthetics of negativity: 'Thus when we find evidence that there developed in Judaism at that time a tendency toward rigidity of belief and religious exclusiveness, with a new note of bitterness toward non-Jews, the setting of such a book as Jonah and the need for it become apparent' (Scott, 'Sign', p. 24). Scott's remark is also a good example of positing an exclusivist post-exilic *Sitz im Leben* for which Jonah can serve as a challenge.

169. Even the outlines of this debate are massive, having at their roots epistemological and aesthetic theory from the classical age up through the present. The reader is referred to the two main works on either side of this issue, Hirsch, *Validity*, and H.-G. Gadamer, *Truth and Method* (Maryknoll, NY: Orbis Books, 1987).

text rather than between reader and author, with the entire burden of finding meaning placed on the reader.[170] In this respect literary critics pride themselves on their freedom from authorial intent and contrast their approaches with the unsuccessful and narrowly restricted methods of historical criticism.[171] Against this claim it can be argued that, rather than a call to renewed critical rigor in the light of the failure of traditional methodologies, these literary approaches constitute instead a 'post-critical' stance that returns to a naive view of the finished text that uproots it from its historical moorings.[172]

Closely related to this naive approach and banishment of the author is the creation of an artificial author in whom is embodied almost divine prerogatives. Brichto's comments concerning Jonah are representative:

> The Book of Jonah is from beginning to end, in form and content, in diction, phraseology and style a masterpiece of rhetoric. It is the work of a

170. Eubanks, 'Cathartic Effects', pp. 8, 24, 39-43, 58. This approach is categorically opposed to Hirsch's view that meaning is encoded into a text by an author via shared literary conventions, of which irony is one.

171. Craig will distinguish poetics from criticism, the former being 'the rigorous application of analytical tools' and the latter 'an intuitive enterprise which lacks methods and objective rules'. Elsewhere Craig opines: 'Historical criticism has by and large failed to provide definitive answers to external questions... while internal issues—the book's art—have often been ignored' ('Poetics', p. 3-5). This distinction is also characteristic of the works of Robert Alter. Trible discusses how rhetorical analysis moves beyond the intent of the author (P. Trible, *Rhetorical Criticism: Context, Method and the Book of Jonah* [Guides to Biblical Scholarship; Minneapolis: Fortress Press, 1994], pp. 228-33).

172. This is Ferdinand Deist's conclusion concerning study of the prophets: 'scholars tended to "side-step" the (socio-anthropological) problem by focussing [sic] more and more on the finished product, the "final/canonical text". The clearer it became that *these questions* [i.e., socio-anthropological] threatened to invalidate the model of rationality the more *that kind of question* was made suspicious or labeled "unanswerable"' ('The Prophets: Are we Heading for a Paradigm Switch?', in V. Fritz, K.-F. Pohlmann and H.-C. Schmitt [eds.], *Prophet und Prophetenbuch* [BZAW, 185; Berlin: de Gruyter, 1989], pp. 1-18 [12]). The term 'post-critical' is from John Barton's critique of the canonical approach in *Reading the Old Testament: Method in Biblical Study* (Philadelphia: Westminster Press, 1983). B.S. Childs reads Jonah canonically ('Canonical Shape', pp. 122-28) as does Elmer Dyck ('Canon and Interpretation: Recent Canonical Approaches and the Book of Jonah' [Ph.D. diss., McGill University; Ann Arbor, MI: University Microfilms, 1986]).

single artist, free from editorial comment or gloss; every word is in place, and every sentence (*Grammar*, p. 68).[173]

In many respects this view is a logical outworking of an aesthetics of negativity, for who but geniuses can create world-subverting works? Yet as in the problem caused by such an assumption, if every author is an artistic genius then the term becomes void of meaning. Such an apotheosis of the author—endowed with such genius and *incapable of any mistakes*[174]—amounts to nothing less than a collapsing of the divine dictation model of scriptural inspiration into the mind of the author, yet another naive, post-critical move. Sternberg's theory of poetical analysis, to which Craig and Brichto are indebted, has come under similar criticism.[175]

Meaning: Message and Purpose of the Book of Jonah
As with so many other issues concerning Jonah discussed above, opinions as to the book's message, occasion and audience present a picture of jumbled multiplicity. Broadly speaking these varying interpretations fall under three headings.[176]

173.   To this can be added Lacocque and Lacocque: 'The author of Jonah could have easily been so provincial in his interests and so narrow in his scope as to render his story unusable for other times and other peoples. But he was a genius' (*Jonah*, p. xxii); Craig, for whom chronological unevenesses or illogicalities are 'one of the signs of artistic genius' ('Poetics', p. 177) and Ackerman ('Satire and Symbolism', p. 228).

174.   This is made patently clear by Brichto: 'poetical analysis cannot admit of superfluous action... without raising questions as to the competence of the literary artist' (*Grammar*, p. 8).

175.   Mieke Bal notes Sternberg's 'ideological commitment to the text and his use of poetics to support it', wherein 'divine omniscience is expressed in omniscient narration' and therefore is no longer clearly seen 'as a religious dogma which may be doubted but a narrative convention which must be accepted as given' ('The Bible as Literature: A Critical Escape', *Diacritics* 16 [1986], pp. 71-79. Eubanks's dissertation, with its discovery of elaborate and wide-ranging allusions in Jonah taken from almost the entire canon ('Cathartic Effects', pp. 125-41), complements the poetical approach of Craig in that Eubanks posits a perfect reader in tune with even the most minute allusion, the ideal counterpart to Craig's perfect author ('Poetics', pp. 34-68).

176.   Compare these three headings to Alexander's four-fold schema of repentance, unfulfilled prophecy, Jewish attitudes towards gentiles and theodicy (*Jonah*, pp. 81-88). Sandor Goodhart ('Prophecy, Sacrifice and Repentance in the Story of Jonah', *Semeia* 33 [1985], pp. 43-63 [44]) distinguishes between an 'old' and a

Jonah as anti-exclusivistic. This by far is the view which has come closest to holding sway in the field,[177] although its heyday has passed. As mentioned above, this approach involves creating a rigid, mean-spirited exclusivist attitude in the post-exilic era (or, for those authors who hold for the historicity of the book, the eighth century), to which Jonah acts as a divine corrective. Unfortunately, some scholars, given free rein in their reconstructions, also give vent to anti-Semitic sentiments which continue to plague the field of biblical studies.[178] These reconstructions, free from any external controls, are rampant with unfounded assumptions and unbridled speculation as commentators create scenarios replete with political, sociological, religious, philosophical and literary parties, movements and ideologies with which and against whom the author of Jonah does battle.[179]

Against this view several criticisms have been raised. Primary is the

'new' reading. All such schemata presuppose a degree of artificiality; hence there is some overlap.

177. This interpretation cuts across the issues of genre, date and methodology which otherwise divide commentators, and is held by those who argue for the book's historicity, for example Alexander, *Jonah*, p. 90; Stuart, *Jonah*, p. 434-35, in addition to other historical-critical studies such as Driver, *Introduction*, p. 323; Bewer, *Jonah*, p. 7; H.G. May, 'Aspects of the Imagery of World Dominion and World State in the Old Testament', in J.L. Crenshaw (ed.), *Essays in Old Testament Ethics* (New York: Ktav, 1974), pp. 60-61; Wolff, *Obadiah and Jonah*, p. 157 and literary analyses of various types such as Wright, 'Book of Jonah', p. 84; Burrows, 'Literary Category', p. 100; Magonet, *Form and Meaning*, pp. 90-112 and Lacocque and Lacocque, *Jonah*, pp. 41-43.

178. As noted above, understanding Jonah to be a condemnation of Judaism goes back at least as early as Augustine and Jerome. Keil and Delitsch represent the extreme example when they speak of the Israelite 'delusion' of their election by God 'which stimulated the inclination to pharisaical reliance upon an outward connection with the chosen nation' (*Minor Prophets*, p. 384). The authors' uncritical ideological bias can be seen in their anachronistic and unfavorable caricature of the concept of pharisaism, a post-Maccabean phenomenon, which they attribute to an outlook they themselves date to the eighth century BCE.

179. To Lacocque and Lacocque must go the distinction of the most complex and fanciful scenario. Their post-exilic period is replete with: 1) Jerusalem ideologues who do not fully reject Hellenism but still reserve Temple privileges and cultic prerogatives to themselves; 2) Hellenists who fully embrace the new cultural *Geist* to a complete abandonment of the old ways; and 3) Universalist Hasidim, perfect in their openness to others and their adherence to tradition. It is this last group which, utilizing the new genre of Menippean satire, offers a corrective to both the Temple ideologues and Hellenistic 'modernists' (*Jonah*, pp. 42-44, 159-60).

simple observation that there is no substantive historical evidence
(apart from a highly irregular reading of Ezra–Nehemiah which
overemphasizes putative ethnic conflicts) to substantiate any Jewish
particularism in the post-exilic era.[180] This lack of evidence only
emphasizes the ever-vexing problem of the paucity of knowledge concerning the period in Israelite/Jewish history from the fifth to the
third centuries BCE.[181] Secondly, the reference to Jonah in 2 Kgs 14.25
does not portray him as a zealous Israelite nationalist, as commentators who hold for the anti-exclusivist approach claim. The text
merely states that Jonah correctly prophesies an expansion of Israel's
borders; it does not say how Jonah feels or thinks about his prophecy,
this particular turn of events, or any other matter.[182] Finally, this
picture of Jonah/Israel as bitter, narrow and petty has resulted from
an overemphasis on and misinterpretation of Jonah's anger in ch. 4[183]
in relation to the rest of the book.[184] Often this exaggeration is due to
scholarly assumptions and preconceptions founded upon confessional
differences.[185] Even though this interpretation is eschewed in more

180. So von Rad, *Theology*, II, p. 292; Clements, 'Purpose', pp. 18-19;
Zimmerman, 'Problems', pp. 586-89; Rofé, 'Classes', p. 155 and Sasson, *Jonah*,
p. 26. Golka classifies Jonah as a 'self-corrective' of Judaism in general and not
directed at any particular group or party (*Song of Songs and Jonah*, p. 72).

181. A problem which, it appears, will continue to be with the field given the
recent attempts to date the origins of the biblical traditions in the Persian period.

182. Pointed out in Trible, 'Studies', pp. 173-74 and Payne, 'Jonah', p. 5.
Grace I. Emmerson adds that, if the prophet of the book of Jonah were an ardent
exclusivist, he would have rejoiced at the opportunity to deliver an oracle of doom to
gentile Nineveh ('Another Look at the Book of Jonah', *ExpTim* 88 [1976], pp. 86-
88 [86]).

183. That the Hebrew text demands that one interprets Jonah's reaction in 4.1 as
anger is critiqued below in Chapter 5.

184. So A.D. Cohen, 'The Tragedy of Jonah', *Judaism* 21 (1972), pp. 164-75
(165-66); and S.D. Goitien, 'Some Observations on Jonah', *JPOS* 17 (1937), pp.
63-77 (66). Keller lists many of the negative appellatives commentators ascribe to
Jonah and remarks: 'In short, one is angry with Jonah but in admiration with the
clearsightedness and liberalism of his "biographer"' (C.A. Keller, 'Jonas' [CAT,
21a; Geneva: Labor et Fides, 1982], p. 329).

185. Discussed in Miles, 'Laughing', p. 178 n. 12, who rightly observes that 'if
the author mocks Jews for their pride, he also mocks the gentiles for their stupidity'.
Other commentators point out specific biases of Christian commentators: 'Assuming
the prophetic books of the Bible are informed, *sui generis*, by a universalist
ethic... most Christian commentators read the book ironically. They separate Jonah's

recent works due to its explicit and problematic correlation with the post-exilic *Sitz im Leben* of Ezra–Nehemiah, the view of Jonah as a corrective against a hypothetical Jewish provincialism is still put forward by exegetes in more abstract terms,[186] in spite of the fact that generalizations do not recommend themselves as more valid interpretations.

Jonah and prophecy. Taking as a cue Jonah's inclusion in the Book of the Twelve, some exegetes hold that the book is a commentary on Israelite prophecy. Beyond this point scholars part company. Among the views held are the following: a prophet cannot escape divinely ordered duty;[187] the honor and validity of a prophet whose message has not come to pass does not matter in light of the divine sovereignty;[188] the book is an explanation of the non-fulfillment of other prophetic oracles (specifically those of an apocalyptic nature);[189] it is a critique

viewpoint from that of an implied author to whom they attribute divine authority' (Elata-Alster and Salmon, 'Deconstruction', p. 41). Norma Rosen sees the purpose of such assumptions as an attempt to 'make what Christian commentators call the "Old Testament God" look good. Vindictive judgment, wrath, devouring punishments are banished. In their place, mercy, pity, love. To which Jonah so perversely objects' ('Jonah', in D. Rosenberg [ed.], *Congregation* [San Diego, CA: Harcourt Brace Jovanovich, 1987], p. 224). Rosen rightly notes the harsh treatment Jonah has suffered at the hands of exegetes: 'the world, scorning Jonah for his lack of mercy, subjects him to a judgment from which mercy is withheld' (p. 227); so also the observation of Rofé (*Prophetical Stories*, p. 162).

186.   Evidence of the enduring allure of the exclusivist approach is Allen's commentary, which sees Jonah's target as a nameless 'community embittered by its legacy of national suffering and foreign opposition' (*Jonah*, pp. 188-91); so also Loretz, 'Herkunft und Sinn', pp. 27-28; Landes, 'Jonah', p. 490 and D. Gunn and D.N. Fewell, *Narrative in the Hebrew Bible* (Oxford: Oxford University Press, 1993), p. 139.

187.   A view held a century ago by Eduard Riehm (cited in Driver, *Literature*, p. 323); Goitien, 'Observations', p. 64; and more recently part of Brichto's 'intraprophetic' aim of the book (*Grammar*, pp. 79-81). Gabriel Cohn interprets more abstractly: the book teaches the necessity to obey divine orders ('Book of Jonah', *EncJud*, X, p. 172).

188.   In itself a revival of an ancient Jewish interpretation; Emmerson, 'Another Look', pp. 86-87 and Berlin, 'Rejoinder', pp. 230-35, are representative.

189.   A view put forward as early as Hitzig (*Jonas*), but maintained more recently in May, 'Aspects', p. 62; Payne, 'Jonah', pp. 11-12; and Day, 'Problems', pp. 46-47, for whom Jonah is a response to the proto-apocalyptic oracles of Joel. For Fretheim

of prophets of woe and those for whom the prophetic word is unconditional;[190] it is a critique of prophecy in general as a decrepit institution of petty practitioners;[191] it is a lesson to its readers of how a city or people ought to respond to a prophetic word.[192]

Jonah and the divine nature. Such a broad category as the divine nature encompasses several subordinate interpretations.[193] The first is that the book deals with the nature of repentance and shows its efficacy in light of the the divine will to save.[194] However, given the use in Jon. 3.10–4.2 of traditions concerning divine mercy found in a variety of biblical texts, it is highly unlikely that the efficacy of repentance is any new idea introduced to Israelite religion in this text.[195]

the book is a questioning of the non-fulfillment of eschatological oracles which promise the ultimate demise of the wicked (T.E. Fretheim, 'Jonah and Theodicy', *ZAW* 90 [1978], pp. 227-37 [228-30]; *idem, Message,* pp. 29-38). Among those who hold that the book deals with the non–fufillment of prophecy in general are Childs, 'Canonical Shape', p. 123; E. Nielsen, 'Le message primitif du livre de Jonas', *RHPR* 59 (1979), pp. 499-507 (502-507) and Rofé, *Prophetical Stories* p. 166

190.   So Bickerman, *Four Strange Books*, p. 43, for whom Jonah is a critique of the unconditional nature of woe oracles found in Jeremiah; J.H. Tigay, 'The Book of Jonah and the Days of Awe', *Conservative Judaism* 38 (1985–86), pp. 67-76 (69); D.F. Rauber, 'Jonah: The Prophet as Schlemiel', *Bible Today* 49 (1970), pp. 29-38 (35-36); E. Wiesel, *Five Biblical Portraits* (Notre Dame, IN: University of Notre Dame Press, 1981), p. 151; and J. Blenkinsopp, who characterizes the book as a 'sapiential critique of prophecy' which 'breaks once and for all the bond of what migh be called prophetic causality by its emphasis on the divine freedom' (*A History of Prophecy in Israel* [Philadelphia: Westminster Press, 1983], pp. 270-71).

191.   Vawter, *Job and Jonah*, p. 101.

192.   T. Collins, *The Mantle of Elijah: The Redaction Criticism of the Prophetical Books* (Sheffield: JSOT Press, 1993), pp. 170-71.

193.   In fact, it is the inclusive nature of his category of theodicy (roughly equivalent to my designation divine nature) that enables Alexander to choose it as the main theme of the book (*Jonah*, p. 89).

194.   Clements, 'Purpose', pp. 21-23; Goodhart, 'Prophecy', p. 53; Porten, 'Baalshamem', pp. 242-43; M.C. White, 'Jonah', in C. Newsome and S.H. Ringe (eds.), *Women's Bible Commentary* (Philadelphia: Westminster Press, 1992), p. 214; and Roffey, 'God's Truth', p. 17. Peckham (*History and Prophecy*, p. 656-57) argues that Jonah is written to refute the Deuteronomistic notion that repentance is sufficient for salvation.

195.   Emmerson also argues that the efficacy of repentance is a presuppostion rather than the aim of the book ('Another Look', p. 86). In addition to the many occurrences of the formula in 4.2 can be added the numerous accounts in the Old

Another view holds that divine sovereignty is the issue, and that Jonah the prophet is taught a lesson in God's freedom both to change a word of destruction and pardon sins that cry out for punishment.[196] Terence Fretheim has one of the more developed approaches of this type. He sees Jonah in light of the debate concerning the question of God's compassionate acts to the evil. That is to say: 'Are God's *compassionate* actions just?'[197] In this way Jonah functions as the logical counterpart to Job, the latter dealing with God's punishment of the innocent. Just as Job upholds God's ultimate sovereignty regardless of any circumstances, so too does Jonah.[198] Still others see the book to reveal the true divine nature as compassionate,[199] loving,[200] suffering;[201] or as an exposition of mutually exclusive viewpoints with

Testament of repentant individuals escaping punishment. The meaning of divine repentance in Jonah and its relationship to that idea in the Old Testament is treated below in Chapters 4 and 5.

196. G.M. Landes, 'The Kerygma of the Book of Jonah', *Int* 21 (1967), pp. 3-31 (28); Burrows, 'Literary Category', p. 100; Magonet, *Form and Meaning*, pp. 90-112; G. Elata-Alster and R. Salmon, 'Eastward and Westward: The Movement of Prophecy and History in the Book of Jonah', *Dor le Dor* 13 (1984), pp. 16-27 (26-27); Mather, 'Comic Art', pp. 285-86; Eubanks, 'Cathartic Effects', pp. 185-86; Schumann, 'Jona und die Weisheit', p. 74; Craig, *Poetics*, p. 154; Golka, *Song of Songs and Jonah*, pp. 125-27; H. Gese, 'Jona ben Amittai und das Jonabuch', *Theologische Beiträge* 16 (1985), pp. 256-72 (repr.; *Alttestamentliche Studien* [Tübingen: Mohr (Paul Siebeck), 1993], pp. 122-38 [134]). The issue of divine freedom is dealt with in more detail below in my treatment of Jon. 3, pp. 132-35. This is also set out in T.M. Bolin, '"Should I Not also Pity Nineveh?"—Divine Freedom in the Book of Jonah', *JSOT* 67 (1995), pp. 109-20.

197. Fretheim, *Message*, p. 23; *idem*, 'Jonah and Theodicy', p. 227. Sasson phrases the question another way: 'Is God godly when acting beyond the comprehension of prophets, let alone ordinary human beings?' (*Jonah*, p. 26).

198. So also Ackerman, 'Satire and Symbolism', pp. 245-46.

199. A.J. Hauser, 'Jonah: In Pursuit of the Dove', *JBL* 104 (1985), pp. 21-37. Hauser's thesis, which holds that the author presents a picture of God as vengeful in Jonah 1–3 only to surprise the reader with divine compassion in light of the Ninevites' repentance and Jonah's anger in 3.10-14, is highly artificial given the longstanding tradition of divine compassion prevalent in the Old Testament which Hauser cites (pp. 22, 34-35). Hauser overlooks the fact that, since the compassion of God is an established theological datum, it cannot function as the element of surprise in a text. Rather, it is an affirmation of the obvious.

200. Trible, 'Studies', pp. 173-74, 263-65.

201. S.H. Blank ('"Doest Thou Well To Be Angry?" A Study in Self-Pity', *HUCA* 26 [1955], pp. 29-41) posits a pattern in biblical texts (first among which is

no resolution.[202] It will be seen below that the book of Jonah is about the theodical issues of divine freedom, but that for the author this divine freedom is not limited in its exercise to forgiveness, mercy or tender concern as typically understood by humankind.[203]

Concluding Remarks

As stated at the outset of the chapter, the purpose of this survey has been to give a representative exposition and analysis of both pre-modern and modern exegesis of the book of Jonah. It has not included all the various types of interpretations gleaned from the book.[204] It

Jer. 45) of human self-pity set over against a divine suffering brought about by the logical conflict between God's justice and compassion:

> A moral necessity demands that in a given situation a just God will act in a certain way. And in the same situation a moral necessity restrains a God committed to a different course from acting in that certain way. The consequences of God's moral nature are at variance with his purpose. And thus the stage is set for conflict, tension, indecision, frustration and hurt (p. 40).

A similar parallel between Jonah and Jer. 45 is drawn in Thoma, 'Enstehung', p. 487.

202. Levine, 'Jonah', pp. 243-44. Among those who argue that the book contains or can support more than one thesis are J. Licht, *Storytelling in the Bible* (Jerusalem: Magnes, 1978), pp. 121-22; Abramson, 'Jonah', p. 45 and Sasson, *Jonah*, p. xi.

203. So also A. Cooper, 'In Praise of Divine Caprice: The Significance of the Book of Jonah', in P.R. Davies and D.J.A. Clines (eds.), *Among the Prophets: Language, Image and Structure in the Prophetic Writings* (JSOTSup, 144; Sheffield: JSOT Press, 1993), pp. 144-63.

204. Among these may be numbered the psychological readings of H.H. Fingert, 'Psychoanalytic Study of the Minor Prophet, Jonah', *Psychoanalytic Review* 16 (1954), pp. 55-65; J. More, 'The Prophet Jonah: The Story of an Intrapsychic Process', *American Imago* 27 (1970), pp. 3-11; C. Lewis, 'Jonah: A Parable for Our Time', *Judaism* 21 (1972), pp. 159-63; U. Steffen, *Jona und der Fisch: Der Mythos von Tod und der Wiedergeburt* (Berlin: Kreuz, 1982); J.L. Bull, 'Rethinking Jonah: The Dynamics of Surrender', *Parabola* 15 (1990), pp. 79-84; Couffignal, 'Le Psaume', pp. 549-52. Zimmerman's typological analysis ('Problems', pp. 582-83) holds that the historical Jonah was part of a Syro-Hellenistic orgiastic cult as a youth and that the story of Jonah represents his being born again into a proselyte stage wherein his sins are forgiven. Karl Henrich's philosophical analysis of Jonah compares it with the ontology of Parmenides and modern Cynicism (*Parmenides und Jona: Vier Studien über das Verhältnis von Philosophie und Mythologie* [Frankfurt: Suhkramp, 1966]). F. Weinreb offers a numerological

neither seeks nor pretends to replace any other overviews, but attempts to complement them.[205] It serves as an introduction to the issues and debates surrounding the book of Jonah; aids in clearing the field of cumbersome or unhelpful assumptions and conclusions; and provides sound methodological guidelines from which the following exegesis proceeds. Consequently, this first chapter ends with a methodological preamble.

Questions of the genre of Jonah will not be examined. As stated above, lack of adequate historical data has given rise to designations which in the end have clouded rather than clarified the meaning and purpose of the book. Instead, an attempt will be made to ascertain the function of Jonah, and to compare it with biblical traditions which work in a similar manner.

A similar lack of historical controls exists for the dating of Jonah. Linguistic, ideological and reconstructive criteria have not proven able to give conclusive support to any date yet proposed. Apart from a fluid and tenuous *terminus ante quem*, a relative date will be assigned to the book on the basis of its use of recognizable pre-existing portions of the biblical tradition.

The recovery of authorial intent, here equated with meaning, is a primary goal, and functions as a methodological control on any conclusions. Labels such as 'genius', 'masterpiece' and 'art' are not founded upon any consensus of method with which to determine their presence or absence, and hence are rendered useless in interpretation. The only assumptions made about the author at this point are a reading and writing knowledge of Hebrew and a familiarity with

---

reading (*Das Buch Jonah: Der Sinn des Buches Jonah nach der ältesten jüdischen Überlieferung* [Zürich: Origo, 1970]); and Attila Fáj attempts to define the book as a Stoic tract ('The Stoic Features of the Book of Jonah', *Instituto Orientale di Napoli, Annali* 34 [1974], pp. 309-45). Fáj sees in the book's universalism a Stoic cosmopolitanism, and in Jonah's submarine journey and return from the depths a symbol of the descending–ascending σπερματίκος λόγος (the seminal logos).

205. Several good reviews of literature are: Wright's Introduction in his volume containing the allegorical reading of Jonah (*Biblical Essays* [Edinburgh: T. & T. Clark, 1886], pp. viii-xxviii); W.W. Davies, 'Is the Book of Jonah Historical?' *Methodist Review* 70 (1888), pp. 827-44 (828-29); J. Döller, *Das Buch Jona* (Vienna: Fromme, 1912), pp. 1-58; Bewer, *Jonah*, pp. 3-27; Burrows, 'Literary Category', pp. 80-105 and Sasson's section entitled, 'Interpretations' (*Jonah*, pp. 323-51).

many elements of the biblical tradition. These will be focused and supplemented as the exegesis progresses.

The two approaches discussed above which understand Jonah solely in terms of the issues of prophecy or the divine nature do not take into account the presence of both these issues in the book. One element is sacrificed for the sake of the other. It is advisable to cast the net wider than heretofore and deal with a matrix that will encompass prophecy, the divine nature and other issues. Thus Jonah will be examined in light of its use and evaluation of elements of Israelite religion in general. This approach will by necessity deal with issues of the distinction between Jew and Gentile, the fate of the good and the wicked, the role and function of prophecy, and the concepts of justice, punishment, repentance, sacrifice, praise, prayer and divine freedom.

Traditional source-critical analysis, based as it is on outmoded criteria of logical coherence and an adherence to limited vocabularies for each hypothetical author, proves itself inadequate for Jonah. Consequently, given the inability to determine any source for Jonah, standard redaction-critical methods are not utilized. Rather investigation of exactly which (if any) portions of the biblical text are being referenced, by citation or allusion, is the key to unlocking the meaning of Jonah.[206] These references will not be an array of phrases and half-verses ranging hither and yon among the biblical corpus, but larger units taken up and used as such in the writing of Jonah. More important is the identification of biblical and extra-biblical motifs and literary traditions utilized in the text. It is in the determination of how these larger units, motifs and traditions inform and comprise the book that the purpose of the author will be discerned. To this end, three of the traditional historical-critical methods are used in the following exegesis: 1) Textual and philological/linguistic analysis in order to establish a text and its semantic range; 2) Form-critical methods which delineate and analyze attested literary units used by the author of Jonah in the writing of the book; 3) Tradition history, in an attempt to determine Jonah's use of biblical traditions, and the place of such usage in the context of a tradition's meaning throughout the Old Testament.

---

206. This type of source-critical work has been done on Jonah most fully by Feuillet, 'Les Sources', and Magonet, *Form and Meaning*, pp. 70-73, both of whose work will be drawn on below.

Jonah is a remarkably well-preserved text. Of the seven scrolls of the minor prophets found in Qumran cave 4, two (4QXII[a,f] dated c. 150–125 BCE and 50 BCE, respectively) preserve fragments of Jonah.[207] A Hebrew copy from Wadi Murabba'at (Mur 88),[208] dating to the early second century CE and a Greek text from Nahal Hever (8 Hev XIIgr) [209] from the late-first century BCE demonstrate the text's remarkable stability. Thorough textual and philological work has been done, upon which is founded a solid basis for exegesis.[210] Although the critical edition of *BHS* is used, many particular textual and trans-lational points are dealt with as part of the task of clarifying the author's purpose.

In sum, the book of Jonah is not history; nor, it appears, is it satire, tragedy or any other known genre. It defies dating, comes from no clearly known historical context, is not written for or against any known group or party. It is not a literary code waiting to be cracked, nor a world beckoning to be entered, nor an object of art to be gazed upon whose magic is to work its subversive power on unsuspecting yet appreciative minds.[211] The book is about prophecy, but it is also about

207. R.E. Fuller, 'The Minor Prophets Manuscripts from Qumran, Cave IV' (Ph.D. diss., Harvard University; Ann Arbor, MI: University Microfilms, 1988), pp. 5-38, 141-50. This book is the first major analysis of Jonah to incorporate readings from these fragments.

208. P. Benoit, J.T. Milik and R. DeVaux (eds.), *Les Grottes de Murabba'at* (DJD, 2; Oxford: Clarendon Press, 1961),.pp. 181-85.

209. E. Tov, *The Greek Minor Prophets Scroll from Nahal Hever* (DJD, 8; Oxford: Clarendon Press, 1990)

210. W. Wright, *The Book of Jonah in Four Oriental Versions, Namely Chaldee, Syriac, Aethiopic, Arabic with Glossaries* (London: Williams & Norgate, 1857); N.H. Snaith, *Notes on the Hebrew Text of Jonah* (London: Epworth, 1945); Levine, *Aramaic Version of Jonah*; work on the Greek text in L. Perkins, 'The Septuagint of Jonah: Aspects of Literary Analysis Applied to Biblical Translation', *BIOSCS* 20 (1987), pp. 43-53 and Almbladh, *Studies*. Trible, 'Studies', pp. 1-65, has by far the most thorough textual analysis utilizing all the versions. Sasson's commentary does an equally wide-ranging philological analysis. Craig, *Poetics*, pp. 19-44, examines more recent English translations.

211. The following observation concerning the interpretation of Homeric texts may be validly applied to biblical exegesis: 'The alien and incomprehensible con-fronts us with our own limited horizons. The result is not some magical, hal-lucinogenic fruit that "fuses" our world with Homer's (H.-G. Gadamer) or that tempts us to "enter" the "world of the text" (Paul Ricoeur)' (G.D. Alles, 'Wrath and Persuasion: The Iliad and its Contexts', *JR* 70 [1990], pp. 167-88 [187]).

the nature of God and repentance. It is the work of a single hand, yet it draws upon that author's literary traditions. The book is a text from the literary strata of ancient Israelite religion, and as such has a point to make and a story to tell about various aspects of that religion, its adherents and their God. To discover these points in this story is the goal of this investigation.

Chapter 2

FLIGHT AND CAPTURE (JONAH 1.1-16)

First count Jonas the friend of God... but yet a young scholar, weak and rude... Nevertheless the God of all mercy... provided for Jonas how all things should be.

—William Tyndale[1]

The heaving sea oft warns of coming storms, when suddenly its depths begin to swell.

—Cicero, *De div.* 1.13[2]

Of simple plots and actions the episodic are the worst.

—Aristotle, *Poetics* 1451b

Aristotle's remark serves as an entrance into exegesis of Jonah, since the book is widely acknowledged to consist of scenes or episodes which correspond to its four chapters (and to which respective chapters of this work will be devoted). In dealing with the first 'episode', Jon. 1.1-16, a few remarks concerning the structure of the entire book are required. Beyond this episodic scheme scholars have produced many diagrams of varying complexity, all of which reveal a subtle, contrived structure in the book. Such analyses began as isolated studies of ch. 1. In 1961 Norbert Lohfink, discussing the original position of Jon. 4.5, attempted to demonstrate that 1.4-16 exhibits a concentric structure whose center is Jonah's 'confession of faith' and the sailors fearful reaction in vv. 9-10a.[3] Lohfink is followed by Rudolf Pesch who, while also centering his chiasm on vv. 9-10a, focuses more on the sailors' expression of fear and its repetition and development in the chapter:

1. From Tyndale's prologue to his translation of Jonah in Daniell (ed.), *Tyndale's Pentateuch,* p. 631.
2. From Cicero's translation of the *Diosemeia* of Aratus, quoted in regard to the value of portents for predicting sea storms.
3. N. Lohfink, 'Jona ging zur Stadt hinaus (Jon. 4,5)', *BZ* 5 (1961), pp. 185-203 (201-202).

the sailors were afraid (1.5)
the sailors were very afraid (1.10)
the sailors were very afraid of Yahweh (1.16).

The first and third statements form the ends of the concentric structure, v. 10 being its center.[4] Peter Weimar attempts a synthesis of the
older source-critical approaches to Jonah, typified in the studies of
Wilhelm Böhme and Hans Schmidt, with the newer literary approaches.
Weimar argues for two centers in the chapter whose presence belies
proof of a redaction of two sources.[5] Many other similar chiastic
patterns have been formulated in the years since Lohfink's article.[6]

In addition to scrutiny of Jonah 1, scholars have long argued for a
larger parallel structure in the two halves of the book. Phyllis Trible
diagrams an elaborate symmetrical structure made up of smaller
chiasms.[7] Much like the flurry of activity following Lohfink's analysis
of Jonah 1, large symmetrical schemata of the entire book can be
found in many commentaries and articles.[8] Duane Christensen's

4.   'Zur konzentrischen Struktur von Jona 1', *Bib* 47 (1966), pp. 577-81
(578). Others, in addition to Pesch, who draw attention to the developing expression
of the sailors' fear are: Magonet (*Form and Meaning,* pp. 32-33) and Good (*Irony,*
p. 46). Pesch's structure has been criticized by Leslie Allen, who observes that the
chiasm requires 1.11b to be read as dialogue (*Jonah,* p. 197).

5.   P. Weimar, 'Literarische Kritik und Literakritik: Unzeitgemässe
Beobachtungen zu Jon. 1,4–16', in L. Ruppert (ed.), *Künder des Wortes: Beitrages
zur Theologie der Propheten* (Würzburg: Echter Verlag, 1982), pp. 271-35 (222, 235).

6.   To mention but a few: Fretheim, *Message,* pp. 73-74; Witzenrath, *Jona,*
pp. 24, 26; Magonet, *Form and Meaning,* pp. 56-58; Alexander, *Jonah,* pp. 106-
107; Nogalski, *Redactional Processes,* pp. 250-51. Recently Raymond de Hoop has
extended the concentric structure to include 1.1-3 on the basis of verbal repetition and
the repetition/expansion of the sailors' fear, all of which de Hoop sees as standard
Semitic poetic technique (R. de Hoope, 'The Book of Jonah as Poetry: An Analysis
of Jonah 1.1-16', in W. van der Meer and J. de Moor [eds.], *The Structural Analysis
of Hebrew and Canaanite Poetry* [JSOTSup, 74; Sheffield: JSOT Press, 1988], pp.
156-71 [158-59, 160-67]).

7.   'Studies', pp. 185-92, 197. The design Trible sets forth in her dissertation
remains unchanged in her book, written thirty years later (*Rhetorical Criticism,*
pp. 110-11).

8.   Again, as a representative sample: Allen, *Jonah,* p. 100; Witzenrath, *Jona,*
p. 45; B. Halpern and R.E. Friedman, 'Composition and Paronomasia in the Book
of Jonah', HAR 4 (1980) pp. 79-92 (88); Weimar, 'Jon. 4.5', pp. 86-109 (105);
Magonet, *Form and Meaning,* pp. 60-62; Elata-Alster and Salmon, 'Eastward and
Westward, pp. 16-27 (22); J.H. Potgeiter, 'Jonah: A Semio-Structuralist Reading of

elaborate analysis is representative of this approach and its results:

> The concentric structure of any one of the four chapters of Jonah is similar
> to the structure of each half of the book, which in turn is but a smaller
> version of the structure of the whole.[9]

Like many of the conclusions in the field, these results become less
plausible as they become more detailed, and agreement on elements
other than the larger relationship of the chapters is not widespread.
Subjectivity abounds. Thus, Trible's analysis has no place for the final
reference to the animals in 4.11. She solves this problem by appealing
to the specious concept of 'symmetrophobia' of 'the Oriental men-
tality'. With this concept as a *deus ex machina* the evidence against her
structure conveniently becomes supporting proof.[10] Raymond de
Hoope's 'neat "onion" structure' of Jonah 1 is based upon mutually
exclusive relationships such as the corresponding occurrences of the
term קום in vv. 2 and 6 alongside its appearance in v. 3 in *contrast*
with שכב in v. 5.[11] Timothy Wilt's efforts to prove the dependence of
Jonah 1 on Josh. 10.1-27 require his speaking of an 'attack' and 'battle
scene' in the storm of Jonah.[12] The storm only lends itself to this
description when one tries to demonstrate its dependence on a text
which speaks of a battle; an *a priori* interpretative move determines
how the relationships within a single text or between texts will be read
or created. Jack Sasson's remark that attempts to find symmetry

a Narrative', *Old Testament Essays* 3 (1990), pp. 61-69 (64); B. Peckham, *History
and Prophecy: The Development of Late Judean Literary Traditions* (ABRL; Garden
City, NY: Doubleday, 1993), pp. 691-94.

9.   'Andrzej Panufnik', pp. 133-40 (140). Elsewhere Christensen puts
forward another symmetrical analysis and argues that Jonah is entirely a metric composition ('Narrative Poetics and the Interpretation of the Book of Jonah', in E. Follis
[ed.], *Directions in Biblical Hebrew Poetry* [JSOTSup, 40; Sheffield: JSOT Press,
1987], pp. 29-48 [30, 33-40]). De Hoope argues similarly ('Jonah as Poetry',
pp. 158-59).

10.   Trible, 'Studies', pp. 199-200, 234; *idem, Rhetorical Criticism,* pp. 117-20.

11.   'Jonah as Poetry', p. 167. Peckham's characterizations of the twelve pairs
of sections he delineates in Jonah are equally subjective: 'silly or humorous... not so
amusing... clever... witty and a little pathetic... serious and ludicrous... not particularly comical... sort of silly... queer... clever... ridiculous' (*History and Prophecy*,
pp. 694-96).

12.   T.L. Wilt, 'Jonah: A Battle of Shifting Alliances', in P.R. Davies and
D.J.A. Clines (eds.), *Among the Prophets,* pp. 164-82 (166-70, 172-75).

between Jonah 2 and 4 are 'farfetched and much too dependent on a highly accommodating analytic language', is equally valid concerning the use of this kind of exegesis in the remainder of Jonah.[13]

In light of the shortcomings of schematic analyses, I do not attempt to derive any exegetical conclusions about Jonah from patterns or designs discovered in its structure. The remainder of this chapter is divided into three sections. The first examines the author's choice of Jonah, the son of Amittai, as the main character of the book. The second analyzes specific exegetical features in Jon. 1.1-16. The final section offers a survey of ancient biblical and extra-biblical sea storm narratives.

Jonah the Son of Amittai

Etymological Significance of the Name 'Jonah'
As mentioned in the previous chapter the Hebrew יונה is also the common noun 'dove', which appears throughout the Old Testament.[14] Personal names derived from fauna are common in Semitic languages, but they are almost exclusively women's names.[15] Most commentaries draw a special significance between the meaning 'dove' and the figure/portrayal of Jonah, particularly in likening his flight and disobedience to the foolishness and cowardice of doves.[16] Hosea 7.11 is often adduced to support the assumption that a dove is a common symbol for Israel, and hence that Jonah=dove=Israel yields derivatively the equation of Jonah and Israel.[17] But this interpretation does

13. *Jonah*, p. 204. Trible's dictum that such schematic analyses should deal only with the *ipsissima verba* of a text, while appearing methodologically sound in theory, yields results which are no less subjective than other attempts.

14. For example concerning temple offerings, or the erotic imagery of Song of Songs.

15. Martin Noth lists several (*Die Israelitischen Personennamen im Rahmen der gemeinsemitischen Namegebung* [BWANT, 3.10; Stuttgart: Kohlhammer, 1928], p. 230). Although as a common noun יונה is feminine, as a proper name it applies to a man. The feminine form of the proper name, ימימה, occurs in Job 42.14.

16. For example, Almbladh, *Studies*, p. 17. Among those who see no significance in the name's meaning is Stuart, *Hosea–Jonah*, p. 431. Jonah's patronymic (בן אמתי) is also seen as significant, being translated as 'son of truth'. Such musings on the relation of the personal name 'Amittai' to the noun 'truth', occur as early as the rabbinic period and are discussed above in Chapter 1.

17. Paul Kahn takes a more circuitous route by citing Lev. 12.8, which allows the substitution of a dove for a lamb. Kahn pairs this concession with rabbinic

not bear scrutiny. The text from Hosea refers only to Ephraim, and at most can be applied to the northern kingdom; apart from this instance, it is not clearly established that a dove was ever widely regarded as a symbol of Israel; finally, the negative connotations applied to doves in this reading are not universally recognized.[18]

The Zohar reads the name as a participle from the root ינה ('to oppress') and, in the context of an allegorical reading of the book, asks:

> Why is she [the soul] called Jonah (aggrieved)? Because as soon as she becomes partner with the body in this world she finds herself full of vexation.[19]

That this interpretation is older than the Zohar is made clear by Jerome's remark that both etymologies of Jonah (i.e., 'dove' and 'the one who suffers') are types of Christ.[20] This latter understanding appears to ignore the fact that the name יונה is the active singular masculine participle of the verb ינה; translating the name as 'he who is aggrieved' requires the passive participial form, ינוי.[21] While possible, Semitic names derived from participial forms are infrequently attested.[22] It is unlikely that the proper name in this instance bears any special etymological significance.[23]

Jonah and 2 Kings 14.25-27

The only other clear reference to Jonah in the Old Testament is in 2 Kgs 14.25:

tradition's equation of the lamb with Israel on the basis of Genesis 22 (*'Jonah'*, pp. 87-100 [89]).

18.   For example the dove is also a symbol of peace or, among Christians, the symbol of the Holy Spirit.

19.   Text in Limburg, *Jonah*, p. 108.

20.   Duval (ed.), *Jerome: Commentaire*, p. 171.

21.   This was pointed out by Johann Carpzov (d. 1767, cited in J. Döller, *Das Buch Jona*, p. 59). E.G.H. Kraeling also notes the active sense of the name in his hypothesis that 'Jonah' is really an apocopated form of יונהיה, 'Yahweh oppresses' ('Evolution', p. 305 n.1).

22.   Noth remarks that such names are 'entirely rare and late' and gives only those derived from participles with the preformative מ (*Die Israelitischen Personennamen*, p. 31).

23.   Mention may be made of John Allegro's attempt to trace the etymology of the name to Sumerian words for fecundity and thereby link it with a universal religious cult centered on vegetation myths (*The Sacred Mushroom and the Cross* [Garden City, NY: Doubleday, 1970] p. 39 n.13).

He [Jeroboam II] restored the border of Israel from the entrance of Hamath as far as the sea of Arabah, according to the word of the LORD, the God of Israel which he spoke by his servant, Jonah the son of Amittai, the prophet who was from Gath Hepher.

The question of the relationship between this text and the book of Jonah has given rise to many explanations. As mentioned in the last chapter, many commentators have understood the reference to Jonah in 2 Kings to be portraying him as a nationalistic prophet. This characterization allows the book of Jonah to be read as an indictment of ethnocentrism. However, Jonah is not an ardent nationalist in either text. Others have seen in the notice of 2 Kings the anchor text for which the book of Jonah is a midrash. Hugo Winckler outlines an elaborate process in which Jonah is written as a midrash on a lost source used to compile the extant 1 and 2 Kings.[24] Otto Eissfeldt claims no relationship between the texts whatsoever, but rather sees in the notice of 2 Kings a prophecy of well-being which is later critiqued by Amos.[25] Some judge that the link between the two texts lies in the verses immediately following mention of Jonah:

For the LORD saw that the affliction of Israel was very bitter, for there was none left, bond or free, and there was none to help Israel. But the LORD had not said that he would blot out the name of Israel from under heaven, so he saved them by the hand of Jeroboam, the son of Joash (2 Kgs 14.26-27).

Thus God's mercy to Israel, even when deserving of punishment (in v. 24 Jeroboam 'did what was evil in the sight of the Lord') is the connecting link and background to the story of God's merciful pardon of the Ninevites, who are equally worthy of punishment.[26]

---

24. 'Zum Buch Jona', pp. 260-65 (260-62).

25. 'Amos und Jona', pp. 11-12. Eissfeldt bases his argument on Amos 6.14 'they will oppress you from the entrance of Hamath to the brook of the Arabah', and sees in the coincidence of geographic terms the response of Amos to the prophecy of territorial expansion of Jonah. The book of Jonah is a later didactic work which has nothing to do with 2 Kings: 'That...the paltry statement of 2 Kings concerning Jonah ben Amittai develops into our book of Jonah is entirely impossible' (p. 12).

26. This is the reasoning of *b. Yeb.* 98b; so also Budde, 'Jonah', p. 229; Clements, 'Purpose', pp. 16-28 (23-24); Fretheim, *Message*, p. 42; and Sasson, *Jonah*, p. 344. If this were in fact the motivation, then it appears the author had little other choice, since Jonah is 'the only prophet highlighted in the Deuteronomistic

While it is difficult to establish any links beyond the common name and patronymic, or on the basis of this alone even to prove a direction of dependence,[27] the following observations show that the author of the book of Jonah utilized the name of the prophet in 2 Kings as the main character of his story.

Written prophecy in ancient Israel was an antiquarian practice from its inception, and the writing of tales and their attribution to otherwise little known figures is both easily explained and demonstrable.[28] Jonah and Ezekiel are the only prophetic books to begin with the apocopated *waw*-consecutive imperfect of היה,[29] but several narrative books in the Old Testament also utilize this introduction in a stative sense with an implied subject.[30] In this fashion, the verb functions as a narrative introduction, much like the English phrases: 'Once there was' or 'and so it happened that'. Those who have thought Jonah to be a midrash, or posited its detachment from an earlier lost source by appeal to the abrupt nature of the introduction, overlook this well-attested usage.

Similarly the phrase, ויהי דבר יהוה אל + personal name/personal pronoun, while not part of the introductions to prophetic books other than Jonah, is found throughout the Old Testament of persons who have previously been mentioned in the text.[31] This datum leads Sasson

history for having announced good news to a bad king' (Peckham, *History and Prophecy*, p. 697).

27.   Brictho judges that the notice of 2 Kings was written after the book of Jonah and added to the text of 2 Kings to give context to the story of Jonah (*Grammar*, p. 87).

28.   On this antiquarian aim see J.L. Crenshaw, *Prophetic Conflict: Its Effect upon Israelite Religion* (BZAW, 124; Berlin: de Gruyter, 1971), pp. 91-109; and J. Barton, *Oracles of God* (New York: Oxford University Press, 1988). Good uses the literary activity centered around the shadowy figure of Enoch as an analogy for arguing that the book of Jonah is derived from the reference in 2 Kings (*Irony*, pp. 41-42).

29.   The opening of Ezekiel uses ויהי as a temporal marker. The LXX of Jer. 1.1 reads τὸ ῥῆμα τοῦ θεοῦ ὃ ἐγένετο ἐπὶ Ιερεμίαν. This is not the equivalent of the MT's דברי ירמיהו, but could plausibly be translating a Hebrew *Vorlage* which begins with ויהי. Even if one deletes the superscriptions in the biblical books, only Jer. 1.3 and Neh 1.1b begin the narrative with ויהי.

30.   Josh. 1.1, Judg 1.1, 1 Sam. 1.1, 2 Sam. 1.1, Ruth 1.1, Est. 1.1. Cf. P. Joüon, *A Grammar of Biblical Hebrew* (2 vols.; repr.; Subsidia Biblica, 14; Rome: Pontifical Biblical Institute, 1990), p. 111 § i.

31.   For example Samuel (1 Sam. 15.10); Nathan (2 Sam. 7.4); Solomon (1 Kgs 6.11); the prophet of Bethel (1 Kgs 13.20); Elijah (1 Kgs 17.2; 21.17); Isaiah

to conclude that 'whatever sources were available...what we now have
of the book are episodes plucked from many Jonah adventures that
apparently circulated in ancient Israel'.[32] Rather than drawing conclusions from hypothetical sources it is methodologically more sound
to say that, since the book of Jonah begins in a manner which presupposes knowledge of the figure of Jonah and, since that figure is
previously introduced in 2 Kings, the figure of Jonah in the book
which bears his name is based on the prophet Jonah from the notice in
2 Kings 14.[33] This argument, drawing on the evidence of the introductory formula and the thematic link provided by the theme of
divine mercy in both 2 Kings 14 and Jonah, is supplemented below in
Chapter 5 by demonstration of a reference made to 2 Kings in Jon. 4.2.

Jonah 1.1-16

Jonah's Call and Flight (1.1-3)
Jonah's commission from God follows a standard form-critical call
narrative pattern, except that the element of protest is exaggerated to
flight. This exaggeration does not function as a means to elicit humor
or shock on the part of the hearers, but rather to set the context for
the following sea storm.[34] While the content of the divine message for
Nineveh is not given here, the preposition על with קרא often is used

(Isa. 38.4) Jeremiah (Jer. 1.4; 2.1; 13.3; 16.1; 18.5; 24.4; 36.27; 37.6; 42.7; 43.8);
Ezekiel (Ezek. 3.16; 6.1; 7.1; 12.1; 13.1; 14.2; 15.1; 16.1; 17.1; 18.1; 20.2; 21.1;
22.1; 23.1; 25.1; 27.1; 28.1; 30.1; 33.1; 34.1; 35.1; 38.1); Zechariah (Zech. 4.8;
6.9; 7.8); and Shemaiah (2 Chron. 11.2). The only figure in the Old Testament of
whom this phrase is used in his first appearance is Jehu (1 Kgs 16.1). The fact that
the phrase is used repeatedly to introduce new episodes in Jeremiah and Ezekiel
merits emphasis due to the similarity to Jon. 1.1. In addition to this verbal contact
between Jonah and the Elijah cycles, Witzenrath notes that Jon. 1.3 and 1 Kgs 17.10
both have imperatives followed by active verbs derived from the same root (*Jona*,
pp. 77-79).

32.   *Jonah*, p. 85.
33.   So also Budde, 'Jonah', p. 229.
34.   Although Hans Walter Wolff emphasizes that 'the reader...knows from the
stories passed down about the prophets that the reaction to Yahweh's "Arise and go!"
is simply "And he arose and went"' (*Obadiah and Jonah*, p. 100). Others who see a
modified call-narrative pattern are I. Nowell, *Jonah, Tobit, Judith* (Collegeville Bible
Commentaries, 25; Collegeville, MN: Liturgical Press, 1986) p. 9; Potgieter, 'Jonah',
p. 67; and Kenneth Craig, for whom the protest element is both Jonah's flight and
his delayed complaint in 4.2 ('Poetics', pp. 77-78; *idem, Poetics,* pp. 79-81).

to denote denunciation.[35] Rather than comply, Jonah attempts to flee to Tarshish. The exact location of this place has never been determined. The majority of commentators favor Tartessos on the Iberian coast, although an inscription found at Nora on Sardinia mentioning Tarshish has led to searches further east in the Mediterranean.[36] That uncertainty concerning the location of Tarshish is not a modern phenomenon is made clear by *Tg. Ps.-J.*, which simply deleted the name and replaced it with 'the sea'.[37] It is uncertain that even the author of Jonah knew where Tarshish was; it is only apparent that it is a place chosen by Jonah because it is far away from Yahweh.[38] Given use of the appellative, 'ship of Tarshish', in the Old Testament with any long-range sea vessel the author is no doubt trying to emphasize the length to which Jonah goes to evade the divine commission.[39]

35.   Sasson, *Jonah*, p. 75. Stuart downplays the divine anger by translating the phrase, כי עלתה רעתם לפני, as 'their trouble is of concern to me'. This allows Stuart to see God's compassion at work from the beginning (*Hosea–Jonah*, p. 449). Martin Luther captures the spirit of the majority opinion: 'In short, God is very angry' (Oswald [ed.], *Minor Prophets*, p. 45).

36.   William F. Albright argues for a site on Sardinia ('New Light on the Early History of Phoenician Colonization', *BASOR* 83 [1941], pp. 17-22). If Tartessos can be shown to be the biblical Tarshish, then the casual remark of Herodotus that Tartessos 'was at that time [i.e., the fifth century] quite unspoilt' (4.152) could provide a *terminus post quem* dating for biblical texts mentioning Tarshish. Gösta Ahlström argues on the basis of the Nora inscription that Tarshish lay somewhere in the eastern Mediterranean ('The Nora Inscription and Tarshish', *Maarar* 7 [1991], pp. 41-49). G. Hüsing holds for a site on the Persian Gulf ('Tarshish und die Jona-Legende', *Memnon* 1 [1907], pp. 70-79).

37.   So also Luther (*Lectures*, XIX, p. 9).

38.   So for Witzenrath, Tarshish 'functions as a code for a place which is removed from Yahweh' (*Jona*, p. 67). Some commentators, drawing on rabbinic tradition, attribute Jonah's flight to the notion that divine messages could only be conveyed to prophets within the borders of Israel. That this concept is not at work in Jonah is made clear by the fact that Joppa would have sufficed for Jonah as a haven outside of Israel. Also, Jonah and God would not have been able to converse outside Nineveh. Discussion and critique in Stuart, *Hosea–Jonah*, pp. 450-51; and Goitien, 'Some Observations', pp. 63-77 (67). Sasson makes the following remark: 'Although it was certainly not an invented place (as are Eldorado or Shangrila), Tarshish seems always to lie just beyond the geographic knowledge of those who try to pinpoint its location' (*Jonah*, p. 79).

39.   *b. Ned.* 38a, elaborating on Jonah's efforts to escape, interprets the phrase 'he paid her fare' in 1.3 as indication that Jonah hired out the entire ship for which he

The felicitous choice of Joppa as Jonah's point of embarkation has been rich fodder for commentators since that city has been the location of the Perseus–Andromeda legend from at least the fourth century BCE.[40] In this story Andromeda, offered to a sea-monster, is chained to a rock overlooking the sea to await her fate. Perseus arrives, does battle with the creature (during which he enters inside of it) and prevails. Pliny and Josephus both relate that the marks of Andromeda's chains are still visible on the rocks. Pliny mentions the cult of the goddess Ceto (a clear borrowing from the Greek κῆτος, the LXX term for Jonah's fish) and recounts that the 40 foot long skeleton of Andromeda's sea-monster was brought to Rome.[41] Strabo also makes reference to the Andromeda legend, in addition to noting that Joppa is the seaport of Judea.[42] Given the superficial thematic contact between the story of Jonah and the Andromeda myth, in addition to Joppa's importance as a Palestinian port, not much should be made of this comparison. In the case of Jonah, the extensive folklore analysis of scholars wishing to prove the contact between such stories, or their dependence upon each other, is its own undoing. The widespread occurrence of similar motifs suggests their independent origin.

Thus in the opening verses the author has begun a story about a prophet which begins with the expected commission-pattern but in which the protest element of the pattern has been elevated to flight. The choice of Tarshish and Joppa as Jonah's point of destination and departure shows how determined Jonah was to flee his divine calling and the means by which he set out to accomplish his intention.

The Storm on the Sea (1.4-16)
Jonah 1.4 begins with an inversion of the normal Hebrew word order:

was the only passenger. Sasson construes לבוא עמהם to mean that Jonah hired himself on and became one of the crew (*Jonah*, pp. 83-84).

40.   John Day cites Pseudo-Scylax as the first to make Joppa the site for the story ('Problems', pp. 32-47 [33]). Hüsing, who places Tarshish in the Persian Gulf and thus is obliged to explain the presence of Joppa in Jon. 1.3, emends the verse by combining וירד יפו to form the *hiphil* of רדפ ('to pursue'). This gives the reading: והרדיפהו and the resulting translation: 'But Jonah arose to flee to Tarshish from the face of Yahweh and he [Yahweh] pursued him' ('Tarshish', p. 72). Given Hüsing's restoration, one must conjecture that the two occurrences of ה have been lost and a ʾ added to yield the present reading from his hypothetical original.

41.   Josephus, *War* 3.420; Pliny, *Natural History* 5.69; 9.11.

42.   Strabo, *Geography* 16.2.28

ויהוה הטיל רוח גדולה אל הים, which, in placing of subject before verb gives special emphasis to the actor.[43] Thus it is emphasized that the storm comes from Yahweh, a fact that will be further developed as it becomes clear that, in spite of the best efforts of the sailors, only appeasement of this particular god can save their lives. Verse 4 ends with the remark that the ship חשבה להשבר. This has been rendered in various ways:

> The ship risked being crushed (LXX).[44]
> The ship sought to break up (*Tg. Ps.-J.*).[45]
> The ship was in danger of breaking up (Vg).[46]
> The schip was in perel for to be al to-brokun (Wycliffe).
> The ship was like to go in pieces (Tyndale).
> The ship was like to be broken (KJV).
> The ship threatened to break up (RSV, JB).
> The ship was on the point of breaking up (NAB).

Sasson captures the sense of חשב in his 'The ship *expected itself* to crack up'.[47] The use of a verb normally reserved for sentient beings (the verb denotes sentience) has been viewed as problematic in its application to an inanimate object. David Noel Freedman, using the presence of ἐκινδύνευε in the LXX, speculates that the original Hebrew *Vorlage* had some form of the verb חוב (probably חבה), which was then corrupted. Freedman's restoration reads: 'And the ship *was in jeopardy* of breaking up'.[48] That personification, so much a common literary feature in many (if not all) languages, should be denied to Hebrew is puzzling. There are other examples of personification in the Old Testament. Most fitting for this context is Isa. 23.1, where Tarshish ships are commanded to wail. Personification of a ship is also found in the early Middle Kingdom Egyptian 'Tale of the Shipwrecked Sailor'. The sailor's ship, caught in a storm, is said to

---

43.   So Sasson, who also notes the occurrence of this syntactical construction in 3.3, 4.11 and the poetic and legal sections of chs. 2 and 3.4, 7 (*Jonah*, p. 93).

44.   καὶ τὸ πλοῖον ἐκινδύνευε συντριβῆναι.

45.   ואלפא בעיא לאיתברא.

46.   Et navis periclitabatur conteri.

47.   *Jonah*, pp. 96-97.

48.   D.N. Freedman, 'Jonah 1.4b', *JBL* 77 (1958), pp. 161-62. B.F. Price and E.A. Nida also argue against seeing any element of personification in this remark about the ship (*A Translator's Handbook on the Book of Jonah* [New York: United Bible Societies, 1978] p. 11).

have 'died'.[49] John Calvin remarks specifically on this phenomenon in his commentary on Jonah: 'the expression corresponds with the idiom of our language, *la navire cuidoit perir*'.[50] The choice of this particular verb also allows the author a play on sounds with the following infinitive, להשבר.

The sailors respond to the storm in three ways: 1) they are afraid; 2) they cry out to their gods; 3) they cast implements from the ship into the sea. Throwing articles overboard in order to lighten the ship was a common practice in storms. Herodotus reports that Xerxes I, caught in a storm off Greece and told by the helmsman that lightening the ship was the only way to save it, ordered a number of the passengers cast overboard until the ship should be light enough to weather the storm.[51] The early second-century CE romance of Achilles Tatius, *Leucippe and Clitophon,* recounts a sea storm and vividly describes how the passengers transfer their baggage numerous times to the side of the ship which lists least until finally, when the storm does not abate, the helmsman orders the cargo jettisoned (3.1). Concerning the sailors in Jonah, the motivation for their utilization of this practice has been seen as piety. Trible notes that the infinitive, להקל has no object, and that the last noun in v. 5 is 'sea'. From this she determines that the sailors are attempting to 'lighten' (i.e., to appease) the sea by using their cargo as an offering. Sasson argues for the same meaning on the grounds that the verb טול with the preposition אל signifies the motivation behind the casting rather than direction. Thus the sailors throw their things towards/at/for the sea, in order to appease it.[52] While the distinction between the two purposes for jettisoning cargo (for practical or religious reasons) may be artificial, the arguments of

49.   W.K. Simpson (ed.), *The Literature of Ancient Egypt* (New Haven, CT: Yale University Press, 1972), p. 52. These examples are also adduced in Sasson, *Jonah*, p. 96.

50.   J. Calvin, *Commentaries on the Twelve Minor Prophets* (Grand Rapids: Eerdmans, 1847), III, p. 32.

51.   Herodotus, *Xerxes* 8.118-19. Herodotus also includes a variant of this account in which the men thrown overboard are Persians, but he goes on to say himself that Xerxes would most likely have chosen the Phoenician rowers.

52.   Trible, 'Studies', pp. 210-11; Sasson, *Jonah*, p. 93. Sasson found more evidence for his view that the sailors reverence the sea in the fact that they use the verbal form of סער in reference to the sea, as if it were causing the storm, while Jonah and the narrator use only the nominal form in speaking of a particular phenomenon which they know Yahweh to have caused (pp. 93-95).

Trible and Sasson for the latter motivation are not compelling.
Trible's interpretation of the object of להקל would be more convincing
if the sailors used that verb in v. 11, when they ask about their options
concerning how to calm the sea. Sasson's argument concerning the
relationship between and the syntactical meaning of טול and אל is
greatly weakened by the fact that the combination only occurs in
Jonah 1. Moreover, in the account from Achilles Tatius, passengers
and crew call out to the gods before the cargo is cast overboard, as the
sailors do in Jonah. Yet in Tatius it is clear that the cargo is thrown
over to lighten the ship, since transferring it from side to side is no
longer of use.

After reporting the activities of the sailors the text next shifts to
Jonah, who has gone down into the ship and fallen asleep.[53] Jonah's
sleep has been subjected to intense analysis. It has been viewed as the
fatigue of despair arising from the fact that Jonah knows he cannot
escape God, or as the smug slumber of the self-satisfied prophet,
secure he has eluded his duty. It has been compared to the divinely
inspired sleep of the first human being in Gen. 2.21, since the terminology in both texts is derived from the same root. For Jonathan
Magonet, Jonah's deep sleep is the first indication of his wish to die,
made explicit in 4.3.[54] The root רדם is also used in the Old Testament
to mean the deep trance which accompanies revelation. Norman Snaith
describes it as 'that deep...sleep which betokens the presence or
influence of Deity'.[55] For example, Abraham is cast into this type of
sleep before the appearance of the burning pot and torch in Gen.
15.12. Job twice speaks of the divine revelations which come to people
in this deep sleep (4.13, 33.15). Noteworthy in these three instances is
the terror which accompanies such sleep and revelation. Yahweh calls
down a tremendous curse upon himself in the oath to Abraham, and
Job knows that divine messages which come in the night do nothing
but trouble and terrify. Such divinely inspired fear fits well the
context of ch. 1, where Yahweh does nothing but frighten the Ninevites,
Jonah and the sailors. This prophetic context for the deep sleep of Jonah
makes more sense than any psychological speculation. Sasson interprets

---

53.   ספינה occurs only in Jonah 1. James Ackerman sees in the phrase ירכתי
הספינה reference to ירכתי צפון in Isa 14.13 ('Satire and Symbolism', pp. 213-46
[229-30]); so also Christensen ('Narrative Poetics', p. 42).
    54.   Magonet, *Form and Meaning*, pp. 67-69.
    55.   *Hebrew Text of Jonah*, p. 14.

Jonah's trance as a response to the storm and a willingness on the prophet's part to submit to the divine will. It is here, for Sasson, that Jonah ceases to run away.[56] Still another factor governing the author's choice of the term lies in the paronomastic relationship the form in Jonah (וירדם) has with the often repeated verb ירד (1.3 [twice], 5) and the cognate accusative phrase וידרו נדרים (1.16).[57]

The captain's[58] speculation about divine concern introduces a central theme in Jonah: the uncertainty of divine care for humankind. Given that the sailors are each praying to a particular god and that Jonah is commanded to pray to his particular god, the context of v. 6 allows reading האלהים as a plural.[59] The captain's 'perhaps' is reiterated by the 'who knows?' of the king of Nineveh in 3.9, although, as is shown below in Chapter 4, the king's remark is informed by the larger biblical tradition in such a way that its uncertainty is mitigated. This affirmation of divine freedom is taken up again by the sailors once they have decided upon Jonah's fate.

The casting of lots is a widespread practice to determine the divine will or to call upon superhuman wisdom in certain vexing situations.[60] Here in Jonah it is coupled with the belief that sea storms are brought about by the guilt of a person on ship. The casting of lots on ship is mentioned by Aristotle, quoting a saying of Socrates:

> If one were to say that magistrates should not be chosen by lot...this would be the same as choosing as representative athletes not those competent to contend, but those on whom the lot falls; or as choosing any of the sailors as the man who should take the helm, as if it were right that the choice should be decided by lot (*Rhetoric* 1393b).

56.   *Jonah*, pp. 99-102. Bruce Vawter also points to the prophetic/ecstatic connotations of the term (*Job and Jonah*, p. 91). Trible contrasts Jonah's deep sleep with the sentient thinking of the ship in 1.5, and maintains that Jonah's repose in the ship's bowels makes him a replacement for the jettisoned cargo (*Rhetorical Studies*, p. 135).

57.   Halpern and Friedman, 'Composition and Paronomasia', pp. 84-85.

58.   רב החבל, literally, 'chief of the ropes'. In spite of its violation of sense in Jonah 1, Kahn takes an alternate meaning of חבל and reads 'master of injury' ('Analysis', p. 90).

59.   Cf. BDB, 43, GKC, 124 g, 145 h–i.; so also Brichto, *Grammar*, p. 69. Allen, noting that the captain does not know Jonah's god at this point, renders the beginning of the captain's rhetorical phrase, 'Perhaps that god' (*Jonah*, p. 203).

60.   Johannes Lindblom has a standard overview ('Lot-Casting in the Old Testament', *VT* 12 [1962], pp. 164-78).

Of the several examples of storms attributed to a guilty traveller, two will suffice. In 411 BCE, the orator Antiphon wrote a defense for a man accused of murdering a companion with whom he had sailed. Antiphon cites as proof of the man's innocence the fact that he has travelled by ship since his accusation and no harm has befallen him:

> I hardly think I need remind you that many a person with unclean hands or some other form of defilement who has embarked on shipboard with the righteous has involved them in his own destruction. Others, while they have escaped death, have had their lives imperilled owing to such polluted wretches.[61]

The argument presupposes the common belief that evildoers who travel suffer misfortune ('I hardly think I need remind you'). Cicero recounts a *chreia* of Diagoras the Atheist:

> On another voyage he encountered a storm which threw the crew of the vessel into a panic, and in their terror they told him that they had brought it on themselves by having taken him on board their ship. He pointed out to them a number of other vessels making heavy weather on the same course, and inquired whether they supposed that those ships also had a Diagoras on board.[62]

Once the lot falls on Jonah he is bombarded with questions. It has long been common to omit the phrase באשר למי הרעה הזאת לנו in v. 8 on the grounds that it does not make sense as a question, because the sailors have just determined the cause of their misfortune by means of the lots. Julius A. Bewer surmises that the phrase had been written into a margin to explain the abbreviation בשלמי הרעה הזאת לנו in v. 7; from there it had been incorporated into the text.[63] Bewer's conjecture

---

61. *Herodes* 82; this text is also cited by Sasson, *Jonah*, p. 91.

62. *De nat. deor.* 3.89. Had the observation of Diagoras been applied to Jonah, a suitable response would have been the remark of *PRE* 10 that the storm affected only Jonah's ship: 'the movement of all the ships passing to and fro was peaceful in a quiet sea, but the ship into which Jonah had embarked was in great peril of ship-wreck' (quoted in Limburg, *Jonah*, p. 105).

63. *Jonah*, p. 37; also Trible, 'Studies', p. 22; Price and Nida, *Translator's Handbook*, p. 17; *BHS* and the NEB. In the LXX, the phrase is omitted in B, א and V. The critical editions of Joseph Ziegler and Alfred Rahlfs attribute the omission to homoioteleuton caused by the two occurrences of ἡμῖν in v. 8 (J. Ziegler [ed.], *Duodecimum Prophetae* [Septuaginta Gottingensis, 13; Göttingen: Vandenhoeck & Ruprecht, 3rd edn, 1984]).

would be valid if the phrase could only be read as a question. It can also be read as a relative clause functioning appositionally: 'Tell us, you on whose account this evil has come upon us'.[64] 4QXII[a] reads בשלמי at Jon. 1.8 and, while partially defective in v. 7, the remaining part of the phrase, ה הזאת..., is clear.[65] M.D. Goldman argues that the Hebrew text is in reality a poor translation of an Aramaic original, which read בדיל מן in both vv. 7-8. The translator, having mis-understood that the Aramaic מן can mean both 'who' and 'what', thus created the redundancy by understanding both as the former.[66] Goldman's thesis is weakened by the fact that this dual meaning for מן in Aramaic is attested only in Syriac translation, and by the use of מן and מא respectively in the *Tg. Ps.-J.* at Jon. 1.7-8.

Taking this first phrase of v. 8 appositionally, the text follows with four questions put to Jonah by the sailors in rapid succession. They concern his purpose,[67] origin,[68] homeland and ethnicity. In many respects these separate questions contain a great deal of redundancy, and Jonah's single response to all of them comes as no surprise. The perceived artificiality of the sailors' questions in the context of the storm has led to alternative explanations of the questions' presence. They have been interpreted as indications of the sailors': 1) kindness in making a full inquiry before they kill Jonah;[69] 2) piety in listening for God's will by means of a prophet;[70] 3) patience in giving Jonah an

---

64.   GKC, 131 o–r. This reading was given as early as the twelfth century by Rabbi David Kimchi (cited in Zlotowitz, *Yonah*, p. 93) and is also maintained by A.B. Ehrlich, *Ezechiel und die Kleinen Propheten* (Randglossen zur Hebräischen Bibel, 5; Leipzig: Hinrich, 1912), p. 265; Brichto, *Grammar*, p. 69; Sasson, *Jonah*, pp. 112-13; Tyndale, KJV and the JPSV.

65.   Fuller, 'Minor Prophets Manuscripts', fig. A. 6. 4QXII[a] has the abbre-viated form, בשלמי, at v. 8, while the MT has it at v. 7. This is analagous to the reversal in the MS of the MT's order, תרשיש... תרשישה in 1.3.

66.   M.D. Goldman, 'Was the Book of Jonah Originally Written in Aramaic?' *Australian Biblical Review* 3 (1953), pp. 49-50.

67.   Halpern and Friedman see a *double entendre* between the term מלאכתך and the term מלאך as designation of a divine messenger ('Composition and Paronomasia', p. 87).

68.   The nature of the question, 'From where do you come?' does not rule out the possibility that the sailors are inquiring into Jonah's nature, if he is a god or a spirit. This is the motivation of Pilate's identical query of Jesus in John 19.9.

69.   Wolff, *Obadiah and Jonah*, p. 114.

70.   Sasson, *Jonah*, p. 127.

opportunity to confess.[71] These explanations stem from the judgment that the questions are superfluous, which in turn arises from reading the first clause of v. 8 as a question. This finally results in discussions concerning the unrealistic scene of a trial or interrogation conducted shipboard in the midst of a storm. Such an interpretation places too much emphasis on the plausibility of the scene and overlooks the fact that plausibility is not an *a priori* criterion for fiction, especially in a work which contains a miraculous survival inside a fish, a magically appearing plant, and an obedient worm. At this point in ch. 1 there is little else left for the sailors to do, as v. 5 demonstrates. They have taken both practical and spiritual measures in the hopes of saving themselves.

Jonah's response tells the sailors all they need to know concerning who he is and what role he has to play in the storm. 'Hebrew' is the preferred word used in the Old Testament when Israelites/Jews identify themselves to foreigners. The LXX has δοῦλος κυρίου, which is probably a misreading of the word עברי as עבד יי, although Larry Perkins implies that the change is deliberate when he observes that the LXX phrase establishes a stronger link with 2 Kings 14, where Jonah is referred to as the servant of the Lord.[72] *Tg. Ps.-J.* substitutes the term 'Jew' for 'Hebrew' (יהודאה אנא). Etan Levine cites a polemical concern as the reason for the change, since Christian exegesis of the book had been used in anti-Jewish polemic.[73] 'God of the heavens', in addition to being the term of choice in identification of Yahweh to foreigners from the Persian period onward, makes clear to the sailors that Jonah's god is the source of the storm. The designation of Yahweh as the creator of both the sea and dry land leaves no room for doubt. Interpreting Jonah's response as some sort of 'confession'[74] is off the mark and no doubt influenced by a tradition of scholarship which looks for—and invariably finds—pithy credal formulae in the biblical

---

71.   John Holbert compares the sailors' questioning of Jonah with God's interrogation of Adam in Genesis 3, and notes that the responses of the sailors and God are identical ('"Deliverance"', pp. 59-81 [67]).

72.   Perkins, 'Septuagint of Jonah', pp. 43-53 (47).

73.   *Aramaic Version of Jonah*, pp. 13, 64-65. Jerome emphasizes that Jonah refers to himself as a Hebrew and not a Jew (Duval [ed.], *Jerome: Commentaire*, p. 201).

74.   So, among others, Wolff, *Obadiah and Jonah*, p. 122; Sasson, *Jonah*, pp. 118-19; Limburg, *Jonah*, pp. 52-53 and Trible, *Rhetorical Criticism*, p. 141.

text. This is not to say that Jonah will not cite stock phrases from the traditions of Israelite piety and religion (e.g., 2.2-10, 4.2), but this particular phrase, not recurrent in the Old Testament,[75] should not be construed as one. The context of the sailors seeking supernatural help so as to survive the storm, coupled with the presence of standard language reserved for foreigners, is sufficient explanation of Jonah's response.

Verses 10-14[76] each end in a clause introduced by כִּי which links them together:

> For (כִּי) the men knew that (כִּי) he was fleeing from the presence of Yahweh because (כִּי) he had told them (v. 10).
> For (כִּי) the sea grew more and more tempestuous (v. 11).
> For (כִּי)[77] I know that (כִּי)[78] it is because of me that this great tempest has come upon you (v. 12).
> For (כִּי) the sea grew more and more tempestuous against them (v. 13).
> For (כִּי) you Yahweh, have done as you desired (v. 14).

Jonah's recommendation that he be cast overboard has been subjected to extensive analysis, grouped by Kenneth M. Craig into the 'Death Wish' and 'Act of Compassion' hypotheses.[79] The first approach interprets Jonah's desire to be thrown overboard as the last desperate attempt of the recalcitrant prophet, disobedient until the end, to flee Yahweh.[80] A variation of this is to say that Jonah has realized that in fleeing the divine command he has committed a capital offense and his

---

75. Yahweh is elsewhere referred to as the creator of the sea and dry land only in Ps. 95.5.

76. Trible treats vv. 10-13 ('Studies', pp. 212-14; *idem, Rhetorical Criticism*, pp. 142-43).

77. William Horwitz uses the apparent redundancy of Jonah's admission of guilt to justify emending the personal pronoun אֲנִי into a term meaning 'ship' by means of placing a *hataph-qameṣ* under the *aleph*. The phrase then runs, 'for the ship knew that it was because of him that this great tempest had come upon them' (W.J. Horwitz, 'Another Interpretation of Jonah I 12', *VT* 23 [1973], pp. 370-72).

78. The presence of a subordinate clause beginning with כִּי in a larger clause also governed by the same particle in v. 11 argues against the excision of the phrase 'because he had told them' in v. 10 as recommended by the editors of *BHS*.

79. Craig, 'Poetics', pp. 256-58; and *idem, Poetics*, pp. 132-33. Craig argues for a 'both/and' view as evidence of the author's ambiguous portrayal of Jonah.

80. So for example Wolff, for whom Jonah is 'intractable' (*Obadiah and Jonah*, p. 118); Eubanks, 'Cathartic Effects', p. 151; and Thorardson, 'Notes', pp. 226-35 (228).

suggestion clearly shows his willingness to 'take his medicine'.[81] The
second approach attributes to Jonah a philanthropic character by
understanding his request as a desire to avoid that innocent sailors
should perish on account of his wrongdoing.[82]

   Similar to this latter view is that which interprets the sailors' futile
attempt to return to shore (1.13) as demonstration of their merciful
desire not to take Jonah's life. Drawing on ancient accounts which
advise against making for shore in a storm, Sasson sees in the deliberate attempt to return to shore a display of sincerity on the sailors'
part: they risk their own lives to show God their desire not to be a
party to Jonah's disobedience.[83] Josephus tells of a fierce storm off the
coast of Joppa during the Roman siege of the city. Known by the
locals as a 'Black Norther' (μελαμβόριον) the storm caused the ships
docked in Joppa to make for the open sea so as to avoid being dashed
on the rocky shore (*War* 3 §§ 423–24). In spite of these examples, it
remains unclear whether this was a standard ancient nautical practice,
and instances attesting the opposite to be the case are readily available.
In Antiphon's account it is clear that the defendant's ship made for
shore during a storm (*Herodes* 21). Similarly, Horace admonishes a
friend:

> You will live a happier life, Licinius, by neither steering always for the
> deep sea nor, in cautious dread of storms, hugging too close a dangerous
> shore. (*Carmina* 10.1)

Concerning the kindness of Jonah to the sailors and their merciful
response to their calamitous passenger, the issue needs to be separated
from any speculation concerning psychological motivation and
directed instead to the ideas that inform the ancient view of sea storms
and baneful travellers: guilt, responsibility and punishment. Questions
of justice and retribution necessarily remove any interpretation
beyond the realm of feeling (e.g., whether Jonah feels despair or

---

   81.   Fretheim, *Message,* pp. 88-89; and Allen, *Jonah,* p. 211.
   82.   A. Feuillet, 'Le sens du livre de Jonas', *RB* 54 (1947), pp. 340-61 (344);
Landes, 'Kerygma', pp. 3-31 (22-23); and Emmerson, 'Another Look', pp. 86-88
(86-87).
   83.   *Jonah,* p. 142. For Stuart the sailors are trying not so much to save Jonah
as to avoid implication in his death (*Hosea–Jonah,* p. 463). Magonet is a good
example of the overinterpretation of the sailors' kindness. He sees in their reference
to Jonah as 'this man' (v. 14) an awareness that 'they are all "fellowmen" tied
together in the same fate' (*Form and Meaning,* p. 97).

concern, whether the sailors are kind) and focus the reader on the only thing the text states the sailors are trying to do: determine the cause of the storm and respond in a way that will save their lives. In light of this it is fitting that legal elements have been noted in vv. 11-16. Robert Ratner adduces the strict penalties enjoined upon those who harbor runaway slaves in several ancient Near Eastern legal corpora, treaties and contracts from the first and second millennia as the background for Jonah 1. Jonah is, in effect, a runaway servant of the god Yahweh and the sailors are accomplices in Jonah's crime through their association with him.[84] The sailors' exclamation at Jonah's confession, 'What is this you have done!' (v. 10) is a stock biblical formula used when one accuses another of wrongdoing (e.g., Gen. 20.9).[85]

Similarly the sailors' final plea to Yahweh in v. 14 is replete with legal overtones.[86] Their request that Yahweh not hold 'innocent blood' against them calls to mind the elaborate apotropaic rite in Deut. 21.1-9. Upon finding a murder victim, and with no hope of discovering the murderer, the elders of a city are to sacrifice a heifer and wash their hands over its corpse saying:

> Our hands did not shed this blood, neither did our eyes see it shed. Forgive, O LORD, thy people Israel, whom thou has redeemd, and set not the guilt of innocent blood in the midst of thy people Israel; but let the guilt of blood be forgiven them. (Deut. 21.7-8)[87]

---

84.   R. Ratner, 'Jonah, the Runaway Servant', *Ma* 5-6 (1990), pp. 281-305; so also T. Harviainen, 'Why Were the Sailors Not Afraid of the Lord before Verse Jonah 1.10?', in E. Grothe-Paulin (ed.), *Studia Orientalia* (Helsinki: Societas Orientalis Fennica, 1988), pp. 77-81.

85.   Ratner, 'Jonah', p. 301.

86.   Craig analyzes the plea as following the 'uniquely...Israelite' prayer pattern of address petition and response and determines it to be a subtle indication of the author's view that gentiles may pray to Yahweh with efficacy. A weakness of Craig's view, which he admits, is the paucity of prayers in ancient Near Eastern literature from which to substantiate a form peculiar to Israel (*Poetics*, pp. 90-93). Trible categorizes the prayer as 'a communal complaint song' (*Rhetorical Criticism*, p. 147).

87.   This is the only occurrence of the phrase אל תתן דם נקי in the Old Testament apart from Jon. 1.14. For Almbladh the spelling נקיא in Jonah (along with קליא in 1 Sam. 17.17 and שיעא in Ezra 6.15) is a late linguistic feature (*Studies*, p. 23). Halpern and Friedman interpret the spelling in Jonah as a pun on the vomiting (ויקא) of the fish in 2.11 ('Composition and Paronomasia', p. 85). Mur 88 omits the א at Jon. 1.14, while the Samaritan Pentateuch includes it in Deuteronomy 21. The only other occurrence of a form of נתן with דם נקי is Jer. 26.15, to which some have

The context of Deuteronomy shows that the purpose of the rite is founded upon the presupposition of communal guilt and responsibility. Since no one malefactor can be found and punished, all are now under threat of punishment, the innocent together with the guilty. The rite recognizes, as do the sailors in Jonah 1, that even though a person may be free from wrongdoing, this is no basis for exemption from divine punishment. God is free to save or destroy apart from any notions of guilt or innocence.

Avi Hurvitz argues for the origin of the Hebrew phrase, 'all that you desire you have done', to be an Aramaic legal formula dealing specifically with the transfer of property, found in contracts from 500 BCE onward.[88] More germane to the context in Jonah is the fact that, in the remaining three occurrences in the Old Testament where it is said that God does whatever he pleases, the context is the condemnation of foreign idolatry. In Isa. 46.6-7 God mocks those who pay to have idols made and then worship them. There then follows the exhortation:

> Remember the former things of old; for I am God, and there is no other; I am God and there is none like me, declaring the end from the beginning and from ancient times things not yet done, saying "My counsel shall stand, *and I will accomplish all my purpose*" (Isa. 46.9-10).[89]

Similarly, in Ps. 115.3-4 one reads:

> Our God is in the heavens; *he does whatever he pleases.*
> Their idols are silver and gold, the work of men's hands.[90]

And again in Ps. 135.5-6, 15:

> For I know that the LORD is great, that our Lord is above all gods. *Whatever the LORD pleases he does*, in heaven and on earth, in the seas and all the deeps... The idols of the nations are silver and gold, the work of men's hands.[91]

In this group of texts two ideas are present. The first is that because Yahweh is the only true god, he can do/accomplish whatever he

argued the text of Jonah is alluding (Golka, *Jonah*, p. 86).

88.   A. Hurvitz, 'The History of a Legal Formula *kol 'aser hapes 'asah*', *VT* 32 (1982), pp. 257-67. Hurvitz's Aramaic formula has no contact with the phrasing of Jon. 1.14 in *Tg. Ps.-J.*.

89.   וכל חפצי אעשה; 1QIsa^a has יעשה.

90.   כל אשר חפץ עשה.

91.   כל אשר חפץ יהוה עשה. Ludwig Schmidt judges the two psalm texts to be the background for Jon. 1.14 ('*De Deo*', pp. 79-80).

wishes. The second is that Yahweh's power extends from the divine
dwelling in the heavens to the furthermost reaches of creation. The
merismus of Ps. 135.6 parallels that of Jonah in v. 9: 'I worship
Yahweh, the god of heaven who made the sea and the dry land'. Put
into the mouth of the foreign sailors the saying continues its function
as a polemic against anything but worship of Yahweh. Placed in the
context of a sea storm narrative the phrase also continues to be illustrated by demonstrations of Yahweh's power over the elements. But
there is more going on here than the reiteration of the futility of
worship of other gods at the expense of the sailors' dignity, and any
humor found here has to be brought to the text rather than from it.[92]
To say that this particular god can do whatever he wishes is to make a
statement about both divine power and divine freedom. It is this latter
aspect which is here emphasized. The sailors have come to know more
than that Yahweh is a mighty storm god, more powerful than their
own deities, and their only hope of salvation. They have also come to
the realization, which they acknowledge in v. 14, that this god is not
only able to accomplish any act, but is capable of accomplishing any
act. There is no doubt concerning the cause of the storm; both divine
(the lot) and human (Jonah's own admission) methods have made it
clear. Thus the request that Yahweh not hold innocent blood against
them, coupled with the statement about divine freedom, reflects no
uncertainty on the sailors' part as to Jonah's guilt. The uncertainty lies
in the possibility that Yahweh may still destroy them even after they
have rid themselves of the malefactor, for this god has both the power
and the freedom at his disposal. This emphasis on the unpredictability
of divine freedom is what the author is emphasizing here, and will
emphasize again in the account of Nineveh in ch. 3.

That this uncertainty haunts them long after Jonah has disappeared
into the waves is apparent in the final verse of the chapter. The sailors
greatly fear Yahweh and offer vows and sacrifices to him. The issue
of sacrifices offered on ship has been a crux of interpretation. *Tg.
Ps.-J.* reads: 'They decided to make a sacrifice', possibly in order to

---

92.   David Payne offers a corrective for those who see the figure of Jonah
satirized while the newfound piety of the sailors is extolled. Payne argues that for the
author, the vows and offerings of the sailors are 'just as much a caricature of reality
as the portrayal of Jonah' ('Jonah', pp. 3-12 [8-9]). The consistency that Payne calls
for can be argued the other way, and require that neither Jonah nor the sailors be seen
as objects of humor.

avoid the problems of the availability of clean animals and the validity of offerings outside of Jerusalem.[93] *PRE* interprets the sacrifice to be the blood of circumcision, for the sailors 'returned to Joppa and went up to Jerusalem and circumcised the flesh of their foreskins'.[94] Modern commentators are divided as to whether the sailors converted or added Yahweh to the gods they worshiped.

Concerning the religious practices of sailors on ship, 'The Tale of the Shipwrecked Sailor' recounts that, after the protagonist sees a passing ship which will rescue him after being marooned, he offers praise to the god who saves him, 'and those who were in the ship did likewise'.[95] More explicit is Antiphon's text. The defendant, on trial for the murder of a companion on ship, recounts that

> the prosecution first of all went on board and conducted a search. On finding the aforementioned bloodstains, they claimed that this was where Herodes had met his end. But the suggestion proved an unfortunate one, as the blood turned out to be that of the animals sacrificed. (*Herodes* 29)

As with Antiphon's argument concerning the misfortune of the wicked when travelling, so here the sacrifice of animals on ship is referred to as a normal practice. Thus the actions of the sailors do not indicate their newfound religion, nor serve as a mockery of non-Israelite worship of Yahweh. The sacrifices and vows of the sailors serve to emphasize their continued fear for their safety when confronted with a god of unlimited power and freedom.[96]

Sea Storms in Ancient Literature

Pamela Lee Thimmes's analysis of several ancient sea storm narratives from both biblical and extra-biblical literature seeks to compare and

93.   Levine, *Aramaic Version of Jonah*, p. 70.
94.   Quoted in Limburg, *Jonah*, p. 107. The text continues by interpreting the vows as the sailors' promise to convert their children and households. Rashi's reading is similar, but the vows concern the sailors' own eventual conversion. For Kimchi the vows are to give alms to the poor (Zlotowitz, *Yona*, p. 104). Stuart follows this interpretation on the issue of a later sacrifice, but denies the sailors converted: 'they merely added Yahweh to the god(s) they already believed in' (*Hosea–Jonah*, pp. 455, 464).
95.   Simpson, *Literature of Ancient Egypt*, p. 56.
96.   De Hoope contrasts the wickedness of the Ninevites which rises up before God in v. 2 from the (implied) pleasing aroma of the sacrifices rising up in v. 16 ('Jonah as Poetry', p. 170).

contrast the two groups in order to find constitutive elements. Unfortunately her sole constitutive element of absence of the loss of life in the biblical accounts, distinguishing them from their Greco-Roman counterparts, is strained and artificial.[97] In attempting to find a background for the storm in Jonah 1 exegetes have had far to look, since the Old Testament contains a paucity of sea storm accounts. The only other extensive references to storms are Ezek. 27.25-36 and Ps. 107.23-32.

Biblical Sea Storm Narratives
Ezekiel 27 is a lament for Tyre, and that Phoenician trading post is symbolized as a great ship. The lament begins with a detailed description of the ship's fittings and moves on to a list of Tyre's trading partners, along with the goods which were exchanged. After this laudatory beginning, the good ship Tyre's demise rapidly follows:

> So you were filled and heavily laden in the heart of the seas.
> Your rowers have brought you out into the high seas.
> The east wind has wrecked you in the heart of the seas.
> Your riches and your wares, your merchandise,
> Your mariners and your pilots... with all your company that is in your midst, sink into the heart of the seas on the day of your ruin.
> At the sound of the cry of your pilots the countryside shakes....
> Now you are wrecked by the seas, in the depths of the waters;
> Your merchandise and all your crew have sunk with you (vv. 25-28, 34).

The numerous verbal contacts between Jonah 1 and Ezekiel 27 have led some to posit the text in Ezekiel as a source for Jonah.[98] Against this it should be emphasized that the storm in Ezekiel is not so much recounted as referenced, the most logical type of demise for a city renowned for trade by sea. While at first glance the common vocabulary speaks for dependence, in many respects the nature of the

97. P.L. Thimmes, *Studies in the Biblical Sea-Storm Type-Scene: Convention and Invention* (San Francisco: Edwin Mellen, 1992), pp. 101-102, 107-108, 113. Thimmes cannot find her criterion of death in all of the Greek examples. She does not treat Ezek. 27.25-36, where a sea-storm results in a large loss of life. Finally, it cannot be said that the scene in Jonah is free from loss of life, as it is clear that this is what the sailors and Jonah intend. Cf. Sasson's section, 'Storms in Ancient Lore' (*Jonah*, pp. 90-92).

98. So Witzenrath, *Jona*, p. 90, who lists the following shared terms: אניה, חבל, זעק, מלחים, שבר, ירד, תרשיש

narrative determines and limits word choice. Thus, in writing about
ships and storms, naturally the terms for 'ship' and 'sailor' are used,
as are verbs signifying 'sinking/going down' and 'crying out'.[99]
Beyond such choices determined by the type of event portrayed, there
is, in fact, surprisingly little contextual contact between Jonah 1 and
Ezekiel 27. John D.W. Watts points out that if the author of Jonah has
used Ezekiel 27, Tyre rather than Joppa would have been the more
likely choice as the point of departure.[100]

Psalm 107 extols the saving power of Yahweh by recounting in succession episodes of danger from which those who cry out to God are
saved. One such dangerous situation is that of being caught in a storm:

> Some went down to the sea in ships, doing business on the great waters;
> they saw the deeds of the LORD, his wondrous works in the deep.
> For he commanded and raised the stormy wind, which lifted up the waves
> of the sea. They mounted up to heaven; they went down to the depths;
> Their courage melted away in their evil plight; they reeled and staggered
> like drunken men, and were at their wits' end.
> Then they cried to the LORD in their trouble, and he delivered them from
> their distress; he made the storm be still, and the waves of the sea were
> hushed.
> Then they were glad because they had quiet, and he brought them to their
> desired haven.
> Let them thank the LORD for his steadfast love, for his wonderful works
> to the sons of men!
> Let them extol him in the congregation of the people, and praise him in the
> assembly of the elders (vv. 23-32).

Here again is a confluence of nautical/meteorological terms which
storm narratives require. The only possible verbal contact between the
two texts is מלאכה ('business') in Jon. 1.8 and Ps. 107.23. There also
is a similar ordering of events in both texts: the description of a
voyage, the raising of a storm by Yahweh, the cry to God for help, the
stilling of the storm, and gratitude.[101] However, as with the similarity
in terminology, such an ordering of events is logically required in

---

99.   E. Strömberg-Krantz discusses the etymological derivations of the nautical
language of these two passages (*Des Schiffes Weg Mitten im Meer* [ConBOT, 10;
Lund: Liber, 1982], pp. 177-88).

100.   Watts, *Jonah*, p. 83.

101.   As is the case concerning Ezekiel 27, these parallels have contributed to
Psalm 107 being cited as a source for Jonah (Thoma, 'Entstehung', pp. 479-502
[492-93]).

narrating a storm, and can be found in extra-biblical narratives as well.

What can be seen from comparing these two remaining sea storm narratives in the Old Testament (Ezekiel 27 and Psalm 107) with Jonah is that the three texts do not depend upon each other so much as draw upon the standard nautical language of their common culture. Joppa is the seaport of Palestine; 'ship(s) of Tarshish' designates any long distance vessel(s);[102] storms are under the command of Yahweh.

Extra-Biblical Sea Storm Narratives

As has been demonstrated by numerous examples cited throughout this chapter, sea storm narratives occur in ancient literature from Egypt, Mesopotamia, Greece and Rome and span a period from the early-second millennium BCE to the second century CE. By the Roman period narratives of sea storms were common enough to be parodied along with other literary motifs by Lucian in *Vera Historia*. They were considered *de rigueur* in the lives of the famous. Luke includes a storm in his life of Paul, as does Josephus in his autobiography.[103] This wide chronological and geographic range for sea storm narratives does nothing to help date Jonah. Thus when André and Pierre-Emmanuel Lacocque write: 'Before the fourth century, no Israelite storyteller would have thought of placing one of his heroes at sea', they completely overlook the presence of sailing and sea storms in ancient texts such as the Gilgamesh epic, 'The Tale of the Shipwrecked Sailor' and 'The Journey of Wen-Amon'.[104] By looking at one of the earliest and one of the most recent examples,[105] the logical constraints which obtained in the three biblical accounts can be seen to apply to the extra-biblical texts as well.

'The Tale of the Shipwrecked Sailor' has long been examined as a background to Jonah.[106] The tale is preserved in an early Middle Kingdom papyrus (early-second millennium). The narrator tells of being caught in a storm with strong winds. The boat in which he is sailing 'dies'. Upon washing up on an island, the sailor makes an

---

102. So 1 Kgs 22.49, 2 Chron. 20.37, Ps. 48.7; discussed by Strömberg-Krantz (*Des Schiffes Weg*, pp. 48-51)

103. Acts 27; Josephus, *Life* 3 §15.

104. Lacocque and Lacocque, *Jonah*, p. 38.

105. Other examples in Thimmes, *Studies*, pp. 40-89.

106. K. Marti, *Das Dodekapropheten* (Tübingen: Mohr [Paul Siebeck], 1904), pp. 246-47.

offering to the gods.[107] These elements appear in Jonah 1 in the same order. The text, a skillful literary work, has a didactic aim. The ship-wrecked narrator meets a serpent-god who admonishes him:

> If you would be brave, regulate your desire. Then you will fill your embrace with our children, you will kiss your wife, and you will see your house (again); for it is better than anything.[108]

Moving forward two thousand years, the sea storm found in Tatius's *Leucippe and Clitophon* has a lengthy sea storm account which strikingly resembles the order of events in Jonah. The passengers find a ship in port preparing to depart (2.31). There arises a wind out of the sea and attempts are made to lighten the boat amid a great wailing (3.1). There is fear that the ship will break and the helmsman[109] orders the cargo jettisoned (3.2). The passengers pray for divine pity and the storm comes to an end (3.5). Much like the Egyptian tale's use of a storm to further a didactic aim, Tatius's account functions as a platform for a lengthy and detailed discussion concerning the respective merits of homosexual and heterosexual love. Of course the storm also provides yet one more adventure for the hero and heroine to endure and to overcome.

It can be seen that the sea storm scene in and of itself maintains a fairly fixed structure, due mainly to logical constraints, and functions in a text in a subordinate manner to an author's larger purpose. This is the case in both the biblical and extra-biblical examples cited above in addition to Jonah 1. The author of Jonah has chosen to utilize a well-established type-scene, and to customize it for his audience by the inclusion of culturally determined geographic and religious features. It is no suprise that an Israelite author, writing a sea storm scene, uses Joppa as a port, Tarshish/ships of Tarshish as destination and means of travel, and Yahweh as cause of the storm.

Conclusion

In bringing together the foregoing remarks, a few broad observations may be made about Jonah 1. First, the author of Jonah is not introducing anything new to Israelite readers in 1.1-16. Jonah the son of

---

107. Translation in Simpson, *Literature of Ancient Egypt*, pp. 50-56.
108. Simpson, *Literature of Ancient Egypt*, pp. 54-55.
109. Tatius uses κυβερνήτης; the LXX of Jon. 1.6 has πρωρεύς.

Amittai is a figure previously mentioned in the Old Testament. Joppa and Tarshish are customary choices for Israelites when referring to a sea voyage. In conversation with foreigners, the terms 'Hebrew' and 'god of heaven' constitute normal usage. The sea storm type-scene is a time-honored literary convention that demands certain features and vocabulary. That in many respects Jonah 1 is rooted in the familiar is a conclusion worthy of emphasis since the tendency of commentators is to exaggerate what is seen as unique, revolutionary or farcical in the text.

A second general observation has to do with the futility of human effort. Magonet points out that in Jonah, every human action introduced with an infinitive verb form is never successfully completed, while every divine action using the infinitive comes to pass.[110] Such human impotence is also illustrated in the failure of a prophet who does not escape his god, a shipload of sailors who cannot escape a storm, and, more indirectly, the polemic against useless gods who are really nothing more than powerless idols. The counterpart to this abject human failure is the boundless power, freedom and authority of Yahweh. By emphasizing human impotence in the face of divine power, the author draws attention to the complete dependence of humans upon God.[111] It should come as no surprise that the sailors' plea for mercy includes an allusion to the apotropaic rite of Deuteronomy 21 that is directed against a divine wrath which does not discriminate between the guilty and the innocent. That the plea ends with the remark that Yahweh does whatever he pleases is all too obvious by this point.

Closely related to Yahweh's power are the terror and menace which he directs towards everyone in ch. 1. He sends Jonah to Nineveh for the purpose of threat and condemnation. He hurls a storm which panics a shipload of sailors. Jonah's sleep may be likened to a prophetic trance wherein God comes and fills the mind with dread. Yahweh is so frightening that the sailors make offerings to him and promise even more after their deliverance. Here the three occurrences of the sailors' fear and its consequent growth and focus offer an insight into the author's purpose. At the outset of the storm the sailors are afraid. Upon learning that Jonah 'fears' Yahweh their fear is heightened. Upon

110. *Form and Meaning*, pp. 30-31.
111. For Sasson, Jonah 1 stresses that submission to the divine will can mean life (*Jonah*, p. 142); for Potgieter the theme is the preservation of life ('Jonah', p. 66).

ridding themselves of Jonah and being delivered from peril, their fear
remains heightened and is clearly said to be the fear of Yahweh. By
playing on the double meaning of ירא as 'fear' and 'worship', the
author's point is clear: the worst of storms or dangers is a small thing
compared to the fierce power and unlimited freedom of the god
Yahweh. This is a thing to be feared more than anything else.

Concerning Jonah and religion, Leslie Allen writes: 'Some stereo-
typed conventions of the Hebrew religious ideology have been thrown
overboard with Jonah'.[112] Many more have remained on board. That
Jonah does not behave as a typical prophet in the Old Testament is a
given and rehearsed in all the articles and commentaries. That the
portrayal of Jonah goes beyond the theological issue of prophecy and
is more earnest than the scholarly weapon of satire is not often discussed in the literature. In the emphasis on an omnipotent god given
only to terrifying helpless creatures, the religious elements in Jonah 1
come under withering scrutiny. In the prophet is seen the hopeless
position of those who know Yahweh, for the god's requirements are
nothing less than quixotic, and failure to accomplish those requirements no less than a capital offense.[113] Jonah is not trapped once the
storm finds him out at sea; his fate is sealed the moment Yahweh's
word is addressed to him. The sailors are the counterpart to Jonah as
individuals who, after coming into contact with Jonah's god, realize
that all their previous practical and religious knowledge is useless
when faced with a world controlled by a capricious, awesome deity.
As the sky clears and their passenger sinks into the sea, the sailors find
themselves in a new world, one in which they will never again be
completely free of fear.[114] In this levelling of ground between Jew
and Gentile the author is not envisioning an all-inclusive utopian ideal,
but demonstrating a pre-determined human condition.

---

112. *Jonah*, p. 212.

113. Vawter sees Jonah portraying Yahweh to the sailors as an animistic deity
desirous of human sacrifice (*Job and Jonah*, p. 93).

114. In a related manner, Jay Holstein argues that Herman Melville subverts the
traditional teaching of Jonah by reading it as 'an affirmation of a paganism which
sees man at the mercy of powers either alien and malevolent (whale)... or indifferent
(sea)... to man' (J.A. Holstein, 'Melville's Inversion of Jonah in *Moby Dick*', *Iliff
Review* 42 [1985], pp. 13-20 [20]).

Chapter 3

PRAYER AND DELIVERANCE (JONAH 2.1-11)

So sacred is any ancient poem.

—Horace, *Ep.* 2.154

The oriental world has a cellar with a pronounced oceanic character.

—Nicholas J. Tromp[1]

In a darkened whale in Ashkelon, a man drank for three days.

—German student song[2]

The psalm that comprises Jonah 2[3] has been one of the most vigorously debated exegetical issues of the entire book. Perceived incongruence between the poem and the surrounding prose text has been remarked upon since antiquity, and it has served as the impetus for the critical study of the book in the last two hundred years. This chapter undertakes several tasks before offering an interpretation of Jon. 2.1-11. The first section of the chapter will sketch the arguments both for and against viewing the psalm as an interpolation. The second section identifies and examines as a foundational issue the question of the psalm's form. In addition to these remarks is an overview of how Jonah fits into the larger debate surrounding the analysis of Hebrew poetry. A third section analyzes key philological and exegetical features of 2.1-11. Finally the question of whether the poem draws directly on the Psalter as a source is considered.

1. N.J. Tromp, *Primitive Conceptions of Death and the Netherworld in the Old Testament* (BibOr, 21; Rome: Pontifical Biblical Institute, 1969), p. 131.
2. Quoted in Haupt, 'Jonah's Whale', p. 154.
3. This chapter follows the Hebrew versification in which the psalm comprises 2.3-10. English versions designate Jon. 2.1 as 1.17, leaving Jon. 2 with ten verses, and the poem as 2.2-9.

The Origins of Jonah's Poem

Jonah's Poem as a Later Interpolation

The main feature of the argument for interpolation is that the psalm of Jonah 2 does not cohere in a logical manner with the prose remainder of the text, the principal violation being that Jonah offers thanks for deliverance while still in the belly of the fish. This is noted as long ago as Josephus (*Ant.* 9.214), who overcomes the inconsistency by rearranging the text and placing Jonah's prayer after his ejection from the fish. Similarly William Tyndale, while affirming that Jonah prays from the belly of the fish, adds:

> But the words of that prayer are not here set. The prayer that here standeth in the text, is the prayer of praise and thanksgiving which he prayed and wrote when he was escaped and past all jeopardy.[4]

Among early historical-critical scholars Johannes G.A. Müller appears to be the first to deny single authorship of the book of Jonah. Müller holds that the psalm dates from the eighth century BCE, the surrounding prose narrative being added during the exile.[5] Wilhelm De Wette reverses this order and formulates what goes on to become the standard position; that is, that Jonah consists of a previously existing prose text to which the psalm has been added.[6] This position holds near unanimous sway for over a century and a half,[7] and in its most

---

4.   Daniell (ed.), *Tyndale's Pentateuch*, p. 635. John Calvin also stresses that the prayer does not contain the exact words of Jonah from inside the fish: 'But we must remember that his prayer was not composed in the words which are here related; but Jonah while in the bowels of the fish, dwelt on these thoughts in his mind' (*Twelve Minor Prophets*, III, p. 75).

5.   Müller, 'Jona', p. 142. Müller was followed by Nachtigal, 'Jonas', pp. 221-73.

6.   W. De Wette, *Lehrbuch der historisch-kritischen Einleitung in kanonischen und apocryphischen Bücher des Alten Testament* (Berlin: Reiner, 1817), p. 298.

7.   A partial listing includes: Budde, 'Vermutungen', p. 42; Bewer, *Jonah*, pp. 21-24; H. Gunkel, 'Jonapsalm', *RGG*[2], pp. 369-70 (369); A.R. Johnson, 'Jonah, II.3-10: A Study in Cultic Phantasy', in H.H. Rowley (ed.), *Studies in Old Tesament Prophecy* (Edinburgh: T. & T. Clark, 1950), pp. 82-102 (83); Trible, 'Studies', pp. 75-82; *idem, Rhetorical Criticism,* pp. 172-73; Keller, 'Jonas', pp. 329-40 (332 n. 18); Eissfeldt, *The Old Testament,* p. 406; Fohrer, *Introduction,* p. 442; Allen, *Jonah,* p. 183; Childs, 'Canonical Shape', pp. 122-28 (125); Licht, *Storytelling,* p. 123; Halpern and Friedman, 'Composition and Paronomasia', pp. 79-82 (80 n. 2); J.A. Soggin, 'Il "segno di Giona" nel libro del Profeta Giona',

developed form is based on the following arguments:

1. Jonah's thanksgiving for deliverance violates the logical consistency of the prose account, as it is prayed during his
   sojourn in the fish.
2. The prayer of thanksgiving is introduced with the *hithpael* of
   פלל, a form which ordinarily (but not exclusively) is used
   for a lament.
3. The pious attitude expressed in the psalm does not correspond to Jonah's recalcitrance in the prose portion.
4. The poem contains no Aramaisms, which are prevalent in the
   prose portion.
5. The poem does not contain any of the *Leitwörter* of the prose
   accounts. Where one would expect the occurrence of such a
   term, synonyms are employed (e.g., שלח ['cast'] in 2.4,
   rather than the repeated טול ['hurl'] of Jonah 1).
6. The text makes good sense if the poem is excised.[8]

Jonah's Poem as Original to the Prose Text

Against this axiomatic conclusion recent exegetical approaches, fueled
by the new literary analysis which emphasizes the text in its final form
over any hypothetical earlier versions, maintain that Jonah's psalm is
original to the book. The first major formulation of this position is the
1967 study of George M. Landes.[9] Landes identifies two prayers in
the psalm: a lament referred to by the perfect verbs in 2.3, 5, 7 and a
thanksgiving into which these references are lodged. He argues that

---

Lateranum 48 (1982), pp. 70-74 (73-74); J.T. Walsh, 'Jonah 2,3–10: A Rhetorical
Critical Study', *Bib* 63 (1982), pp. 219-29 (219); F.M. Cross, 'Studies in the
Structure of Hebrew Verse: The Prosody of the Psalm of Jonah', in H. Huffmon and
F. Spina (eds.), *The Quest for the Kingdom of God: Studies in Honor of George E.
Mendenhall* (Winona Lake, IN: Eisenbrauns, 1983), pp. 159-67 (167); Weimar,
'Jon 2.1–11', pp. 43-68 (64-68); D. Daube, 'Jonah: A Reminiscence', *JJS* 35
(1984), pp. 36-43 (41); Wolff, *Obadiah and Jonah*, pp. 129-31; Day, 'Problems',
pp. 32-47 (41); Couffignal, 'Le Psaume', p. 548; Nogalski, *Redactional Processes*,
pp. 254-55; Collins, *Mantle of Elijah*, pp. 172-73.

8.   Summaries of these arguments can be found in Bewer, *Jonah*, pp. 21-25;
Trible. 'Studies', p. 75-82; Wolff, *Obadiah and Jonah*, pp. 129-31; and Ackerman,
'Satire and Symbolism', pp. 213-46 (213-14).

9.   'Kerygma', pp. 3-31. While André Feuillet held the psalm to be original
twenty years prior to Landes's study, he did not develop his position ('Livre de
Jonas', p. 344)

this flashback feature of the psalm matches that of Jonah's prayer of
4.2, which also refers to prior utterances of Jonah. This structural and
thematic link between the psalm of ch. 2 and the prayer of ch. 4
complements a similar correspondence that has long been noticed by
scholars between elements in chs. 1 and 3, and yields an overall
pattern in Jonah wherein portions of every other chapter are related.[10]
Jonathan Magonet stresses the verbal contact between קרא and ירד in
both the poem and prose portions. Unlike the pattern maintained by
Landes, Magonet charts a complex inverted step pattern which links
chs. 2 and 3.[11]

   In the years since Landes's study, the argument for the integrity of
Jonah's psalm has gained adherents.[12] In spite of this, the issue
remains at an impasse because proponents of both opinions have failed
to deliver 'the knockout punch'. Peter Weimar's elaborate three-stage
redaction of Jonah, which posits the addition and subsequent editing of
the psalm, is as unrealistically convoluted, overly-analytical and speculative as Magonet's subtle wordplays and elusive descent–ascent
pattern which seeks to argue for the text's integrity. From the standpoint of logic and chronology, the psalm does not fit. Yet, as has
already been mentioned, to attribute such inconsistency to redaction is
to operate from an unfounded assumption that biblical authors exhibit
a superhuman level of sophistication and rigidity matched only by an
equally extreme incompetence on the part of redactors. The circular
argument that redaction is identified through inconsistencies because
redactors do not skilfully use or edit their sources has been an implicit
assumption in both source and tradition-history analysis, and serves as
a springboard for the widespread construction of hypothetical sources,
authors, redactors, historical crises and movements. All textual

   10.   'Kerygma', pp. 13-17. Along the same lines, Terence Fretheim argues that
the absence of identical vocabulary between the psalm and prose texts matches a
similar incongruence in Jonah's prayer of 4.2–3 ('Jonah and Theodicy', 234 n. 17).

   11.   *Form and Meaning*, p. 61.

   12.   Among scholars of this opinion are : Cohn, 'Book of Jonah', p. 170-71;
Emmerson, 'Another Look', p, 87; Fretheim, *Message*, pp. 58-60; Price and Nida,
Translator's Handbook, p. 34; Ackerman, 'Satire and Symbolism', p. 215;
Christensen, 'Narrative Poetics', p. 43; Stuart, *Hosea–Jonah*, pp. 438-39; Golka,
Jonah, pp. 93-94; A. and P.-E. Lacocque, *Jonah*, p. 98; Woodard, 'Death in Life',
p. 9; Brenner, 'Jonah's Poem out of and within its Context,' in D.J.A. Clines and
P.R. Davies (eds.), *Among the Prophets: Language, Image and Structure in the
Prophetic Writings* (JSOTSup, 144; Sheffield: JSOT Press, 1993) pp. 183-92 (186).

evidence for Jonah, beginning with the earliest extant MSS, includes the psalm in the same place.[13] That the text reads better, or has a better fit (whatever this may mean) if the psalm is removed, is more a matter of taste than an exegetical observation.[14]

Background Issues: The Gattung *of Jonah's Psalm* and its Analysis as Poetry

Thanksgiving or Lament?

Of the reasons cited above for viewing Jon. 2.3-10 as a later inter-polation, the first is that the prayer of thanksgiving does not fit with Jonah's situation. In addition to the excision of the psalm, and the solutions of Josephus and Tyndale noted above, this problem is dealt with in a variety of ways. The LXX changes several of Jonah's asser-tions to wishes or questions.[15] Ibn Ezra appeals to the prophetic perfect, the prophet's recital of future events in the perfect tense through means of divinely granted foresight.[16] Some view the fish as a rescue from drowning and therefore a suitable setting for gratitude.[17] Still others, following Landes, hold that there are two prayers in the psalm, references to a past lament made in the context of a thanks-giving.[18]

Two issues perceived to be problematic by commentators need to be addressed: 1) the presence of both lament and thanksgiving elements

---

13.   Codex A includes the psalm both in the odes collected at the end of the Psalter and in its customary place immediately following Jon. 2.2 (Trible, 'Studies', p. 82).

14.   So also Stuart: 'An ability to excise does not equal, however, a warrant to excise... Excisability is never a legitimate indication of lack of integrity in a literary work' (*Hosea–Jonah*, pp. 438-39).

15.   Listed in Perkins, 'Septuagint of Jonah', pp. 43-53 (48-50). These changes will be treated in the following section.

16.   Quoted in S. Goldman, 'Jonah', in A. Cohen (ed.), *The Twelve Prophets* (Hindhead, Surrey: Soncino, 1948) pp. 137-50 (142).

17.   Representative of this approach is T.T. Perowne, *Obadiah and Jonah* (Cambridge: Cambridge University Press, 1905), p. 68. Conversely, Scott interprets the fish as an instrument of divine punishment ('Sign of Jonah', p. 22).

18.   So J.W. Woodhouse, 'Jesus and Jonah [Matt 12.39-40; Matt 16.4, Lk 11.20]', *Reformed Theological Review* 43 (1984), pp. 33-41 (38-39); Eubanks, 'Cathartic Effects', p. 157; and Craig, 'Poetics', pp. 80-81. Stuart argues against this interpretation (*Hosea–Jonah*, pp. 476-77).

within the poem; 2) the presence of a thanksgiving within the distressed setting of Jonah 2. In both of these cases, any apparent incompatibility is derived from the application of overly strict logical categories. Form-critically the song is a thanksgiving.[19] Yet the combination of thanksgiving and lament features in psalms is a standard occurrence (e.g., Isaiah 38, Psalms 22, 116)[20] and poses no obstacle. Concerning the second issue, John D.W. Watts notes that, because Hebrew poetry embedded in prose has no significant bearing on the plot, its excision will not leave a noticeable gap. As such, excision should not be a criterion in determining secondary features. More importantly, Watts points out that these poems often violate the chronological order of the prose account, specifically in their praise or thanks for a promise yet to be fulfilled.[21] Thus Hezekiah's prayer comes after he has been told God will allow him to live, but before he has been healed (Isa. 38). Daniel praises God for the received vision prior to his audience with the king that will save his life (Dan. 2). Hannah's song comes before the birth of Samuel (1 Sam. 2). In light of this, Jonah's thanksgiving from the innards of the fish is not premature gratitude, but another example of this feature. Given this, along with the combination of lament/thanksgiving as a common

19.   Gunkel categorizes it as a Thanksgiving Song of the Individual (*Danklieder des Einzelnen*; in *The Psalms* [repr.; Philadelphia: Fortress Press, 1967 [1930] pp. 15-17) as does S. Mowinckel, *The Psalms in Israel's Worship* (2 vols.; in 1, Nashville: Abingdon Press, 1962), II, pp. 34-35. Hartmut Gese adds that the psalm is specifically a thanksgiving of a proselyte. As such it addresses the exclusivity of salvation from Yahweh ('Jona ben Amittai', p. 272=*Alttestamentliche Studien*, p. 138).

20.   Mowinckel observes that lament formulae are a pronounced element in thanksgiving songs (*Psalms*, II, p. 142) and Gunkel points out that laments often end with the certainty of future rescue and thanksgiving (*Psalms*, pp. 36-37).

21.   J.D.W. Watts, '"This Song." Conspicuous Poetry in Hebrew Prose', in J.C. de Moor and W.G.E. Watson (eds.), *Verse in Ancient Near Eastern Prose* (AOAT, 42; Neukirchen–Vluyn: Neukirchener Verlag, 1993), pp. 345-58 (352-55). Jack Sasson also notes some poetry's loose attachment to a prose plot and its freedom from the constraints of chronology (*Jonah*, pp. 202, 206). Most recently S.P Weitzman has attempted to demonstrate that the presence of poetic passages in prose is an Old Testament compositional technique developed in pre-exilic texts which is then consciously imitated by post-exilic authors ('"Sing to the Lord a New Song": The Role of Songs within Biblical Narrative and their Resonance in Early Biblical Interpretation' [PhD diss., Harvard University; Ann Arbor, MI: University Microfilms, 1993]).

element in Hebrew poetry, reasons for excluding 2.2-11 as a later interpolation lose their merit.

Jonah and the Analysis of Hebrew Poetry

As is the case with the discussion of the language, date and genre of Jonah in Chapter 1 above, specific issues concerning the poetry of Jon. 2.3-10 serve as a reflection on and concrete example of larger methodological debates in the field. There is little agreement as to what is the constitutive element of Hebrew poetry. Divergences flourish in regard to the presence and identification of meter. The counting of letters, syllables, stresses, morae and syntactical units leads to numerous charts, diagrams and graphs, each in competition with the others. They generate more heat than light. In the face of this lack of consensus, James L. Kugel and Michael O'Connor each separately proposes that Hebrew verse has no meter, and that the search for one should be abandoned.[22] Against Kugel and O'Connor, Wilfred G.E. Watson argues analogously from the lack of consensus concerning meter in English, and holds that Hebrew poetry has a meter which is not continuously maintained throughout a poem.[23] Kugel holds the determining feature to be parallelism, and Sasson observes: 'Beyond agreeing that poetry features parallelism as a major element, scholars spiritedly debate whether it also exhibits other components'.[24] Yet this view has its detractors as well.[25]

22.   J. Kugel, *The Idea of Biblical Poetry: Parallelism and its History* (New Haven, CT: Yale University Press, 1981); M. O'Connor, *Hebrew Verse Structure* (Winona Lake, IN: Eisenbrauns, 1980); so also D.L. Petersen and K.H. Richards, *Interpreting Hebrew Poetry* (Guides to Biblical Scholarship; Minneapolis: Fortress Press, 1991), pp. 38-43. Similar discussions concerning Hebrew poetry are those of Sasson, *Jonah*, pp. 161-67, 201-15; Craig, *Poetics*, pp. 103-109; and D.L. Christensen, 'The Song of Jonah: A Metrical Analysis (Jon 2.3-10)', *JBL* 104 (1985), pp. 217-31 (218-22).

23.   W.G.E. Watson, *Classical Hebrew Poetry: A Guide to its Techniques* (JSOTSup, 24; Sheffield: JSOT Press, 1984), pp. 88, 92, 98. These remarks occur in Watson's chapter on meter, which summarizes all the different approaches (pp. 87-113). Watson opts for a stress-based analysis.

24.   *Jonah*, p. 162.

25.   So Petersen and Richards, *Interpreting Hebrew Poetry*, pp. 26-31. Watson argues that if parallelism is the sole key feature of Hebrew poetry, then it has no 'distinctive character' since parallelism may be seen in translation. For Watson there must be 'some additional "native" component' (*Classical Hebrew Poetry*, p. 109).

Jonah's song has been subjected to metrical analysis of every kind. Frank Moore Cross counts syllables and produces a structure based upon alternating short and long cola, but he is required to emend the text in vv. 3, 7 in order to reach his conclusions.[26] Such emendation *metri causa* confuses the goal of the metrical analysis (i.e., explication of a poem's structure) with the means employed towards that goal (i.e., counting syllables). The unhappy result of this confusion is that the text to be interpreted becomes the means used to prove the validity of the method. Sasson subjects Cross's analysis and the method itself to a sustained critique and sums up the shortcomings incisively:

> I think it would be worth our while occasionally to step back and ponder the consequence of manipulating what we have into something that can never be proved... Where does it all lead, after all, this reconstruction of texts by maneuvering this or that element and by modifying metrical counts through the exchange of this or that syllable? Are we resurrecting thereby an 'original' text?... Are copyists and scribes alone to blame for the metrical irregularities in our received Hebrew text?... Is it insensitivity, mischief, or perversion that drove them to do so?[27]

Representing the opposite end of the spectrum from Cross, Kenneth Craig eschews any attempt to find a meter in Jonah's psalm and concentrates on grammatic and semantic parallelism. While this seems a promising approach at first glance, Craig's reader is frustrated to find the main conclusion to be, after 27 pages of analysis, that 'with verse, a terseness of expression is observed at the semantic–grammatic–phonological level'.[28] Looking closer at Craig's work, arbitrariness is evident. An example is his treatment of 2.7, 9:

> Waters encompassed (my) neck;
> (The) deep swirled around me.

> I descended to the underworld;
> Bars were upon me forever.

26.   'Studies', pp. 161-66.
27.   Sasson, *Jonah*, p. 212. This quote occurs at the end of Sasson's extended critique (pp. 209-12).
28.   Craig, 'Poetics', p. 139, analysis from pp. 112-39. This is equally lengthy in Craig's book (*Poetics*, pp. 109-23). There, the conclusion is rewritten to read: 'this investigation has shown that parallelisms of equivalence or contrast are found at semantic–grammatic–phonological levels, and that the innovative imagery...is characterized by action, simplicity and concreteness' (p. 122).

Craig designates the first couplet (v. 7) as an example of 'focusing, heightening', while the second (v. 9) is 'complementary'. One may just as easily argue that both verses represent an intensification of imagery: water—the swirling deep; the underworld—its eternal bars.[29] Craig's conclusions rest upon subjective criteria couched in abstract language.

What is patently evident among the many attempts to delineate a structure to Jonah's psalm[30] is that no two offerings are alike,[31] which justifies the suspicion that there is no recoverable structure to be found. As is the case with the emendation method of Cross, other approaches have blurred the line between the use of a method to explicate a text and the use of texts to justify methods.[32] The lack of consensus and absence of reasonably plausible results serve as the reasons why this study will not offer a chart or diagram of Jonah's poem, but will rather attempt to understand it through grammatical observations, comparison of similar passages in the Old Testament and analysis of imagery.

---

29.   *Poetics*, pp. 109-10; the translation and layout is Craig's. It should also be noted that Craig overlooks the quasi-alliteration between מגּד and נגרשׁתּי (v. 5) in his table of sound patterns (p. 118). Stanislav Segert finds a true parallelism only in 2.3 ('Syntax and Style', 129).

30.   In addition to the works discussed in this chapter are the divisions of Landes, 'Kerygma', p. 26; Walsh, 'Jonah 2,3-10', p. 220; Almbladh, *Studies*, p. 30; Sasson, *Jonah*, p. 166; M. Barré, 'Jonah 2.9 and the Structure of Jonah's Prayer', *Bib* 72 (1991), pp. 237-48 (242-43); Nogalski, *Redactional Processes*, pp. 252-53 and Trible, *Rhetorical Criticism*, pp. 163-64. Such extreme divergence and the subjectivity it presupposes is also evident in attempts to delineate other structures in Jonah discussed above in Chapter 2.

31.   So Barré: 'The disagreements in these studies—all from accomplished scholars—only serve to show that interpreting the structure of a Hebrew poem is still far from an exact science' ('Jonah 2.9', p. 237); so also Craig, 'Poetics', pp. 118-19.

32.   This is clear in the statement of Walsh: 'The option chosen in this paper—that of counting stress groupings rather than syllables—is an entirely pragmatic one: for this particular psalm, syllable count does not seem to yield useful results (e.g., consistent patterns and significant divergencies therefrom) whereas stress count does' ('Jonah 2.3-10', p. 220 n. 2).

To this may be added Sasson's observation that 'charting the structure of some compositions can be a private and artificial enterprise, guided solely by taste and experience' (*Jonah*, p. 165).

The setting for Jonah's psalm is quickly sketched: a three-day sojourn within a large fish.[33] The gender of Jonah's fish changes twice in the course of its appearance in the book. First a male fish (דג, 2.1) is commanded to swallow Jonah and he stays in its belly for three days and nights. When Jonah prays in the fish, the feminine is used (דגה, 2.2). Finally, when God commands the fish to eject Jonah, the masculine reappears (2.11). *Tg. Ps.-J.* maintains this shift. The LXX lodges Jonah in a sea–monster (τὸ κῆτος) which, by means of the New Testament citation of the LXX, is the origin of the association of Jonah with a whale. Conveniently the Greek term is a third declension neuter, and thus poses no problem concerning gender; it may be surmised whether its ability to translate both the Hebrew forms is the motivation behind its selection. The Vg renders the term with *piscis*, a third declension masculine noun.

This change in the Hebrew has been explained by examples where the feminine is used to signify a single example of a class normally designated by the masculine (*nomen unitatis*).[34] While this gives grammatical grounds for the presence of the feminine form, it leaves unresolved the reason for the shift in gender. Karin Almbladh argues that the feminine form is used to create a parallel structure between the phrase ממעי הדגה and מבטן שאול in the following verse.[35] Sasson holds that the shift is a vernacular phenomenon, and cites as support a Mari letter in which 'lion' and 'lioness' are indiscriminately inter-

33.   Karl Marti argues that the fanciful account of an entire ship being ingested by a whale found in Lucian's *Vera Historia* 2 is a satire on Jonah (*Dodekapropheton*, p. 247). This is refuted by Schmidt, *Jona*, p. 63.

34.   BDB, p. 185, GKC, 122s-t, and Trible, 'Studies', pp. 31-32. GKC, also cites the feminine אניה in Jon. 1.3 as another example of a *nomen unitatis*.

35.   Almbladh, *Studies*, p. 25. She cites as another example the single occurrence of the feminine מחנה in Ps. 27.3 in relation to מלחמה. Almbladh's argument would be stronger if מלחמה occurred in the masculine elsewhere in Psalm 27. Her remark on this issue is vague, and can be construed to mean that the term does occur in the masculine in Psalm 27: 'So also e.g. *mhnh* in Ps 27.3, where it is in the feminine, i.e. to the parallelism with *mlhmh* in the sequel, *although it otherwise is in the masculine*' (p. 25 n. 52, emphasis added). That מחנה is written identically in both the masculine and feminine (BDB, p. 334) makes it a poor choice to help shed light on the phenomenon in Jonah.

changed.[36] The merit of Sasson's example from Mari is minimal because of the time span—over a millennium between the letter and Jonah. That he goes so far to find an example speaks to the unlikelihood of the explanation.

At this juncture the possibility of textual corruption should be entertained.[37] It can be argued that the feminine appears here because it is in a construct relationship with מעה הדגה (ממעי), which can mean 'womb'. Or one could say that an orthographic confusion resulted from the prefixed definite article, and so הדג becomes הדגה. The first explanation overlooks that דג and מעה occur in the identical construct relationship in 2.1 (הדג במעי, although this phrase is governed by a different preposition) with the noun in the masculine. The second line of reasoning has no MSS witnesses to support it. Mur 88 reads exactly as the MT.[38]

None of the explanations previously offered has much evidence upon which to draw support. Perhaps we should change our understanding of the fish incident in Jonah and, in the wonder of the fish that went from male to female and back again, see an act of divine power which eclipses the survival of a human being in its belly. Along these lines, the *Midr. Jon.* offers an innovative explanation of this puzzling feature: God saw that Jonah was comfortable inside the roomy confines of the male fish. Therefore he appointed a second fish to swallow Jonah, a female, pregnant with 365,000 of her young. The male fish spat Jonah into the female's mouth. In his new surroundings, Jonah was so cramped and miserable that he prayed for forgiveness and release. God relented, had Jonah spat back into a male fish, and then vomited upon shore.[39]

Landes argues that the three days and nights Jonah spends in the fish are to be seen as a standard ancient Near Eastern time span used to

36.   Sasson, *Jonah*, pp. 156-57. The only examples from Hebrew that Sasson can cite are 2 Sam. 19.27, where a masculine noun is subsequently referred to by a feminine pronoun, and Ps. 42.2, where a masculine noun takes a feminine verb (so also GKC, 122-23). There is no instance in the Old Testament apart from Jonah where a noun changes gender midstream, as it were.

37.   To my knowledge, none of the commentaries argues for corruption, nor is the verse annotated in *BHS*.

38.   4QXII^a and 4QXII^f are defective for these verses.

39.   Texts quoted in Zlotowitz, *Yonah*, p. 108 and Limburg, *Jonah*, pp. 108-11. Rabbinic tradition is replete with vivid accounts of the spacious accommodations of Jonah's fish, and the marvelous places to which it takes him. Cf. Chapter 1.

denote a journey to the netherworld. He appeals to the Sumerian 'Descent of Inanna', in which the goddess Inanna, before her voyage to the underworld, orders her servant to sing a lament for her only after she has been gone three days.[40] Although provocative, Landes's position does not withstand scrutiny. One could argue that the three-day motif illustrates the practice in which a period of waiting is observed after death to ensure that the individual truly is dead and to prevent premature burial. Thus, the three-day wait before the lament is raised for Inanna can signify the realization that she has gone down to the land of no return.[41] But this approach is too specific. Johannes Bauer analyzes the occurrences of three-day/three-day and night time spans in the Old Testament and, due to the wide variety of contexts in which they occur, determines the phrase to be a circumlocution used to denote varying lengths of time.[42] Bauer's position is supported by the 'three days' in Jon. 3.3 used to speak of the size of Nineveh.

Indicative of poetry in any language, Jonah's song exhibits an elasticity of grammar and vocabulary, and consequently more lexical observations are required than in the analysis of the prose portion of the text. The poem begins with a formula recounting the supplicant's cry to God and the wish/assertion that it will be heard (so also Pss. 120.1, 130.1). There follows a description of Jonah's plight utilizing a cluster of vivid water imagery. Sasson notes that the *polel* form of סבב in vv. 4, 6 is used in its two other occurrences in the Old Testament (Deut. 32.10, Ps. 32.10) to signify being surrounded in a protective manner.[43]

Verse 5 presents the first major textual issue in Jonah. The MT (followed by the *Tg. Ps.-J.*) introduces the second clause with the particle אך, and makes the phrase an assertion: 'but I will again look upon your holy temple'. The LXX has ἆρα, which functions interrogatively at the beginning of a clause, and thus gives the reading:

40. G.M. Landes, 'The "Three Days and Three Nights" Motif in Jonah 2.1', *JBL* 86 (1967), pp. 446-50; *idem*, 'Kerygma', pp. 11-12.

41. To paraphrase Benjamin Franklin: 'Fish and dead visitors stink after three days'. Sasson critiques Landes's reading on the grounds that it 'risks turning the psalm into a travel guide to hell and back' (Sasson, *Jonah*, p. 153 n. 19).

42. J.B. Bauer, 'Drei Tage', *Bib* 39 (1958), pp. 354-58; Bauer notes modern equivalents in German ('ein paar Tage') Italian ('un paio di giorni') and English ('a couple of days').

43. *Jonah*, p. 176.

'how shall I again gaze upon your holy temple?'[44] On the basis of the LXX many have emended אך to איך.[45] This solution is untenable when one observes that the LXX has changed other assertions in Jonah's psalm into questions or wishes:

1. In 2.7b the MT reads 'You have brought up my life from the pit, Yahweh my God'. The LXX reads 'the corruption of my life' (φθορὰ ζωῆς μου) and makes this phrase the subject of the clause. The verb is rendered in a third-person imperative which casts the phrase as a wish: 'Let the corruption of my life ascend, O Lord, my God'.
2. In 2.8b the optative is employed (ἔλθοι), which changes the MT's 'my prayer came to you in your holy temple' to 'may my prayer come to you'.[46]

In this larger setting of contextual changes of the exact same nature, it seems more plausible to hold that the LXX rephrased the assertion of 2.5b into a question. Mur 88, although partially damaged at this point, also supports the MT. Next to the *aleph,* the long downward stroke of the final *kaph* can be read. There is no room between these two letters for a *yodh*.[47] Thus the reading of the MT should be retained.[48]

The structural and thematic center of the psalm lies in vv. 6-7. Jonah's descent reaches the extreme depths and he then begins his return upward by means of divine aid.[49] Magonet argues that these verses are filled with 'unfamiliar terminology', in contrast to the borrowing from the Psalter evident in the other verses of poem. This unfamiliarity is a means through which the author stresses Jonah's

44. Theodotion has πῶς. 8 Hev XIIgr is not preserved at this point. Jerome comments that ἄρα can be rendered as 'therefore' (*igitur*): 'as a final conclusion... which does not convey the incertitude of one who hesitates, but the assurance of one who asserts' (Duval [ed.], *Jerome: Commentaire*, p. 238. Jerome is no doubt referring to ἄρα, which is an inferential particle designating 'then'.
45. So Mowinckel, *Psalms*, II, p. 34; Cross, 'Studies', p. 164; Couffignal, 'Le Psaume', p. 544; *BHS*, RSV, JB and JPSV. Arnold B. Ehrlich emends the text to read אכן, which retains the assertive sense of the phrase (*Ezechiel*, p. 267).
46. Perkins, 'Septuagint of Jonah', pp. 48-49.
47. The editor of the scroll reads אך (Benoit [ed.], *Grottes des Murabba'at*, p. 190, pl. 15). 4QXII [a,f] are defective at this point.
48. So the versions of Wycliffe, Tyndale, KJV, NAB.
49. So also Sasson, *Jonah*, p. 182; Trible, *Rhetorical Criticism*, p. 169 n. 37.

arrival at the absolute furthest point from his world and his God.[50] Magonet's interpretation is undermined by inspection of other uses of this terminology, which shows that it is not unique to Jonah:[51]

> Waters have encompassed me up to my neck (אפפוני מים עד נפש, Jon. 2.6).
>
> Save me O God! For the waters have come up to my neck (מים עד נפש באו, Ps. 69.1).
>
> For evils have encompassed me without number (כי אפפו עלי ראות, Ps. 40.13).

> I went down to the land whose bars closed upon me forever (הארץ ברחיה בעדי לעלם, Jon. 2.7).
>
> Who shut the sea with doors... when I... prescribed bounds for it, and set bars and doors (ואשים בריח ודלתים, Job 38.8, 10).[52]

In v. 9, משמרים has been pointed as a *piel* participle; the RSV reading, 'Those who pay regard to vain idols forsake their true loyalty', is representative.[53] Ps. 31.7 is often cited in support. Michael Barré argues against this translation for the following reasons:

1. Jon. 2.9 is the only occurrence of the *piel* participle of שמר in the Old Testament. In Ps. 31.7 the verb is a *qal* participle.
2. Participles followed by finite verbs, as is the case in Jon. 2.9, have a relative force.
3. שמר and עזב occur often in opposition to each other.

---

50. Magonet, *Form and Meaning*, p. 51; this is also the opinion of Golka, *Jonah*, p. 97. Walsh points out the correspondence in the psalm between descent and the Yahweh's absence. Here, at the nadir of Jonah's downward plunge, Yahweh is not mentioned ('Jonah 2,3-10', p. 227).

51. The correspondence between language in Jonah's psalm and other psalms in the Old Testament is treated more fully below.

52. Tromp has traced the usage of ארץ for the netherworld, and the image of Sheol as a fortified city with bars and gates (*Death*, pp. 27-28, 46, 154). Although grammatically awkward, RSV places v. 7a with 6b, and reads: 'weeds were wrapped around my head at the roots of the mountains'. This reading is also favored by Snaith, *Hebrew Text of Jonah*, pp. 27-28; Johnson, 'Jonah II.3-10', p. 84 n. 13; Cross, 'Studies', p. 164; Almbladh, *Studies*, p. 28 and Craig, *Poetics*, p. 110. Grammatical arguments against this transposition are in Sasson, *Jonah*, pp. 186-87 and Price and Nida, *Translator's Handbook*, p. 44.

53. Although cf. JPSV: 'They who cling to empty folly forsake their own welfare'. The editors note that the verse is uncertain in the Hebrew. *Tg. Ps.-J.* liberally expands with its 'Not as the nations, who worship idols, who do not understand the source of their well-being' (Levine, *Aramaic Version of Jonah*, pp. 79-80).

4. שמר never takes a deity as an object.

5. Understanding the מ-prefix of משמרים as a preposition, rather than a participial construction, establishes a pattern in Jonah's poem in the alternation of the prepositions מן and אל.[54]

Barré's revised reading casts the entire verse as a prepositional phrase modifying the clause of v. 8b.[55] While inelegant, this translation is grammatically sound. It requires the *waw*-conjunctive which begins v. 10 to be read paratactically ('*and* I'), rather than disjunctively. Contextually, however, the sense of the poem is strained. In the standard reading, the verse gives the sense of an aside that fits well in vv. 9-10, as Jonah emphasizes his faithfulness through contrast with those who worship false gods and promises to intensify his worship of the true god, Yahweh, by means of the fulfillment of vows he has made along with the promise of future sacrifice. Barré's translation maintains this contrast, but the nameless idolaters are no longer only a reference in Jonah's musings. Instead they form the setting for Jonah's prayer; it is from among them that Jonah makes his appeal. Read this way, v. 9 forms a nonsensical shift in the midst of a well-established dual setting of the supplicant's placement in the underworld and Yahweh's abode in the temple.[56] Moreover, while the new translation does complete (or rather, creates) a pattern in the occurrences of מן in the psalm, these prior uses of the preposition all refer to the respective portions of the dual setting, underworld/temple. Thus, Jonah cries out to Yahweh *from* his distress (v. 3); he is heard *from* the belly of Sheol (v. 3); he is cast *from* Yahweh's presence (v. 4); Yahweh brings him

---

54. Barré, 'Jonah 2.9', pp. 239-41, 247.

55. 'And my prayer came to you, to your holy temple, from (among) those who hold to faithless practices, who abandon/disregard their covenant fidelity' (Barré, 'Jonah 2.9', p. 243). Aquila tranlsates similarly: ἄπο φυλασσοντῶν, but Symmachus captures the intensive sense of the *piel* with ὅτι παραφυλασσόντες. Gordon R. Clark renders חסדם in 2.9 by 'the one who extends חסד to them' (*The Word Ḥesed in the Hebrew Bible* [JSOTSup, 157; Sheffield: JSOT Press, 1993], p. 200). Clark's reading is consonant with translations and commentaries. It establishes a contrast between the pious Jonah and those idolaters who forsake divine mercy. Rabbi David Kimchi translates חסד in Jon. 2.9 as 'shame' on the basis of Lev. 20.17. Kimchi's revision gives the opposite sense: those who worship idols abandon their shame (their idolatry) and come to worship Yahweh (quoted in Zlotowitz, *Yonah*, pp. 116-17).

56. Christensen argues erroneously that in v. 8 Yahweh comes down to Jonah and makes the fish his temple ('Song', pp. 227-30).

up *from* the grave (v. 7). These internal features, in addition to the absence of MSS variants for the term, and the near unanimity (save Aquila) of the versions for the standard reading are strong reasons not to accept Barré's argument.

From the foregoing analysis it becomes clear that Jonah's song has many affinities with the poetry found in the book of Psalms. The question of its relation to the Psalter is another issue to be investigated in the exegesis of Jonah 2.

Jonah's Psalm and the Psalter

Nearly every article, monograph and commentary on Jonah includes a listing of relationships between Jon. 2.3-10 and the Psalter.[57] In earlier debates surrounding the book these relationships often are used to argue for a date for Jonah but, given the uncertainty of dating the psalms, such a method is nothing but an exercise in explaining the obscure by means of the enigmatic.[58] An important fact that often gets lost in such long lists of psalm citations is that only one exact verbal correlation exists between Jonah and the Psalter: 'all your breakers and waves swept over me' (Jon. 2.4b=Ps. 42.8).[59] Ninety years ago

57.   Wilson, 'Authenticity', pp. 434-36; Feuillet, 'Livre de Jonas', pp. 181-82; O. Kaiser, 'Wirklichkeit, Möglichkeit und Vorurteil: Ein Beitrag zum Verständnis des Buches Jona', *EvT* 33 (1973), pp. 91-103 (97 n. 22); Allen, *Jonah*, p. 184; Fretheim, *Message*, pp. 94-95; Ackerman, 'Satire and Symbolism', p. 221 n. 15; Magonet, *Form and Meaning*, p. 50; Vawter, *Job and Jonah*, p. 99; Cross, 'Studies', p. 160; Nowell, *Jonah*, pp. 11-12; Craig, 'Poetics', p. 100 n. 30; *idem*, *Poetics*, p. 93 n. 27; Brenner, 'Jonah's Poem', p. 185. Daube, 'Jonah', p. 41 and Couffignal, 'Le Psaume', p. 545 both refer to Jonah's psalm as a cento of the Psalter. Meinrad Stenzel lists similarities in the text of the Vg and points out how vocabulary between Jonah and the Psalter was made to conform to each other ('Zum Vulgatatext des Canticum Jonæ: Prälat A. Allgeier zum 70 Geburtstag', *Bib* 33 [1952], pp. 356-62 [358-59]). P. Kyle McCarter finds the traces of an ancient near Eastern legal practice of a river ordeal in Jonah 2 and similar Psalms ('The River Ordeal in Israelite Literature', *HTR* 66 [1973], pp. 403-12). Nogalski points out the similar terminology in Jonah 2 and Mic. 1.1-7 in the context of his discussion of the formation of the Minor Prophets collection (*Redactional Processes*, p. 248).

58.   Thus Keil and Delitzsch will use their Davidic dating of the psalms to argue for an eighth century BCE date of Jonah (*Minor Prophets*, I, p. 381 n. 1). Charles H. Wright uses the same method to argue for an exilic date ('Book of Jonah', p. 61). Haupt reads a Maccabaean background ('Jonah's Whale', pp. 163-64).

59.   Pointed out by Price and Nida, *Translator's Handbook*, p. 39 and Sasson,

Julius A. Bewer held that Jonah's psalm is not so much the result of a direct borrowing from the Psalter, but rather demonstrates,

> that the author was steeped in the religious language of the post-exilic community. That he should have worked these 'quotations' together into a psalm, taking them from these various other psalms, does not seem likely... The phrases it has in common with the other psalms were the common property of the religious language of the author's day.[60]

Recently Thomas L. Thompson has argued that the entire Old Testament is comprised of separate traditions that are themselves a combination of even smaller literary segments.[61] While maintaining that this type of process is what lies behind the formation of all of the biblical texts, Thompson draws particular attention to the prominence of this compositional strategy in biblical poetry.

> In a quite substantial way, larger tradition units are created through the joining or selecting of smaller units. In biblical poetry, for example, it is commonplace to recognize that the independent quality and mobility of a poem's segments can be easily exchanged as they take part in one of many psalms and songs.[62]

An examination of several psalms with similar phraseology to the psalm of Jonah 2 bears out the remarks of Bewer and Thompson, but with a significant added feature. Jonah 2.3-10 is more than just an elaborate patchwork of quotations/motifs/segments drawn from widely divergent areas of the Psalter and representative of the repertoire of

Jonah, p. 176. Luther also notes the verbatim correspondence and remarks: 'It is possible that Jonah borrowed this speech from that psalm' (Oswald [ed.], *Lectures*, XIX, p. 76).

60. Bewer, *Jonah*, p. 24. Bewer is followed by Johnson, 'Jonah II.3-10', p. 83 n. 6. Although holding that Jonah's poem does borrow from the Psalter, Perowne, similar to Bewer, writes that the song is 'drawn from the well–stored memory of a pious Israelite... giving vent to his feelings in the cherished forms' (*Obadiah and Jonah*, p. 69). Cf. also the methodological caveat of Sasson concerning the rush to conclude that a text borrows from another (*Jonah*, p. 23). Magonet makes the distinction between 'quote' and 'reminiscence', but this does not stop him from arguing for a dizzying patchwork of borrowing at work in Jonah (*Form and Meaning*, pp. 65-67).

61. T.L. Thompson, '4QTestimonia and the Composition of Texts: A Copenhagen Lego Hypothesis' (forthcoming): 'All biblical genres are what might be described [as] segmented genres; that is, they are complex units of tradition that are composed of multiple smaller segments of material' (p. 10).

62. Thompson, '4QTestimonia', p. 10.

biblical poets. Jonah's song also exhibits evidence of how *certain stylized combinations* of these segments—recognizable patterns of clustered motifs—are used freely in biblical composition. The number of psalms quoted here serves to emphasize the prevalence of these motifs occurring together.

> The cords of death encompassed me; the torrents of perdition assailed me; the cords of Sheol entangled me...
> In my distress I called upon the LORD; to my God I cried for help.
> From his temple he heard my voice and my cry to him reached his ears.
> Then the earth reeled and rocked; the foundations also of the mountains trembled... (Ps. 18,4-7).[63]

Here we see the same motifs as are found in Jon. 2.3-7:[64] death as a surrounding presence compared with raging water, a cry to Yahweh from a hopeless situation, Yahweh's presence in and response from his temple, reference to the foundations of the mountains. However, the order is not identical between Psalm 18 and Jonah 2. Psalm 18 first describes the menacing presence of death and the underworld before the poet calls upon Yahweh for help. In the psalm the foundations of the mountains tremble as a result of Yahweh's angry response, while in Jonah they mark the place of Jonah's final descent from the divine presence.

> O LORD, my God, I call for help by day; I cry out in the night before thee...
> Let my prayer come before thee...
> Thy wrath lies heavy upon me, and thou dost overwhelm me with all thy waves...
> They surround me like a flood all day long; they close in upon me together (Ps. 88.1-2, 7, 17).

Here again is the cry for help and the desire that the psalmist's prayer come to Yahweh. Here again death is construed by water imagery and understood as instrument of Yahweh's punishment ('your wrath', 'your waves', vv. 7, 17). This last feature is a further thematic contact with Jon. 2.4, where the waves and breakers are understood as Yahweh's.

---

63. See also the variant in 2 Sam. 22.5-7, 16. Although this chapter uses the Hebrew numbering for Jonah 2, verse numbers in the Psalm citations follow the RSV. Some of the passages are cited in Sasson under the heading, 'Illustrative Passages', pp. 168-200, *passim*.

64. Note the presence of אפף ('encircle'), שאול ('Sheol'), סבב ('surround') and היכל ('temple') in both Ps. 18 and Jon. 2.

> The snares of death encompassed me; the pangs of Sheol laid hold of me;
> I suffered distress and anguish. Then I called on the name of the LORD...
> I will pay my vows to the LORD... I will offer to thee the sacrifice of
> thanksgiving... I will pay my vows to the LORD... in the courts of the
> house of the LORD (Ps. 116.3-4, 14, 17-19).

In Psalm 116 again are the motifs of endangerment by encircling
death and the cry to Yahweh for help but in the opposite order of their
occurrence in Jonah 2. In Psalm 116 too we find segments regarding the
fulfillment of vows and the offering of a sacrifice connected with
thanksgiving as they are found in Jon. 2.10.[65]

> Offer to God a sacrifice of thanksgiving, and pay your vows to the Most
> High; and call upon me in the day of trouble; I will deliver you, and you
> shall glorify me...
> He who brings thanksgiving as his sacrifice honors me; to him who
> orders his way aright I will show the salvation of God (Ps. 50.14-15, 23).

As in Psalm 116 we have here the clustered motifs of the payment of
vows and the sacrifice of thanksgiving. However coupled with these
segments are phrases which understand Yahweh as the giver of deliverance and salvation, the same motif with which Jonah ends his poem
(Jon. 2.11).[66]

> I will come into thy house with burnt offerings, I will pay thee my vows,
> that which my lips uttered and my mouth promised when I was in
> trouble... I cried aloud to him, and he was extolled with my tongue...
> Truly God has listened; he has given heed to the voice of my prayer...
> Blessed be God, because he has not rejected my prayer or removed his
> steadfast love from me (Ps. 66.13-14, 17, 19-20).

Here we see the combination of the cry to Yahweh from distress,
Yahweh's response to the cry and the psalmist's promise to fulfill his
vows. In addition we find here also the notion of Yahweh's mercy (חסד,
v. 20) not being removed from the faithful psalmist. This same idea is
represented in its antithetical form in Jon. 2.9: those who have no faith
forfeit the חסד of Yahweh.

> Thou hatest those who pay regard to vain idols; but I trust in the LORD.
> I will rejoice and be glad for thy steadfast love...
> I had said in my alarm, 'I am driven far from thy sight'.
> But thou didst hear my supplications. (Ps. 31.6-7, 22)

---

65. Note the usage of נדר ('vow'), שלם ('pay'), זבח ('sacrifice') and תודה
('thanksgiving') in both Ps. 116.14, 17 and Jon. 2.10.

66. Cf. בישע אלהים in Ps. 50.23 with ישועתה יהוה in Jon. 2.10.

In Psalm 31 are three motifs also present in Jonah 2, although in a different configuration: the comparison between the sorry fate of those who worship false idols and the psalmist's faith in Yahweh's חסד, both linked with the conjunctive phrase 'but I' (ואני, Ps. 31.6; Jon. 2.9); the psalmist's distress at being far from Yahweh expressed in the form of an internal quote and introduced with 'and I said' (ואני אמרתי, Ps. 31.22; Jon. 2.5);[67] and Yahweh's favorable response to a cry for help.

Similar to the discussion above in Chapter 2 of the relationship between Jonah 1 and the sea storm accounts of Ezekiel 27 and Psalm 107, what is at work in Jonah's song is not a direct dependence or borrowing of a text or texts by another, but evidence of an established method of literary composition in which certain motifs occur in the same clusters within the larger, differing contexts of several Hebrew poems. Bewer is not far off the mark in his observation that Jonah's psalm shows more of the repertoire available to a Hebrew poet and not his sources. However, instead of understanding these similarities as the stock religious language of the pious Israelite we should, following Thompson, view them as highly stylized literary language which forms the compositional building blocks of biblical authors.[68] Jonah's poem, along with several other examples of biblical poetry: 1) speaks of trouble and distress in terms of encircling, raging water; 2) has calls to Yahweh out of such distress that are answered; 3) understands Jonah's divine rescue as no less than a return from the grave; 4) acknowledges that the only proper response after such an ordeal is fervent gratitude and renewed piety which separates the faithful Israelite from the idolater who has no hope of Yahweh's mercy. The use of these motifs in many examples of ancient Hebrew poetry, occuring as they do grouped together but with differences in order

---

67.   There is a striking verbal similarity between the motifs: השמרים הבלי שוא (Ps. 31.6) and משמרים הבלי שוא (Jon. 2.9); נגרזתי מנגד עיניך (Ps. 31.22) and עיניך הבלי שוא נגרשתי מנגד (Jon. 2.5). Note closely how these two motifs occur in the opposite order in their respective poems.

68.   Thompson's analogy references the Lego block, a popular children's toy ('4QTestimonia', p. 10). Sasson hints at this kind of understanding of Jonah's psalm when he notes: 'Because of their floating nature, the expressions and imagery of Jonah's poem... may be available at all periods of Israel's history' (*Jonah*, pp. 207-208). It should also be noted that Sasson's examples of 'Illustrative Passages' can function as further examples of the use of these clustered motifs.

and configuration, provides evidence not of a biblical author's sources but of his literary tradition and method of composition.

The Interpretation of Jonah 2.3-10

Jonah: Reformed or Mocked?

Among those who hold Jon. 2.3-10 to be a later insertion, the question that naturally follows is: 'Why is such a psalm put into Jonah's mouth?' The explanation is that a later reader or copyist inserts the poem in order to recast the rebellious Jonah in a more favorable light. As such, the psalm converts or rehabilitates Jonah by its attribution to him of cherished pious sentiments.[69]

For those who argue the song to be an original part of the narrative, the task is to resolve the tensions that arise from the divergent portrayals of Jonah. This is done by appeal to notions such as satire, parody and irony. Thus Jonah's prayer serves to mock and satirize prophecy,[70] the Psalter,[71] or Jonah himself.[72] A key argument in this view is that the metaphorical water imagery from which Jonah's psalm draws is rendered literal on the lips of a man in the belly of a fish; this in turn is seen as humorous.[73] Similar to this approach is that which reads the poem ironically. Such a reading invariably impugns

69. Soggin, 'Il "segno di Giona"', pp. 73-74; and Nogalski, *Redactional Processes*, pp. 263-65.

70. Vawter, *Job and Jonah*, pp. 98-101. Vawter will go on to add that Jonah is 'not only...a caricature of prophecy, he is also a mockery of Israelite piety' (p. 101).

71. Miles, Jr., 'Laughing', p. 174. Ironic perhaps in its own right, Miles holds the psalm to be a later insertion (p. 173), but his interpretation has been taken up by those who argue against this position.

72. Eubanks, 'Cathartic Effects', p. 156.

73. Judson Mather remarks that the psalm's 'moving, metaphorical language is burlesqued by being rendered literal'. This language thus becomes 'pious stock phrases comically appropriated by the literal-minded Jonah in his most comic fix' ('Comic Art', pp. 284-85). Following Miles, Brenner holds that the song 'offers the most articulate and extravagant use of water and pit imagery in biblical poetry'. As such, it is evidence of the poet's deliberate use of hyperbole, which serves to reduce Jonah to an absurd character: 'Factuality and image cancel each other out' (Brenner, 'Jonah's Poem', pp. 184, 189-90). Lacocque and Lacocque consider whether to read the psalm as a satire, but instead choose to see in it a psychological transformation in Jonah which involves his turning outward toward God (*Jonah*, pp. 99, 103-104).

Jonah's character, as the psalm is then seen as his self-righteous musings on true piety when, in fact, the only truly pious people are the sailors and the Ninevites.[74] John Holbert, noting the preponderance of second-person endings and passive verbs used in relation to Yahweh in vv. 3-4, argues that Jonah is wrongly blaming Yahweh for his predicament. In his recalcitrance, the prophet thinks God to be the cause of his troubles, when in reality it is he who has fled from his commission and the sailors who have cast him into the sea.[75]

The validity of such readings 'against the grain' is severely tested by the fact that its practitioners cannot seem to agree exactly at what Jonah's psalm wants its readers to laugh. Satire/parody/humor is effective only insofar as it can unambiguously designate the target of its attack for all to see; otherwise it becomes an 'inside joke'. The lack of consensus concerning Jonah's target speaks to the absence of humor altogether in the text. The opinion that Jonah wrongly attributes his predicament to Yahweh is a gross oversight of key features of Jon. 1.1-16. The sea storm account goes to great lengths to stress that Yahweh is the cause of the tempest (1.4) and the only action that can ease the storm is the sailors' offering of Jonah (1.12). Their prayer to Yahweh underscores that he is in control of all that is occurring (1.14).

Conclusion

This chapter has argued that the psalm of Jon. 2.3-10 is original to the book of Jonah on the basis of MSS evidence, as well as the prevalence of inset poetry in the Old Testament which ostensibly violates the logical sense of a prose account. Attempts to scan the prayer as poetry have only served to delineate scholarship's lack of data concerning the constitutive elements of ancient Hebrew verse, and consequently no schema has been outlined here as another sample to the many offerings already available. Upon closer inspection, 'borrowings' from the Psalter are seen rather to be clusters of common images and

74.   Golka, *Jonah*, p. 99.
75.   '"Deliverance"', pp. 71-73: 'the hypocrite is skewered on his own words' (p. 73). Ackerman also comments on Jonah's mistaken notion that Yahweh has cast him into the sea ('Satire and Symbolism', p. 223); so also Trible, *Rhetorical Criticism*, pp. 168-72. Such a view of Jonah's so-called false attribution of his situation to Yahweh may be the motivation behind the change in Jon. 2.4 from second to third-person endings in *Tg. Ps.-J.* (Levine, *Aramaic Version of Jonah*, p. 73).

motifs which Hebrew poets used to describe distress and salvation. Finally, attempts to view the psalm as either the rehabilitation or the pillorying of Jonah are seen to be founded upon the assumption that a tension exists between the psalm and the prose text. That a coherent reading can be given free of this assumption now serves as the bridge to a concluding interpretation.

The psalm can be read as a continuation of the themes set out in Jonah 1.[76] In this respect Jonah's final words from the fish, 'Deliverance belongs to Yahweh' (2.10), are illuminating. The importance of the phrase is emphasized in its placement as both the climax of vv. 9-10, and as Jonah's final remark before Yahweh releases him from his confinement.[77] David Gunn and Danna N. Fewell translate the verse, 'Victory is Yahweh's', and read it as evidence that Jonah has ceased struggling with God and agrees to follow the divine will.[78] Gunn and Fewell are correct in seeing a concession to divine power in the psalm, and this acknowledgment of Yahweh's power functions as both a summary of the song's theme and a reiteration of Jonah 1.

In the preceding chapter, it was shown that the sailors with whom Jonah travelled are brought into a new understanding of their world through an encounter with Yahweh. They come to know this god as creator of all, who exacts a terrible price for disobedience and allows no boundaries to be set on the completely free exercise of his limitless power. Alone with his thoughts, Jonah echoes this lesson in his poem. In the same way that the author drew upon an established narrative motif of the sea storm and made it uniquely Israelite through the choice of port, destination and divinity, so here does the author draw upon the common Israelite literary practice of poems inserted into prose combined with the standard imagery used for distress, appeal and salvation. Jonah does not wrongly blame God for his predicament but acknowledges the reality of the situation: Yahweh has brought him to this place, and only Yahweh can bring him out again. Referring to the breakers and the waves as belonging to Yahweh reiterates the

76. Various thematic contacts between 1.1-16 and 2.3-10 have been noted by Allen, *Jonah*, p. 219 and Ackerman, 'Satire and Symbolism', p. 226.

77. Sasson designates the phrase a doxology (*Jonah*, p. 199). For Fretheim it is 'the key verse of the book' as it anticipates Jonah's joy at his deliverance in 4.6 (*Message*, p. 103).

78. D. Gunn and D.N. Fewell, *Narrative in the Hebrew Bible* (Oxford: Oxford University Press, 1993), p. 136.

statement of 1.9 that he is the creator of the sea and the dry land. The affirmation that salvation comes only from Yahweh echoes the sailors' affirmation that he does whatever he pleases. It is hardly an accident that both these acknowledgments come as the final words before Yahweh relents (1.14, 2.10). Phyllis Trible disparagingly describes Jonah's psalm as a 'self-righteous religiosity [which] seeks to flatter the deity'. [79] Faced with a deity of unbounded power and freedom, flattery is a reasonable option for human beings. Some might dare to call it praise. Like the sailors, Jonah's only hope is to state the painfully obvious fact that Yahweh alone has the power and freedom to cast whomever he wills from his presence, and to bring that person back again. Put another way, Jonah's complete abandonment is necessary (but not sufficient, lest divine freedom be compromised) for his salvation. In this respect, the Koran rightly remarks of Jonah: 'had he not been one of those who glorify God, he would have tarried in the fish's belly until the day when they are raised' (37.143-44). Like the sailors, once Jonah admits that he is bound, that he has no control, then is he given a reprieve. In Jonah 3 the author will again restate this idea, but with the added factor that even the reprieve is subject to Yahweh's freedom.

79.   *Rhetorical Studies*, p. 172.

Chapter 4

A CITY'S FATE (JONAH 3.1-10)*

Divine anger is slow to mete out justice, but in its severity it makes up for
the delay.
                           —Valerius Maximus, *Memorable Words and Deeds* 1.1.3

Release me from the fast. Haven't I observed it long enough?... I shall
eat! I shall drink wine!
                           —Esarhaddon, in a letter to his astrologers[1]

With Jonah's efficient, if not graceful, exit from the fish, the story
progresses to the goal he has so desperately been trying to avoid.
After a recommissioning from Yahweh, Jonah expeditiously fulfills
his role as messenger, and then disappears as attention is shifted to the
city of Nineveh. Accordingly, this analysis of Jon. 3.1-10 will for the
most part be devoted to Nineveh both as a historical place and a literary tradition. Jonah, although present for a small portion of this
scene, offers several intriguing exegetical issues himself. I will first
look at the linguistic and textual features of Jon. 3.1-10. There follows
an investigation of four differing portrayals of Nineveh: the historical
city revealed by archaeological research, the great city described in
Jonah 3, the rapacious enemy of the remainder of the Old Testament,[2]
and finally the long-lost exotic city of Greek/Hellenistic literary tradition. Exploration of similar motifs of divine repentance, along with
use of the rhetorical phrase, 'Who knows?' in the Old Testament
serves as a final area of inquiry before concluding remarks are offered.

---

* A portion of this chapter has appeared in Bolin, '"Should I Not Also Pity
Nineveh?"'

1. Quoted in J.B. Schaumberger, 'Das Bussedikt des Königs von Ninive bei
Jona 3, 7.8 in Keilschriftlicher Beleuchtung', *Miscellenea Biblica* 2 (1934), pp. 123-
34 (130-31).

2. The only other substantial references to Nineveh in the Old Testament are
found in Nahum and Zephaniah.

Jonah 3.1-10

Jonah 3.1-2 is so similar to 1.1-2 that the author specifies that Yahweh's word to Jonah is the second communication of this kind (3.1). While at first glance the divine commission appears to be a reiteration of the command of 1.1-2, a divergence emerges in the change in prepositions from 1.2 to 3.2. In the first command, the verb קרא takes the preposition על, while in the second אל follows. Jack Sasson observes that when קרא takes על, the connotation is negative (e.g., Deut. 15.9, 1 Kgs 13.2, Jer. 25.29, 49.29, Lam. 1.15, Ps. 105.16).[3] This shift in Jonah from על to אל denotes a change in the content of the two messages: whereas in 1.2 Jonah is to denounce the city, now in 3.2 he is to announce to it an as yet unspecified message from God. Sasson's argument is based on several sound examples and is a valid explanation of the change of prepositions in Jonah. However, it should be noted that the Old Testament is not consistent in its use of קרא with על as a circumlocution for denunciation. Exceptions are Isa. 34.14, where קרא + על describes animals calling out to each other, and 2 Chron. 20.3, which uses the phrase to denote the proclamation of a fast. Another mitigating circumstance is the fact that, while the change in the meaning of the two commissions is carried over in rabbinic tradition and modern translations,[4] ancient versions did not read such a difference. *Tg. Ps.-J.*, while consistently rendering the Hebrew אל with the prefix ל, reads על for both Jon. 1.2 and 3.2. This makes the element of denunciation present in both commands.[5] In the LXX,

---

3.   Sasson's definition is 'to impose an (unpleasant) fate upon something' (J. Sasson, 'On Jonah's Two Missions', *Henoch* 6 [1984], pp. 23-30 [26]). See also the discussion of Jon. 1.2 above in Chapter 2. Others who note a shift in meaning are Witzenrath, *Jona*, p. 7; Wolff, *Obadiah and Jonah* (Minneapolis: Augsburg, 1986), p. 139 and Gunn and Fewell, *Narrative*, p. 137. Gunn and Fewell do not read קרא על as denoting judgment, but rather as a reference to the Ninevites' evil. Cyrus Gordon sees in the repetition of Jon. 1.1-2, 3.1-2 an example of a feature he calls 'Buildup and Climax', a combination of parallel narratives which further a plotline ('"This Time", [Genesis 2.23]', in M. Fishbane and E. Tov [eds.], *Sha'arei Talmon* [Winona Lake, IN. Eisenbrauns, 1992], pp. 47-51 [50]).

4.   The thirteenth-century Rabbi, Bachya ben Asher, notes the difference (quoted in Zlotowitz, *Yonah*, p. 119). It is also reflected in the KJV, RSV, NAB, JPSV.

5.   Levine, *Aramaic Version of Jonah*, pp. 55-56, 83.

neither command bears any negative connotation,[6] and Jon. 3.2 is formulated as a reiteration of 1.2 by use of the phrase, 'according to the former message'.[7] This is Jerome's rendering as well, and he is clear that both his Greek and Hebrew texts had this additional phrase specifying the second message to be the same as the first.[8] The only witness to the Hebrew text quoted by Jerome is 4QXII[a], dated 150–125 BCE. The text, with restored portions in brackets, reads

[הקרי][אה כזות אשר אנכי ד[בר] [9]

These textual differences yield three different interpretative possibilities:

1. Jonah is first told to condemn Nineveh, and then to convey to it an as yet unspecified message (MT, Vg, modern translations).

2. Jonah is told to condemn Nineveh in both of his commissions (*Tg. Ps.-J.*).

3. Jonah is twice commanded to convey to Nineveh an as yet unspecified message (LXX, Jerome, 4QXII[a]).

From an exegetical standpoint what is at stake in this matter is the notion of divine forgiveness in Jonah. If one accepts the first example, then it can be argued that as early as 3.2 God relents from a proposed destruction of Nineveh. With the remaining two selections, God's

---

6.   In the examples cited above which use קרא + על to denote denunciation, the LXX uses βοάω + κατά (Deut. 15.1), ἐπικαλέω + πρός (1 Kgs 13.2), and καλέω + ἐπί (Jer. 24.29=LXX 32.29, 49.29=LXX 30.24, Lam. 1.15, Ps. 105.16). The LXX uses κηρύσσω, a verb which carries no negative connotations, in Jon. 1.2, 3.2. This verb is also used to render קרא + על in the proclamation of the fast in 2 Chron. 20.3. קרא + אל is never used to denote denunciation; see BDB, pp. 895-96.

7.   κατὰ τὸ κήρυγμα τὸ ἔμπροσθεν. For ἔμπροσθεν used to refer to a previous occurrence, see LSJ, s.v. ἔμπροσθα, p. 548.

8.   Jerome translates both his Hebrew and Greek texts with 'et praedica in ea juxta praedicationem priorem' (Duval [ed.], *Jerome: Commentaire*, p. 258). Critical editions of the Vg delete this phrase and follow the MT: 'et praedica in ea praedicationem quam ego loquor ad te' (*Liber Duodecim Prophetarum ex Interpretatione Sancti Hieronymi* [Biblia Sacra Iuxta Latinam Vulgatam Versionem ad Codicem Fidem, 17; Rome: Libreria Editrice Vaticana, 1987], p. 166).

9.   Fuller, 'Minor Prophets Manuscripts', fig. A. 8. זות appears for זאת elsewhere in 4QXII[a]. For כזאת as a reference to a previous occurrence, see BDB, s.v. זה 6c, p. 262. Sasson's remark concerning the LXX reading demanding a 'wholesale alteration of our consonantal text' fails to take into account the evidence of 4QXII[a] (*Jonah*, p. 227). There is similar terminology in the JB of Jon. 3.2. 'preach to them as I told you to'.

forgiveness of the city comes upon seeing the repentance of the Ninevites. Concerning which reading is the original, the MT has the strongest case for pre-eminence. The distinction between אל and על eventually becomes blurred in Hebrew.[10] Thus the explanatory phrase found in the LXX and 4QXII[a] can be read as a gloss arising out of the scribes' unawareness concerning the distinction between the two prepositions.[11] This beginning of a divine reprieve hinted at in the MT of 3.2 is further intimated in the ambiguity of Jonah's announcement discussed below.

Jonah's 'oracle', arguably the shortest prophetic utterance in the Old Testament,[12] presents yet another textual divergence between the MT and the LXX. In the former, the time until Nineveh's destruction is 40 days, in the latter three days.[13] Jerome marvels at the discrepancy, 'for in Hebrew, neither the letters, nor the syllables, nor the accent, nor the word presents any common point'.[14] Some exegetes have argued for the priority of the LXX on the grounds that it makes better

10.   BDB, pp. 41, 757 discusses occurrences of one preposition where the other is expected; it attributes most of these examples to copyists' errors. Mur 88 is defective at Jon. 3.2, but reads על at 1.2. As an example of this later blurring of meaning between the two prepositions, the scroll also reads ויקראו על אלהים at Jon. 3.8—a context which cannot mean 'denounce' (Benoit [ed.], *Grottes de Murabba'at*, pls. 60-61).

11.   Whether the gloss originates in the LXX or the Hebrew is uncertain. It is equally likely that similar glosses arose independently of each other. In the MT, where כזאת is used to refer to previous events, it is never translated in the LXX by ἔμπροσθεν. I do not wish to argue that, in Jon. 3.2, the LXX is translating a Hebrew *Vorlage* identical to that found in 4QXII[a]; so also Fuller, 'Minor Prophets Manuscripts', p. 37.

12.   Jonah's laconic nature has led some commentators to see him as deliberately distorting or attempting to impede God's will concerning the Ninevites. This is the opinion of Kaiser, 'Wirklichkeit, Möglichkeit und Vorurteil', p. 99; Fretheim, *Message*, pp. 108-10; and R.J. Lubeck, 'Prophetic Sabotage: A Look at Jonah 3.2-4', *Trinity Journal* 9 (1988), pp. 37-46. Sasson sees in Jonah's beginning to announce on his first day in the city an indication that Jonah is eager to fulfill his inescapable mission and have done with it (*Jonah*, p. 236). This position is similar to Jerome's, who attributes Jonah's quick delivery to a newfound zeal (Duval [ed.], *Jerome: Commentaire*, p. 263).

13.   The Arabic agrees with the LXX. Codices Marchialanus and Syrohexaplaris, the recensions of Aquila, Symmachus, Theodotion, Theodoret, Theophylact, and 8 Hev XIIgr read 'forty'.

14.   Duval (ed.), *Jerome: Commentaire*, p. 265.

sense of the plot—it is more realistic for Jonah to sit outside of the city for three, rather than 40 days, to observe its fate.[15] But, as noted previously, notions of what is or is not more 'realistic' are governed by a strict logic which has little validity in a fabulous book such as Jonah. Indeed this explanation, that the plot is more plausible with the shorter time span, can be used as the rationale behind the LXX changing the reading from 40 days to three. The many examples of the 40-day time span in the Old Testament used to denote periods of penance or trial can be adduced as support of this observation. The three day phrase of the LXX is easily explained as a compositional variant arising from the desire for Jonah's oracle to correspond with the play of events in the remainder of the book. The use of a three–day time span to denote the size of Nineveh in the preceding verse provided an alternative to MT's 40 days.

While at first glance Jonah's utterance appears unequivocally to be an announcement of imminent destruction, the author's use of the *niphal* participle of הפך has a wider semantic range. Although הפך is used often in the Old Testament to speak of cities' destruction,[16] it is for this sense always in the *qal*. In the *niphal*, הפך can mean, 'to change oneself', and is used to denote any radical change from one extreme to the other, including that of the heart or mind.[17] In Hos 11.8 it signifies divine repentance:

> How can I give you up, O Ephraim! How can I hand you over, O Israel!
> How can I make you like Admah! How can I treat you like Zeboim!
> My heart recoils (נהפך) within me; my compassion grows warm and
> tender.

Such a semantic range gives Jonah's oracle a tautological nature, for when he announces, 'In forty days Nineveh turns over', regardless of whether the city is destroyed or repents and is spared, his oracle is true. This ambiguity is carried over in *Tg. Ps.-J.*, where מתהפכא is used, and in the discussion of Jon. 3.4 in *b. Sanh.* 89b.[18] Augustine acknowledges the double meaning of the term, as does the sermon of Pseudo-Philo, which states that

15. So Bewer, *Jonah*, p. 52; Jepsen, 'Anmerkungen zum Buch Jonah', pp. 297-98 and Kraeling, 'Evolution', pp. 308-309.

16. BDB, p. 245. It is most often used in this sense to speak of Sodom and Gomorrah.

17. BDB, p. 245, e.g., Exod. 14.5.

18. Levine, *Aramaic Version of Jonah*, pp. 84-85; Zlotowitz, *Yonah*, p. 122.

> The city has truly been overturned, as it was proclaimed, but in its hearts
> and not its walls. It is no longer the same city.[19]

Exegetes are divided as to whether the dual sense is intended in Jon.
3.4.[20] It seems more than coincidence that, in an account wherein a
city slated for destruction is spared, the author would choose a con-
jugation that makes Jonah's announcement ambiguous when a different
form from the same root is commonly used to describe the destruction
of cities. This ambiguity is heightened even more when one also notes
that the author chooses a city which at the time of writing was already
destroyed. This issue will be examined below in the section concerning Nineveh.

Immediately upon hearing Jonah's word, the Ninevites stage a mass
repentance which encompasses the entire populace.[21] Word then
comes to the king,[22] who engages in standard behavior signifying

19.   Augustine cited in Fáj, 'Stoic Features', p. 313. Ps.-Philo quoted in Duval,
Livre de Jonas, I, p. 81. John Wycliffe captures the dual meaning well with his
translation, 'yet fourti daies and Nynyue schal be turned upsodoun'. Scholars who
argue for the historicity of Jonah point out that this double meaning also obtains in
the Assyrian verb *abaku*. So Wiseman, 'Jonah's Nineveh', p. 49 and Stuart, *Hosea–
Jonah*, p. 489.

20.   For Sasson the discrepancy, caused by the fact that God (and the author)
understand הפך as transformation while Jonah takes it to mean destruction, is the
source of Jonah's distress in ch. 4 (*Jonah*, pp. 234, 267-68). Others who see a
deliberate *double entendre* in the term's use are Ackerman, 'Satire and Symbolism',
pp. 225-26; Good, *Irony*, pp. 48-9; Magonet, *Form and Meaning*, p. 109; Eubanks,
'Cathartic Effects', pp. 31, 165; Trible, *Rhetorical Criticism*, pp. 184 n. 23, 190 (this
is a reversal of her position in her 'Studies', p. 269); and Kahn, 'Analysis', p. 96.
Among those who argue that the author limits Jonah's oracle exclusively to an
announcement of destruction are Allen, *Jonah*, p. 222; Price and Nida, *Translator's
Handbook*, p. 55; Wolff, *Obadiah and Jonah*, p. 149; Golka, *Jonah*, pp. 104-105;
and Lubeck, 'Prophetic Sabotage', pp. 44-45.

21.   The Ninevites' repentance is but one of many episodes in the Old Testament
of the repentance and sparing of cities. Sasson discusses the various types of such
repentance in his section, 'Divine Clemency' (*Jonah*, pp. 241-43). Allen and Stuart
each describe a recurring pattern of threat–repentance–reprieve (Allen, *Jonah*, p. 223;
Stuart, *Hosea–Jonah*, p. 489). Trible lists the accounts in the Old Testament of cities
that repent ('Studies', pp. 222-25; *idem, Rhetorical Criticism*, pp. 191-93).

22.   Some see 3.6-9 as a flashback; so Wolff, *Obadiah and Jonah*, p. 145; and
Brichto, *Grammar*, p. 75. This viewpoint relies on a subtle reading and strict logical
binding of a text that makes sense as it is, and is critiqued by Sasson (*Jonah*,
p. 247). The figure of an all-powerful king who reacts to situations, rather than

repentance. The *piel* of כסה (which forms a wordplay with מכסאו four words prior) is used in v. 6 to describe the king's dressing himself in sackcloth, whereas in v. 5 לבש, and in v. 8 the *hithpael* of כסה are used to denote the same action. Sasson points out that, while the *piel* is an odd choice to describe the reflexive action of clothing oneself, this form of the verb in the Old Testament signifies the covering over of transgressions or of being covered in righteousness.[23] Such nuances fit here given the mass repentance.

The king's decree is presented in two differing versions. In the MT, it encompasses vv. 7b-9. The LXX reflects an understanding of the first verb of v. 8 as a *waw*-consecutive + imperfect (rather than the *waw*-conjunctive + jussive of the MT). Consequently, the king's decree ends in v. 7 and vv. 8-9 are presented as the reaction of the populace.[24] Use of מטעם in the introduction of the royal order is not an Aramaic term denoting 'decree', but rather carries the standard Hebrew meaning of 'taste'. It therefore forms a pun with the command that the people not eat (אל יטעמו).[25] This pun corresponds with a second wordplay between the following command in v. 7 that the animals not feed (ירעו אל) and the repeated use of רעה ('evil') in 3.9–4.1.[26] Attempts by many scholars to read a farcical and humorous tone into the royal decree are based more on an inability to acknowledge vast differences between epochs and cultures concerning what is and is not funny.[27]

acting upon them is a favorite one in the Old Testament. L.K. Handy analyzes these figures in 'The Great Ruler of the World: Variations on a Stock Character in Old Testament Short Stories' (Paper presented at the annual meeting of the Eastern Great Lakes Midwest Society of Biblical Literature, Notre Dame, IN, February, 1992).

23.   Sasson, *Jonah*, p. 251. For example, Job 31.33, Prov. 17.9, Pss. 32.5, 40.11. *Tg. Ps.-J.* elaborates on the king's opulence by speaking of his 'royal seat' and 'precious robe' (Levine, *Aramaic Version of Jonah*, pp. 86-87). Cf. Ezek. 26.16.

24.   So too the Vg. Both of these versions were then forced to add a plural subject to the rhetorical question of v. 9 (λέγοντες, *dixerunt*). These changes are noted in Trible, 'Studies', pp. 45-46; Perkins, 'Septuagint of Jonah', pp. 44-46; and Sasson, *Jonah*, pp. 252-65. Especially helpful is Sasson's chart comparing the MT with the LXX (*Jonah*, p. 265).

25.   So Sasson, *Jonah*, p. 256; Halpern and Friedman, 'Composition and Paronomasia', p. 83; and Trible, whose translation captures the pun well: 'The taste of the king and his nobles is that the people not taste' (*Rhetorical Criticism*, p. 185).

26.   So D.L. Christensen, 'Anticipatory Paronomasia in Jonah 3.7-8 and Genesis 37.2', *RB* 90 (1983), pp. 261-63 (262); *idem*, 'Andrzej Panufnik', p.139; and Sasson, *Jonah*, p. 256.

27.   Among those who see humor in the decree, Brichto, *Grammar*, p. 268 n.

Clothing animals in garb of mourning and penitence is a common practice from the Assyrian through to the Roman periods.[28] In fact, rather than attempting to paint a silly scene in the mass repentance of all the Ninevites, the author has constructed a tightly structured decree that focuses in turn on people, animals, then both.

> *people*
> Not to eat (verb specific to humans, wordplay between אל יטעמו and מתעם).

> *animals*
> Not to feed (verb specific to animals, wordplay between אל ירעו and רעה).

> *both*
> Not to drink.[29]

The notice that God repented of the pronounced doom upon seeing the repentance of the Ninevites has caused consternation among those who hold that no causality exists between human action and divine response.[30] However, 3.10 is clear that Yahweh changes his mind only after seeing how the Ninevites change their ways. The same term

17, is representative. Martin Luther pauses in his commentary to remark that, 'Sackcloth is a strange clothing for beasts of burden' (Oswald [ed.], *Lectures*, XIX, p. 24). Bewer, *Jonah*, pp. 54-55, and Stuart, *Hosea–Jonah*, p. 485, deny the presence of humor.

28.   Herodotus 9.24 is often cited in relation to Jon. 3.8 to argue for a Persian period provenance of the book, although the practice occurs both earlier and later. Jdt. 4.10 offers another biblical example of animals joining an entire population in mass repentance. John Day discusses the inadequacy of the example from Herodotus ('Problems', p. 34).

29.   Discussion in Trible, 'Studies', pp. 90-91); and Sasson, *Jonah*, pp. 254-55.

30.   John Calvin stresses that the Ninevites' deeds did not save them, but rather the fact that they had repented from a sense of fear, which necessarily implies faith (*Twelve Minor Prophets*, III, pp. 113-14). Contrary to Luther's exegesis of the Ninevites' repentance (treated above in Chapter 1), Calvin does not cite Jon. 3.5 as proof of his assertion. Wolff's characterization of God's repentance in 3.10 in relation to his freedom 'God does not specifically take notice of any good work... all he regards is the turning away from evil' (*Obadiah and Jonah*, p. 155) makes the author of Jonah a good Lutheran pastor and Jonah a 'mulish... inhibited theologian' (pp. 176-77). Among others who deny any causal link between the Ninevites' repentance and their forgiveness are Fretheim, *Message*, pp. 56-57; Cooper, 'In Praise of Divine Caprice', pp. 156-57; and Trible, *Rhetorical Criticism*, p. 187.

(שוב) is used to speak of both Yahweh's and the Ninevites' change.[31] Yet even though the text is clear that Yahweh relented due to the city's repentance, it will be shown that the author of Jonah is concerned to maintain the absolute sovereignty of divine freedom in a way more radical than those who would deny any link between repentance and forgiveness. This divine freedom at work in ch. 3 makes itself known by investigation of the city chosen as the site of Jonah's mission.

Nineveh the Great City

The Historical Nineveh

Nineveh's ruins lie on the the east bank of the Tigris river opposite the modern Iraqi town of Mosul. The two tells of Kouyounyik and Nebi Yunus ('the prophet Jonah') contain the ancient citadel and monuments, respectively. Paul Emil Botta was the first, in 1842, to dig at the site. Between the summer of 1846 and May, 1847, Austin Henry Layard sank a series of trenches 20 feet deep and uncovered nine royal chambers. A series of investigators dug throughout the following century and a half, through 1990.[32] Earliest occupation on the site is from the fourth millennium, with an uninterrupted sequence beginning in the third millennium. The name 'Ninua' occurs on Ur III period tablets (2112-2004 BCE) and twenty-first century inscriptions from Kultepe.[33] The city achieved its greatest glory at the beginning of the seventh century BCE when Sennacherib made it the capital of the Assyrian empire. He enclosed what would be known as the mounds of Kouyounyik and Nebi Yunus in a trapezoidal wall twelve kilo-

31. Christensen points out that the two plural occurrences of שוב in regard to the Ninevites frame two singular forms of the verb in reference to God ('Narrative Poetics', p. 44).

32. Layard published his account of work at Nineveh in *Nineveh and its Remains* (repr. and abridged; New York: Praeger, 1970 [1849]). A detailed survey of nineteenth-century excavations at Nineveh is R.C. Thompson and R.W. Hutchinson, *A Century of Exploration at Nineveh* (London: Luzack, 1929). A good overview of the city and its history can be found in M. Roaf, *Cultural Atlas of Mesopotamia and the Ancient Near East* (New York: Facts on File, 1990), pp. 186-87.

33. T. Madhloum, 'Excavations at Nineveh: A Preliminary Report (1965–67)', *Sumer* 23 (1967), pp. 76-82 (76). Many of the early modern work on Jonah made much of the fact that the cuneiform sign for Nineveh is the compound of a fish in a house; so A. Parrot, *Nineveh in the Old Testament* (London: SCM Press, 1955), p. 24.

meters in circumference with fifteen gates. Its glory was not long lived, as the Medes and Babylonians combined forces and besieged the city in 612 BCE, utterly destroying it.[34] Excavations revealed the extent of the destruction. In the Shamash gate on the city's eastern wall, a crude incision of a burning tower and a man with a bandaged head was found.[35] More violent evidence was found in the Halzi gate, also in the eastern wall. There excavators discovered poor, hastily built brickwork which narrowed the gate's opening from seven to two meters. Immediately in front of the gate they uncovered more than a dozen skeletons surrounded by bronze and iron arrowheads. One skeleton, that of a thirteen year old boy, still had an arrowhead buried in its leg bone.[36] After the Babylonian destruction, the site never again had a substantial population and, as will be seen below, quickly passed into the realm of legend.

Nineveh in the Book of Jonah

Jon. 3.3 offers three pieces of information about Nineveh; each poses an exegetical problem:

> Now Nineveh *was* (הִיתה) a city *great to God* (עִיר גְדוֹלָה לֵאלֹהִים), *a journey of three days.*

Use of the *qal* of הִיה in reference to Nineveh has long been viewed as proof that Jonah is written long after the city had been destroyed.[37] G.S. Ogden's analysis of the use of חיה in the Old Testament shows that, in the *qal* the verb always carries a strict sense of past or completed action. A stative or continuing sense in the *qal* is observable only in its use in direct speech.[38] To argue that the expression 'Nineveh was...' is merely part of the narrative past tense, one needs to explain why the author did not use the apocopated *waw*-consecutive form of הִיה, as is normally the case in Jonah (1.1, 4, 2.1, 3.1, 4.8).[39]

---

34. Babylonian text of Nabopolassar in *ANET*, pp. 304-305. 'the city was seized and a great defeat inflicted upon the entire population... The city they turned into ruin—hills and heaps of debris'.

35. Madhloum, 'Excavations at Nineveh', p. 78.

36. D. Stronach and S. Lumsden, 'UC Berkeley's Excavations at Nineveh', *BA* 55 (1992), pp. 227-33 (231-32).

37. So Bewer, *Jonah*, pp. 28-29.

38. 'Time and the Verb הִיה in O.T. Prose', *VT* 21 (1971), pp. 451-69 (451-53). Among those who argue for a stative sense of the verb in Jon. 3.3 are Perowne, *Obadiah and Jonah*, p. 74; and Wilson, 'Authenticity', p. 55.

39. This would give the reading וַתְּהִי נִינְוֵה. Although not as frequent as the

Many explanations have been offered for the phrase, נדולה לאלהים עיר. In the twelfth century, Rabbi David Kimchi observes that, when-ever the Old Testament wishes to emphasize the greatness of a thing, it often attaches it to the noun 'God'.[40] D. Winton Thomas, in an analy-sis of the use of the superlative in Hebrew, concludes that the divine name is used to express the superlative insofar as it brings something into comparison with God.[41] Sasson, in a critique of Thomas, notes that only in Jon. 3.3 is a noun not in the construct in a comparative relation to a word for God. On this basis he argues against reading the super-lative in Jon. 3.3, and rather understands the phrase to signify that Nineveh belongs to God.[42] Other interpretations read the phrase as reference to the number of temples in the city,[43] Nineveh's status as a divine residence (great enough for a god),[44] or its importance to God.[45]

Concerning the remark that Nineveh was a journey of three days, whether one understands it to mean traversing in a straight line across the city or meandering in its streets, it in no way corresponds with the historical city whose walls are twelve kilometers in circumference and whose widest point across is no more than five kilometers. As mentioned above in Chapter 1, some who argue for the historicity of Jonah contend that the text is referring to the larger urban area formed by the cities of Nineveh, Calah and Dur Sharrakin. Alternatively, Donald Wiseman holds that the three days refer to a diplomatic process—a day for arrival followed by one for accom-

---

masculine, the apocopated feminine form ותהי occurs over ninety times in the Old Testament. It should also be noted that in this clause of 3.3, the subject, Nineveh, occurs before the verb. This is contrary to normal Hebrew syntax and is used else-where in Jonah to draw attention to the subject (1.4, 4.10).

40. Quoted in Zlotowitz, *Yonah*, pp. 120-21.

41. D.W. Thomas, 'A Consideration of Some Unusual Ways of Expressing the Superlative in Hebrew', *VT* 3 (1953), pp. 210-24 (210-15). The superlative with the divine name occurs in Gen. 23.6, 30.8, Exod. 9.28, 1 Sam. 14.15, Pss. 36.7, 80.11 and Job 1.16. Only in Jon. 3.3 is the preposition ל prefixed. Thomas also cites Acts 7.20, which describes Moses as ἀστεῖος τῷ θεῷ; this text is also refer-enced in BDB, p. 513 in regards to Jon. 3.3. Day renders the superlative in a collo-quial sense: 'a godalmighty big city' ('Problems', p. 34).

42. Sasson, *Jonah*, pp. 228-29. This is the also the position of A. Rofé, who reads the phrase genitivally: 'God's great city' (*The Prophetical Stories*, p. 165).

43. Wiseman, 'Jonah's Nineveh', p. 36.

44. Trible, 'Studies', pp. 42-43.

45. Stuart, *Hosea–Jonah*, p. 437.

plishment of business and finally the day of departure.[46] Emil G.H. Kraeling hypothesizes that Jon. 3.3 originally spoke of a journey of one day, which was changed to three in the Hellenistic period to accord with the growth of cities then.[47] Helpful in clarifying this issue is Johannes B. Bauer's analysis of the time span 'three days' in the Old Testament cited above in Chapter 3.[48] It will be recalled that Bauer concludes that the phrase is a circumlocution denoting an appreciable passage of time. Thus, its use in Jon. 3.3 can easily be read as a standard way of simply saying that Nineveh was a very large city, without attempting to reconcile it with speculation as to whether it refers to Nineveh proper, to the surrounding area, to the city's circumference, or to a journey through its streets. The phrase, together with 'a city great to God', functions to form a hendiadys used to convey the enormity of the place. William Tyndale observes:

> And as for the three days' journey of Nineve [sic], whether it were in length or to go round about it or through all the streets, I commit unto the discretion of other men. But I think that it was then the greatest city of the world.[49]

Thus in the description of Nineveh in Jon. 3.3, it is apparent that for the author Nineveh is a city of an incredibly large size that no longer exists. The book of Jonah is not attempting to refer to the historical Nineveh, but rather portrays the city in a legendary fashion.

Nineveh in the Old Testament

Jonah contains the most references to Nineveh in the Old Testament. The city is also mentioned in an aetiology concerning the origin of several Mesopotamian cities in Gen 10.8-10 in addition to the references to the city in Nahum and Zephaniah. Both of these prophetic books emphasize Nineveh's role as symbol of the Assyrian empire, the mortal enemy of Israel, renowned for brutal conquest and cruelty.[50] Accordingly, many scholars, regardless of their particular stripe,

46. 'Jonah's Nineveh', pp. 37-39.
47. 'Evolution', pp. 308-309.
48. 'Drei Tage', pp. 354-58.
49. Daniell (ed.), *Tyndale's Pentateuch*, p. 636. Wolff also righty observes that 'the reader is not supposed to do arithmetic. He is supposed to be lost in astonishment' (*Obadiah and Jonah*, p. 148).
50. The Assyrians were ruthless in the subjugation of peoples, as their own records and reliefs vividly illustrate.

understand the Nineveh of the book of Jonah to be informed by the concept of Nineveh found in Nahum and Zephaniah which depicts the city as the antithesis to all that is civilized, God-fearing and in a word, Israelite. Thus, in a stunning hyperbole, André and Pierre-Emmanuel Lacocque, in elucidating Jonah's mission to Nineveh, ask:

> Where is the Auschwitz survivor who would go to Berchtesgaden or Berlin carrying God's salvation?[51]

Phyllis Trible, attempting to move away from this approach, interprets Jonah's Nineveh as more of a type of the great city.[52] Yet even Trible is compelled to admit that Jonah contrasts itself with a concept of Nineveh as 'the symbol of cruelty par excellence'.[53] Others refuse to read Nahum and Zephaniah into Jonah's Nineveh, and argue that the city is a symbol for any great city of the distant past,[54] or of generic moral lawlessness.[55]

51.   *Jonah*, pp. 121-22. Elsewhere Lacocque and Lacocque emphatically state. 'To go to Nineveh is not very different from going to hell' (p. 37); so also the views of Bewer: 'Nineveh was the capital of... the bitterest enemies of Israel in pre-exilic times' (*Jonah*, p. 29); Hart-Davies, for whom 'the Assyrians were the Huns of ancient days' ('Book of Jonah', p. 237); Wolff: 'The author and the reader have before their eyes, what the lament of Nahum 3 understands... Nineveh is for the author a symbol of evil and wicked grandeur' (*Studien zum Jonabuch* [Biblische Studien, 47; Neukirchen–Vluyn: Neukirchener Verlag, 1965], pp. 50-51; cf. *idem*, *Obadiah and Jonah*, pp. 100, 148); For Eubanks, the Assyrians represent 'the epitome of all that is evil to Jews', although to Jonah's post-exilic audience, Assyrian brutality would be 'cruel enough to stir the emotions, yet far enough away that the emotions would not be too intense' ('Cathartic Effects', pp. 122, 178); Sasson refers to 'a Hebrew audience who remembers Nineveh's conniving minds no less than its bitter weapons' (*Jonah*, p. 315); Limburg maintains that 'No matter when the story may have been written, we need to understand it in the context of the ancient Near Eastern world of the eighth century B.C.' (*Jonah*, p. 22). This is against Limburg's statement elsewhere that 'at the time the book of Jonah was written, Nineveh had been long destroyed... [it] functions as a symbol for the great cities of the world' (p. 78).

52.   'The burden of cities hangs heavily on the consciousness of ancient Israel... To understand our particular story it is perhaps best not to read too much of the historical Nineveh into it. Through the portrayal of a legendary Nineveh our author shows God's mercy upon great cities' (Trible, 'Studies', pp. 270, 272).

53.   Trible, 'Studies', p. 271.

54.   'Jonabuch', *RGG*[2], p. 369; Schmidt, '*De Deo*', p. 37; and Rofé, *Prophetical Stories*, pp. 158-59.

55.   H. Orlinsky, 'Nationalism–Universalism and Internationalism in Ancient Israel', in H.T. Frank and W.L. Reed (eds.), *Translating and Understanding the Old*

When one compares the portrayal of Nineveh in Jonah on the one hand with those of Nahum and Zephaniah on the other, there are no common points, especially in regard to the nature of the city's wrongdoing. In Jon. 1.1, Nineveh is accused of evils (רעה) which rise up before God. In 3.8 the Ninevites follow an evil path and practice violence (דרך הרעה, חמס). This description contrasts with the more graphic atrocities found in Nahum and Zephaniah. Neither רעה nor חמס occur in the latter two books in reference to Nineveh. Rather, the city is described in Nah. 3.1 as bloody (דמים), full of deceit (כלה כחש) and plunder (לא ימיש טרף). In Zeph. 2.13-15, Nineveh is the exultant city (העיר העליזה), once secure but now desolate (לשמה היושבת לבטח היתה).[56] There is no similar vocabulary between Jonah and Nahum or Zephaniah to warrant any supposed relationship or dependence of Jonah upon the other texts,[57] or even that Jonah is drawing upon notions of Nineveh as a brutal military power. On the basis of these observations it appears that the author of Jonah views Nineveh as a legendary great city of the past. But such notions do not arise in a vacuum, and it does not suffice to leave the matter here without first investigating ancient traditions concerning Nineveh which might help provide a context for Jonah's portrayal of the city. It will be seen

---

Testament: Essays in Honor of Herbert G. May (Nashville: Abingdon Press, 1970), pp. 206-36 (231); Cohen, 'Tragedy of Jonah', pp. 164-75 (172-73); May, 'World Dominion', p. 61; Witzenrath, *Jona*, p. 61; Good, *Irony*, p. 48; M. Walzer, 'Prophecy and Social Criticism', *Drew Gateway* 55 (1984–85), pp. 13-27 (17-18); Tigay, 'Book of Jonah', p. 70.

56. חמס (the more specific of the two terms found in Jonah) is seldom used to describe the actions of an invading military force, but rather denotes the 'rude wickedness of men, their noisy, wild, ruthlessness' (BDB, p. 329). Orlinsky points out that רעה and חמס are the terms used to describe the general lawlessness and evil of the pre-deluge generation in Genesis 6 ('Nationalism–Universalism', p. 231).

57. But the use of the phrase 'the oppressing city' (העיר היונה) in Zeph. 3.1 immediately after the description of Nineveh, utilizing a synonym with Jonah's name (in addition to a grammatical structure similar to the repeated reference to Nineveh in Jonah as העיר הגדולה) can be understood as evidence that Zephaniah is using Jonah. At best a weak relationship can be drawn between the use of יונים in Nah. 2.8 in reference to the women of Nineveh and another possible etymological derivation for the proper name יונה. The lack of verbal contact between these three texts, which are the only references in the Old Testament to the destruction of Nineveh, further distances Jonah from any supposed standard Israelite view of Nineveh based on any known biblical traditions.

then, that the legendary portrayal of Nineveh in Hellenistic authors provides common elements with Jonah and offers an interpretative matrix in which to understand the larger message of the book.

Nineveh in Greek and Hellenistic Literary Traditions
The earliest Greek reference to Nineveh comes from the sixth-century BCE *Sentences* of Phocylides, and contrasts a city governed by virtue to Nineveh: 'A city on a peak ruled in accordance with nature is more powerful than senseless Nineveh'.[58] The historical proximity of Phocylides to the destruction of Nineveh by the Babylonians in 612 allows for the possibility that his comment stems from knowledge of the destruction as indication of the city's lack of reason. What is important to note here is that for Phocylides, Nineveh is a powerful city (hence its use in a rhetorical comparison with another nameless city) and that it is not governed by reason. In the following century, Herodotus is clear that Nineveh is a great city of the Assyrians, destroyed by the Medes. *History* 1.102.9 mentions 'the Assyrians who held Nineveh' and 'had formerly ruled all of Asia'.[59] This latter text testifies to Nineveh's greatness, for in speaking of the power of the Medes, Herodotus relates that they took the cities of the Assyrians 'among them even Nineveh' (1.185.6). Roughly a century later Plato also makes it clear that Nineveh no longer exists. In the *Laws*, Socrates speaks of the Illians who brought about the Trojan war, partly due to their reliance on Assyrian aid. Plato writes 'of the Assyrian power which was in Nineveh; and still the remainder of this kingdom was not small, even as now we fear the great king' (685c). In Plato it can be seen that: 1) Nineveh is the capital of the Assyrian empire; 2) it no longer exists; 3) even in its waning years it was still a force to be reckoned with, even as the Persians ('the great king') are in Plato's day. Xenophon speaks of Cyrus's army passing the city: 'a great stronghold, deserted and lying in ruins' (*Anabasis* 3.4.10). He also mentions the impressive height of the walls: foundations 50 feet wide and equally as high, a main wall 50 feet wide and 100 feet high. For Xenophon the city was so impregnable that it only fell to the Persians due to intervention from Zeus.[60] In the first century BCE, Strabo

---

58.   4.2. πόλις ἐν σκοπέλῳ κατὰ κόσμον οἰκεῦσα σμικρὴ κρέσσων Νίνου ἀφραινούσης.
59.   The fall of Nineveh is also mentioned in *History* 1.106.
60.   *Anabasis* 3.4.11-12. Xenophon thinks the city to have fallen to the Persians

critiques Eratosthenes' geographic divisions because the latter divides the region of Syria and thus places Nineveh and Babylon in two separate regions. These two cities are part of the same region, both of their inhabitants being called Syrians (here Strabo confuses this term with Assyrian), and Nineveh was clearly the capital of the region (*Geography* 2.1.31). Elsewhere Strabo clarifies that the country of the Syrians was once that of the Assyrians, and in speaking of their capital, Nineveh, he is clear that it was 'much greater' than Babylon and destroyed by the Medes (*Geography* 16.1-3). Diodorus of Sicily has a lengthy account of the history of Nineveh, based on the work of the fourth-century BCE author Ctesias, which deserves to be closely examined. The city's eponymous founder Ninus, after stunning military victories, 'was eager to found a city of such magnitude, that not only would it be the largest of any which then existed in the whole inhabited world, but also that no other ruler of a later time should, if he undertook such a task, find it easy to surpass him' (2.3.1). The city was 150 by 90 stades in circumference, the wall a height of 100 feet and wide enough for three chariots to ride it abreast, with 1500 towers, each 200 feet tall. And thus Ninus, 'was not disappointed in his hope, since a city its equal, in respect to either the length of its circuit or the magnificence of its walls, was never founded by anyone after his time' (2.3.2-3). After his death, Ninus's widow raised a huge burial mound for him in the city, visible for many miles, and still visible in Diodorus's day, even though the city 'was razed to the ground by the Medes' after having stood for 1300 years (2.7.1-2).[61]

In the first century CE Dio Chrysostom quotes the old maxim of Phocylides and uses it to show both that Phocylides is as great a poet as Homer, if not better due to his brevity, and that a city, no matter its greatness, is not worthy of the name if it is not virtuous. Thus Dio asks whether

> a small city on a rugged headland is better and more fortunate, if orderly, than a great city in a smooth and level plain, that is to say, if that city is conducted in a disorderly and lawless fashion by men of folly? (*Discourses* 36.13)

rather than the Babylonians. Kraeling argues that Xenophon mistook the ruins of Mespila for Nineveh, and thus has recorded the accurate dimensions of the former city ('Evolution', p. 313 n. 1).

61.   In 28.7 Diodorus reiterates that the city 'was levelled to the ground'.

Thus, since the term 'city' cannot be applied to a place not ruled by reason, 'consequently not even in referring to Nineveh could the poet use the term "city", since Nineveh is given over to folly' (36.20).[62]

Moving further into the common era, it will suffice to list briefly authors who mention the city. They are unanimous in their descriptions of Nineveh as a great city now destroyed. Thus Arrian speaks of the Tigris which runs 'past the city of Ninus, which once was a great and rich city' (*Indica* 42.3). In his *Life of Apollonius*, Philostratus always uses the adjective 'ancient' (ἀρχαία) when referring to Nineveh, the hometown of Apollonius's companion, Damis (e.g., 1.3.2, 19.1). Lucian, in a famous quote has Hermes tell Charon 'as for Nineveh, ferryman, it is already gone and there is not a trace of it left now; you could not even say where it was' (*Inspectors* 23).[63] Lucian is clear as to the fact that the ruins of Nineveh are irrecoverably lost, whereas other Greek writers had been confident of its location, albeit some of them erroneously so.[64] Aristides, in a listing of famous conquests mentions among others that 'Ninus was captured by the Medes' (*In Defense of Oratory* 240). Athenæus quotes another authority telling wrongly of Cyrus besieging and destroying the city (*Deipnosophistæ* 12.529 e-f).[65]

With this brief overview it is clear that for at least seven centuries in Greek literary traditions Nineveh is seen as one of the great cities, if not the greatest city there has ever been. The traditions are also clear that this great city no longer exists. Of the two authors who do not make explicit reference to Nineveh's destruction (Phocylides and Dio Chrysostom) both of them are clear that Nineveh is a city given over to lawlessness and madness.

62. In 62.5 Dio calls Nineveh and Babylon 'the greatest cities that had yet existed'.

63. An instance much earlier than that of Lucian which may belie ignorance about the location of Nineveh is the book of Tobit. C.C. Torrey argues, on the basis of Tobiah's itinerary in the book, that the author has mistaken Nineveh for the twin cities of Seleucia-Ctesiphon further down the Tigris ('Nineveh in the Book of Tobit', *JBL* 41 [1922], pp. 237-45 [241-43]).

64. For example, Diodorus places the city on the Euphrates rather than the Tigris (2.3.2) and Strabo does not mention it as being on any river (*Geography* 16.3).

65. Xenophon is also erroneous in attributing the destruction to the Persians (3.4.11-12).

These major themes used of Nineveh: its greatness, its lawlessness and its destruction, converge in the Greek traditions of Sardanapallus,[66] Nineveh's last king. Herodotus recounts that he was fantastically wealthy, and stored his treasures underground (2.150). In the *Nichomachean Ethics* Aristotle cites Sardanapallus as an example of licentiousness:

> The generality of mankind then show themselves to be utterly slavish, by preferring what is only a life for cattle; but they get a hearing for their view as reasonable because many of those in power share the feelings of Sardanapallus (1095b).

Strabo identifies him as the last king of Nineveh (*Geography* 16.1.2).

Diodorus has a very detailed account of Sardanapallus and the fall of the city. The king, thirtieth in line from the founder of the empire Ninus,

> outdid all his predecessors in luxury and sluggishness... he lived the life of a woman... he had assumed the feminine garb and so covered his face and indeed his entire body with whitening cosmetics... that he rendered it more delicate than that of any luxury-loving woman... He also took care... at his carousals not only to indulge regularly in those drinks and foods which could offer the greatest pleasure, but also to pursue the delights of love with men as well as with women; for he practiced sexual indulgence of both kinds without restraint (2.23.1-2).

When news of the king's behavior reaches his subjects a conspiracy and revolt is instigated by the Medes, Persians and Babylonians. They besiege Nineveh for two years, finally taking the city with the aid of a flood. Sardanapallus, realizing all was lost

> built an enormous pyre in his palace, heaped upon it all his gold and silver as well as every article of the royal wardrobe and then, shutting his concubines and eunuchs in the room... he consigned both them and himself and his palace to the flames (27.2).[67]

Traditions about Sardanapallus were so widespread in the Greek

---

66.   Equated by some with the historical (and biblical) Ashurbanipal (668–630 BCE). Such an equation is problematic both on semantic and historical grounds. Ashurbanipal was not the last king of Assyria and, in addition to his military prowess, is noted for the foundation of a large library at Nineveh, an achievement hardly to be equated with licentiousness.

67.   This dramatic scene is the subject of Eugène Delacroix's 'The Death of Sardanapallus'.

world that Dio Chrysostom calls him a 'byword' (θρυλούμενος) and says of his statesmanship 'to kingship he could lay no more of a claim than some rotting corpse' (*Discourses* 62.5). Elsewhere Dio compares the true trophies of kingship—the arms of defeated enemies—to the opulent jewels with which Sardanapallus decorated his palace (*Discourses* 2.35).[68] Aristides refers to his self-immolation (*In Defense of Oratory* 240). Athenæus, basing his account on that of Ctesias (although he may be using Diodorus and embellishing the account) speaks of the king's transvestism and his fiery death. Athenæus reports that the king heaped 10,000,000 talents of gold and 100,000,000 of silver onto his pyre which then burned for 15 days (*Deipnosophistæ* 12.529c).[69] There are several variants to Sardanapallus's epitaph, preserved in Nineveh (how this can be so when the city was destroyed did not bother our authors). The heart of the epitaph runs:

> Knowing well that you are mortal, lift up your heart; take delight in feasts.
> You will have no more pleasure when dead.
> For I am dust, who once ruled great Nineveh—and these things I had which gave me joy—what I ate, my desires and what I found through passion.
> But many happy things are left behind.[70]

Thus in the Greek literary tradition Nineveh is acknowledged to be the capital of the great and ancient Assyrian empire, but the focus in Greek culture in not so much on the city's political or military prowess, but rather on the magnitude of its opulence. This opulence becomes personified in the figure of Sardanapallus, an individual so wealthy and eccentric as to be the ancient world's symbol of unbridled hedonism. The excesses of Sardanapallus and Nineveh are not merely consigned to a far distant and fictitious antiquity, but are bound up in the universally recognized fate of the city: its utter destruction. This Greek focus on Nineveh as wealthy, powerful and destroyed is different from what is seen as the standard view of the city in the Old Testament, which portrays it as the worst of Israel's enemies and the

---

68. Dio as well has a detailed and lurid description of the king's transvestism (62.6) in addition to that of Diodorus.

69. Athenæus also calls him 'the most prosperous man of all' (12.529d).

70. Diodorus (2.23.3), Dio Chrysostom (*Discourses* 4.135) and Athenæus (*Deipnosophistæ* 8.336a).

evil of the gentile world. With this Greek picture acting as a template, it can be seen how much it helps in reading Jonah.

The lack of historical accuracy found in Jonah matches that of the Greek traditions. Thus the title, 'king of Nineveh', which the Assyrian kings never used for themselves, is found both in Jonah and the Greek writings.[71] Similarly, the king of Nineveh in Jonah 3 who, following the lead of his citizenry, rises from his throne and casts off his robe to sit in ashes, only to order all in the city to fast, wear sackcloth and pray to God (actions instigated by the populace itself) matches well with the wealthy but witless Sardanapallus who exercised great power over people and things but had the sense to rule neither. The king's wholehearted repentance in Jonah provides a jarring contrast, given Sardanapallus's love of luxury and unbridled hedonism.[72] Finally, the Greek emphasis on the city as utterly destroyed creates an entirely new interpretation of God's attitude towards it. It was observed above that the author phrased Jonah's oracle in such a way that it would be seen as true regardless of the Ninevites' reaction to it. While this is correct, the author's choice of Nineveh, and the influence of well-attested traditions concerning that city during the Hellenistic era, reinterpret Jonah's message. What is present in the statement, 'Yet forty more days and Nineveh turns over', is neither the claim that the city will be destroyed nor that it will repent. Rather, in the author's choice of a city whose traditional identity never fails to mention it as irrevocably destroyed, the statement encompasses both meanings: Nineveh repents and then it is destroyed. This bringing together of what previously have been seen as two mutually exclusive options is also at work in the phrasing of the king's rhetorical question in Jon. 3.9. The biblical context of this question and of all of Jon. 3.1-10 is the next area of inquiry.

---

71. This lack of historical accuracy present in the title 'King of Nineveh', is found nowhere else in the Old Testament. All other references to Nineveh and Assyria either refer to a 'king of Assyria' who lives in Nineveh, or make clear that Nineveh is the first city of Assyria; see Gen. 10.11, 2 Kgs 19.36, Isa. 37.37, Nah. 3.18, Zeph. 2.13.

72. Any comic/satiric nature in this or the remainder of Jonah should not be overemphasized, as is done by scholards such as Miles, Jr, 'Laughing', pp. 168-81; Holbert, '"Deliverance"', pp, 59-81; and Mather, 'Comic Art', pp. 280-91. Sasson offers a critique and a caveat against a zealous hunt for humor in the book (*Jonah*, pp. 331-34).

The Biblical Context of Divine Repentance

Jonah and God's Repentance

In Jeremiah 18, Yahweh commands the prophet to observe a potter in his workshop destroying and reshaping clay on the wheel. This serves to illustrate Yahweh's message:

> If at any time I declare concerning a nation or a kingdom, that I will pluck up and break down and destroy it, and if that nation, concerning which I have spoken, turns from its evil, I will repent of the evil that I intended to do to it. And if at any time I declare concerning a nation or a kingdom that I will build and plant it, and if it does evil in my sight, not listening to my voice, then I will repent of the good which I had intended to do it. (vv. 7-10)

The verbal and thematic links between Jer. 18.7-10 and Jon. 3.5-10 have been noticed for centuries.[73] Many scholars argue that the text from Jeremiah is the background for the scene in Jonah,[74] their reason being that the former text functions as a narrative illustration of the abstract ideas in the latter. This is a weak reason to argue for dependence, in light of the absence of other examples in the Old Testament where a story is created to explain a separate, non-narrative text. This opinion also overlooks the context of Jeremiah 18, where Yahweh's statement is already linked to, and arises out of, a narrative illustration, the visit to the potter's house.[75] While both Jonah 3 and Jeremiah 18

---

73.   The Christian commentator Einhard (770–840) understands God in Jonah to be acting upon the principles set out in Jeremiah 18 (Bowers, *Legend of Jonah*, p. 42). The medieval Muslim commentator Tha'labi narrates a legend in which God, in response to Jonah's anger, commands him to go to a potter's house and demand the potter smash his pots. The potter refuses on the grounds that he cares about his creations. This protest is then analogously applied to God's care for Nineveh (Komlós, 'Jonah Legends', p. 60).

74.   Driver, *Introduction*, p. 324; Feuillet, 'Livre de Jonas', pp. 169-76; Andrew, 'Gattung and Intention', p. 17; Allen, *Jonah*, p. 193; Fretheim, *Message*, pp. 105-106; Vawter, *Job and Jonah*, p. 107; Magonet, *Form and Meaning*, pp. 102-103; Wolff, *Obadiah and Jonah*, p. 154; and White, 'Jonah', p 213.

75.   Lacocque and Lacocque deny any dependence of Jonah 3 on Jeremiah 18 on the specious criterion that the statements of Jeremiah apply only to Judah (*Jonah*, p. 130). Further relationships are drawn between Jonah 3 and Jeremiah 26 and 36, and it is argued that Jonah uses the wicked Jerusalemites and their wicked king in Jeremiah as a foil to the repentant Ninevite king and populace; so Kaiser, 'Wirklichkeit, Möglichkeit und Vorurteil', p. 100; Witzenrath, *Jona*, pp. 86-89; Magonet, *Form and*

may be understood to mean that God is free to repent from promised destruction if the threatened group mends its ways, this is an idea repeated in the prophetic corpus (e.g., Isa. 38; Jer. 5–6; 42; Ezek. 18; 36).[76] As such, it can be argued that Jonah is drawing upon a common theme in the Old Testament, and it is to the larger biblical context surrounding the theme of divine repentance that the investigation should now turn.

Looking at the texts in the Old Testament where God is said to repent (נחם), it quickly becomes apparent that, although the possibility of repentance is admitted, in the majority of the cases this change of mind is followed by or linked with an act of divine destruction.

Genesis 6.6: God's sorrow at the creation of humanity leads to its almost complete annihilation in the flood.

Exodus 32: At the urging of Moses, Yahweh repents of his desire to destroy the Israelites after their worship of the golden calf (v. 14). Yet even after Moses requires an internecine slaughter as punishment for the offense, Yahweh sends a plague (v. 35).

Judges 2.18: Yahweh repeatedly punishes the Israelites in anger at their apostasy, only to repent and save them before punishing them again.

1 Samuel 15.35: Yahweh repents of his choice of Saul as king when the latter fails to kill the entire population of the Amalekites. This withdrawal of divine favor from Saul precipitates his madness and the bloody struggle with David.

2 Samuel 24: Yahweh incites David to order a census of the people. David then inexplicably begs forgiveness from God, who requires him to choose one of three devastating punishments. David chooses three days of pestilence. Yahweh repents of the pestilence before it reaches Jerusalem (v. 16), but only after it has killed 70,000 Israelites.[77]

Amos 7.1-9: Amos is shown visions of marauding locusts and devouring fire. He intercedes for Jacob, whereupon Yahweh repents of these plans. He then shows Amos the vision of the plumbline, signifying the destruction of Israel.

Meaning, pp. 76-77; Wolff, *Obadiah and Jonah*, pp. 146, 151; Golka, *Jonah*, p. 108; and Eubanks, 'Cathartic Effects', p. 168.

76.   Jer. 26.18-19 cites a precedent of divine repentance in the context of an appeal to Jerusalem.

77.   The parallel account of 1 Chronicles 21 attributes the instigation of the census to Satan rather than to Yahweh.

Similarly, of the five instances in the Old Testament where it is said that Yahweh never repents of his word, three (1 Sam. 15.29, Jer. 4.28, Ezek. 24.14) refer to Yahweh not relenting from a promised curse or punishment. One (Num. 23.19) speaks of Yahweh remaining constant to a word of blessing.[78] Only four texts (Pss. 106.45, 135.14, Jer. 31.19, Joel 2.14) mention divine repentance with no hint of destruction or punishment. Given this juxtaposition in the Old Testament of divine repentance with the carrying out of acts of destruction, when Jon. 3.10 recounts that God 'repented of the evil which he said he would do' to the Ninevites, it cannot be assumed that Nineveh does escape destruction because it cannot be assumed that when Yahweh repents he will forego an act of destruction. The traditional notion of Nineveh as a destroyed city of the distant past, examined in the previous section, corresponds with the idea prevalent in the Old Testament that Yahweh truly does not change his mind in deciding against an act of retribution.

God's Repentance and the Expression 'Who Knows?'
In an analysis of the ten occurrences of the phrase מי יודע ('Who knows?') in the Old Testament, James L. Crenshaw groups them into two categories. In the first, the phrase admits the possibility of a change in a situation for good. Those in the second group deny any such possibility, and in these instances the expression functions as the equivalent of 'No one knows'.[79] Of the five which Crenshaw groups in his first category, four (including Jon. 3.9) use the phrase in reference to God. These merit a closer look.

2 Samuel 12.22: When the child of David and Bathsheba's adulterous union is taken ill, David justifies his fasting and prayer with the observation, 'Who knows whether Yahweh will be gracious to me, that the child may live?' The child dies.

---

78. The remaining text (Ps. 110.4) refers to Yahweh's not relinquishing a vow. Zech. 8.14 mentions Yahweh's never relenting from punishment of Israel in days long past in the context of a promise of salvation. One can also argue that Yahweh's promises of repentance in Jeremiah (chs. 18, 26, 42) should be grouped with these texts, given that Jerusalem is destroyed in Jeremiah.

79. J.L. Crenshaw, 'The Expression *mi yodea'* in the Hebrew Bible', *VT* 36 (1986), pp. 274-88 (274-75). Crenshaw describes these two categories as 'An Open Door' and 'A Closed Door' respectively. All five occurrences in the second category are in Proverbs and Qoheleth.

Psalm 90.11: The psalm is a meditation on the fragility and transient nature of human life. This condition is attributed to the fierce
anger of Yahweh, which consumes humankind and pushes it back into
dust (vv. 3-10). Immediately following this description, the author
asks, 'Who knows the power of your anger and your wrath, according
to the fear of you?'

Joel 2.14: Joel asks, in the course of an oracle of restoration, 'Who
knows whether he (Yahweh) will not turn and repent and leave a
blessing behind him?' It is clear in Joel that divine blessing does
follow.[80]

Jonah 3.9: The king of Nineveh asks, 'Who knows? Yahweh may
turn and repent from his anger, and we will not die'.[81]

Apart from Jonah, two of the three remaining texts which use the
expression 'Who knows?' in reference to God do so in a way that
highlights divine punishment and anger. Thus the answer to David's
question of whether Yahweh will relent and save the child is negative.
The child dies. Similarly, after describing the effects of divine anger
on human existence, the psalmist still feels obliged to use the phrase to
emphasize further the intensity of Yahweh's punishment. Even in the
face of the pain and shortness of life, who knows the completeness of
God's anger? The implied answer, that no one knows, serves to stress
the psalmist's point that all the suffering of this life still does not
plumb the depths of God's wrath. In this context, along with the
dependence of Joel 2 on Jonah, [82] the king's question in Jon. 3.9 can
be understood with the sentiments of 1 Samuel 12 and Psalm 90. Thus,
when the king muses as to whether God will indeed repent and spare
the city, the answer is that God will not; Nineveh is doomed. This
corresponds to and complements the author's use of the notion of

---

80.   Crenshaw argues that Joel 2 is uncertain as to whether God will relent
('The Expression *mi yodea*'', p. 276). This overlooks the clear imagery of utopian
restoration that begins with Joel 2.14 and extends to the end of the book.

81.   *Tg. Ps.-J.* reinterprets the king's question as a command. 'Whoever knows
that he has guilt on his hands will turn...' (מַן ידע דאית בידיה; Levine, *Aramaic
Version of Jonah*, pp. 88-89). The Massoretes place a strong disjunctive accent
(*zaqep qaton*) on the word ישוב which yields a reading similar to that of the Targum.
'The one who knows will turn (repent), and God may repent from his anger...'
(Sasson, *Jonah*, p. 266).

82.   A position argued fully below in Chapter 5.

divine repentance in the Old Testament in which the presence of God's forgiveness is most often linked with an act of divine wrath.

Conclusion

Writing about proper and poor dramatic technique, Aristotle remarks that one of the worst devices is 'to intend the action with full knowledge and not perform it; that outrages the feelings and is untragic' (*Poetics* 1453b). At first glance, Yahweh's *volte face* in Jon. 3.10 in response to the Ninevites' penance would appear to be a prime example of Aristotle's maxim. However, as the foregoing analysis has shown, the author of Jonah has drawn upon biblical and extra-biblical traditions so as to stress the freedom of God throughout the episode with the Ninevites.

1.   Through use of the *niphal* form of הפך in 3.4, what appears to be an unequivocal announcement of impending destruction is in reality an open-ended statement that will be fulfilled regardless of Nineveh's fate.

2.   The Nineveh in Jonah 3 is not informed by the view of the city condemned by Nahum and the picture of the cruel Assyrian empire portrayed in the Old Testament and in Assyrian historical texts, but by traditions about the city which are prevalent in the Persian and Hellenistic periods and well-attested in Greek writings. An investigation of Greek traditions surrounding the history of Nineveh has shown that Jonah makes better sense with a Hellenistic background as the context for its conception of Nineveh than with a Near Eastern one. Thus, instead of representing the zenith of the cruel Assyrian empire, Israel's bitter enemy, Nineveh is the idyllic great city of long ago, full of gross excess, exotic opulence—and utterly destroyed. The author and original readers, living in a culture informed by traditions which do not fail to mention Nineveh as a city that no longer exists,[83]

---

83.   In a curious *non sequitur*, Lacocque and Lacocque also assume the readers know of the city's destruction, but see this knowledge as helping to highlight God's mercy (*Jonah*, p. 125). David Payne realizes that the first readers' knowledge of Nineveh's ultimate fate would color the way the ending of Jonah was received. Payne determines such a reception to be 'quite the wrong audience-reaction' from what the author intended. Thus, in an even more curious exegetical move, Payne infers 'an already existing tradition' of a historical (albeit temporary) repentance of Nineveh at the preaching of Jonah ben Amittai ('Jonah', p. 7). Others who hold that

do not see a loving God who is free to forgive whom he wills, but rather a God who may forgive at will and revoke that forgiveness as well.[84] This accords well with the equivocal nature of Jonah's oracle.

3.   The biblical texts which speak of Yahweh's repentance, as well as those that utilize the phrase, 'Who knows?' in reference to divine punishment, do so in a way that still allows for acts of retribution to follow. Thus, when the king asks, 'Who knows if God will repent... and we will not die?' the answer given by the Old Testament is clear: Yahweh's repentance, should it occur, is no guarantee that the Ninevites will escape punishment, since this divine change of mind is most often followed by an act of destruction. The author's choice of a city renowned for the fact that it is destroyed further emphasizes this.

All of these elements at work in Jonah 3 serve the author's larger purpose, prevalent also in Jonah 1–2, of emphasizing an absolute divine freedom capable of forgiveness or destruction (or both for the same situation), and whose messages are phrased accordingly so that God is never proven false. In the account of Yahweh's dealings with Nineveh, the author is not concerned to stress Yahweh's freedom to love Gentiles,[85] or to change his mind for the sake of mercy.[86] Such

Jonah's audience knows of Nineveh's destruction are Coote, *Amos among the Prophets*, p. 132; and Orth, 'Genre in Jonah', p. 270. Ancient interpreters of Jonah deal with the contradiction between Yahweh's sparing of the city and its historical destruction by concluding that the Ninevites reverted to their evil ways after the pardon and were subsequently (and justifiably) punished; so Jerome (Duval [ed.], *Jerome: Commentaire*, p. 167) and *PRE* (quoted in Komlós, 'Jonah Legends', p. 55 n. 99).

84.   Alan Cooper argues the same thesis for Jonah on the basis of an intertextual analysis ('In Praise of Divine Caprice', pp. 144-63). C.A. Keller writes

> He [God] will not always relent. The threat continues to hang over Nineveh. Jonah's message... is not annulled. The day will come when the message will be realized. Jonah has spoken the truth. At the time the poet wrote his account, the great city did not exist. it was a vast field of ruins where jackals howled ('Jonas', p. 340).

85.   So Bewer, *Jonah*, p. 7; Trible, 'Studies', pp. 273-79; Lacocque and Lacocque, *Jonah*, pp. 41-43; Wolff, *Obadiah and Jonah*, pp. 85-88; Stuart, *Hosea–Jonah*, pp. 434-35; and Limburg, *Jonah*, p. 98.

86.   So, for example, Sasson, *Jonah*, pp. 315-320. 'For God, however, there remained the burden of making Jonah understand that justice and mercy are not necessarily synonymous in God's lexicon and that no one issue can be framed solely in terms of a prophet's personal satisfaction' (p. 316); Landes, 'Kerygma', pp. 3-31; Fretheim, 'Jonah and Theodicy', pp. 227-37; Emmerson, 'Another Look', pp. 86-88; and Mather, 'Comic Art', pp. 280-91.

'freedom', in reality a human constraint put upon Yahweh in order to compel forgiveness, is one of the views the author of Jonah refutes.[87]

In the three episodes of Jonah thus far analyzed, the author has repeatedly stressed the absolute power of Yahweh over all creation coupled with a complete license concerning any act or behavior, beyond human categories of justice or logic. Having slowly constructed this complex picture of an inscrutable God, the author will confront the issue directly in the dispute between Yahweh and his unhappy servant which serves as the final scene of the book of Jonah.

87.   So also Cooper, 'In Praise of Divine Caprice', pp. 150-51.

Chapter 5

THE MESSENGER AND THE MESSAGE (JONAH 4.1-11)

Let me have silence and I will speak, and let come on me what may...
Behold, he will slay me; I have no hope, yet I will defend my ways to his
face.

—Job 13.13, 15

Look! You have something greater than Jonah here.

—Mt. 12.41

If one were to argue for a climax to the book of Jonah, a case can be
made for the confrontation between Jonah and Yahweh which comprises the entirety of ch. 4. The book's plot, which from the outset
encompasses such far-flung settings as Tarshish in the extreme west,
exotic Nineveh to the east, and the depths of the netherworld, now
centers on a bare patch of earth under the hot sun as the arena for a
divine messenger's debate with the one who sent him. Much like ch. 2,
Jonah 4 is occupied only by Yahweh and Jonah. But, in a manner
distinct from Jon. 2.1-11, here Jonah does not engage in a pious
monologue with God. Instead there is a debate as, for the first time,
the two main characters in this story speak and respond to each other.
The following analysis of Jon. 4.1-11 examines grammatical and lexical
issues, the relationship between the formulaic utterance of Jon. 4.2 and
its occurrence elsewhere in the Old Testament, especially Joel 2.14, and
Jonah's request for death in the context of that motif's biblical usage.

Jonah 4.1-11

As with every other portion of Jonah, ch. 4 has been subjected to a
literary analysis which searches for and finds elaborate schemata
hidden within the text.[1] However, unlike these other patterns which

---

1.   For example, the charts of Fretheim, *Message*, pp. 117-18; H. Witzenrath,

have been read into the text, Jon. 4.1-11 does exhibit a contrived feature, constructed by the author, which consists in the allotment to Jonah and Yahweh of the exact same amount of dialogue:

Jonah (vv. 2-3) 39 words
Yahweh (v. 4) 3 words
Jonah (v. 8) 3 words
Yahweh (v. 9) 5 words
Jonah (v. 9) 5 words
Yahweh (vv. 10-11) 39 words[2]

It is important to point out that this correspondence not only exists in the sum total of words spoken by the two parties, but also is evident in the relationship of dialogue between them. Thus, when Yahweh is given a remark of three or five words, Jonah also has dialogue of the exact same length, and both utter long speeches of 39 words. The importance of this pattern lies specifically in the fact that this parity of dialogue occurs in the context of a debate between Jonah and Yahweh. This careful attention to the amount of speech in this dispute indicates that for the author there is no clearcut victor in the debate between Jonah and Yahweh over the latter's actions. Each side is given 'equal time', as it were, to set forth its position, but in the end the topic remains insoluble. Thus, God's final remarks in vv. 10-11 should not be seen as an example of a subtle, gentle, yet irresistible logic which brings Jonah to a crushing silence. Unlike in Job, there is no indication given in the text that either God or Jonah wins this dispute. Instead, for the author of Jonah, the intractability of the issue in light of divine freedom serves to render irrelevant any hope of resolution to the debate.

Verse 1 records Jonah's feeling at the sparing of Nineveh with the use of the verb רעע and its cognate accusative, רעה. This creates a link between Jonah's reaction to the Ninevites' temporary good fortune and their repentance in ch. 3. Thus, the Ninevites turn away from evil (רעה) in 3.8, 10, which in turn prompts Yahweh to do likewise (3.10),

---

Jona, p. 40 and Nowell, *Jonah*, pp. 14-15.

2.   Keller sees a pattern of 39–8–8–39 ('Jonas', pp. 333-34). Jack Sasson makes the further elaboration of 3–3–5–5 (*Jonah*, p. 317) and is followed in this by Trible, *Rhetorical Criticism*, p. 224. Further indication of a heightened literary artificiality is the extensive soundplay at work in the preponderance of gutturals in the vocabulary of Jonah 4; see Halpern and Friedman, 'Composition and Paronomasia', pp. 86-87.

whereupon it immediately comes upon Jonah in 4.1.[3] This construction, along with the use of חרה, has contributed to the interpretation that Jonah is angry, and that his anger stems from God's pardon of the evil, Gentile Ninevites. This reading in turn helps support the understanding that Jonah represents the ethnocentric, selfish, narrow-minded Israel of the post-exilic era.[4] That this construction of ancient Judaism owes more to Julius Wellhausen and the Law–Gospel bias of Christian exegetes than to historical study has already been observed above in Chapter 1. The only ancient version to read Jonah's reaction as anger is Jerome's Vulgate.[5] This is not surprising, given Jerome's vilification of Jonah, and his making of him into a symbol of and target for Jerome's anti-Semitic sentiments. Hans Walter Wolff sustains this interpretation another way by reading the subject of רעע to be Jonah himself. Thus, the phrase reads 'But Jonah became very evil, and he was angry'.[6] Against Wolff's position, G.I. Davies points out that in the remaining two instances in the Old Testament where רעע *qal* occurs without a subject and is followed by ל or אל + noun or suffix, the subject is always an implied impersonal pronoun and רעע does not denote wickedness.[7] Thus, v. 1 should be understood to read,

---

3.   Trible, 'Studies', p. 229. Kenneth Craig notes that רעה is used in Jonah in relation to every character ('Poetics', pp. 55-56). Halpern and Friedman note the pun between וירע רעה גדולה in 4.1 and וייראו יראה גדולה in 1.10, 16 ('Composition and Paronomasia', p. 88). Sasson observes that, while רעה is a frequent term in Jonah, only in 4.1 is the noun qualified with גדולה, and the verbal form רעע found (*Jonah*, p. 272).

4.   For example, Jerome (Duval [ed.], *Jerome: Commentaire*, p. 287); Keil and Delitzsch, *Minor Prophets*, I, p. 411; Bewer, *Jonah*, p. 57; and Craig, 'Poetics', p. 43. An explanatory note in the 1990 *Catholic Study Bible* remarks that Jonah becomes angry 'because of his narrowly nationalistic vindictiveness'. The medieval Muslim commentator Tabari attributes Jonah's anger to the fact that God so hurried him to carry out his mission that he had no time to mount his steed or even to put on his shoes (Komlós, 'Jonah Legends', p. 57).

5.   Observed by Sasson (*Jonah*, p. 275). Jerome has 'iratus est'. The LXX reads Jonah's reaction as distress and grief ἐλυπήθη... συνεχύθη (L. Perkins, 'The Septuagint of Jonah, p. 46). Similarly *Tg. Ps.-J.* emphasizes extreme displeasure ובאיש... ותקף (Levine, *Aramaic Version of Jonah*, p. 90). Wycliffe, Tyndale, KJV, RSV, JB and NAB all render Jonah's response as anger.

6.   Wolff, *Obadiah and Jonah*, p. 165.

7.   G.I. Davies, 'The Uses of *R''* Qal and the Meaning of Jonah IV 1', *VT* 27 (1977), pp. 105-110 (107). Craig critiques Wolff's position on the same grounds ('Poetics', pp. 166-67).

'But this displeased Jonah greatly, and he was grieved'.[8]

Jonah begins his long speech to Yahweh with reference to an earlier remark made in his homeland before he fled his divine commission. Yet even a reader with the shortest of memories knows that Jonah makes no utterances at all on his native soil in the book of Jonah. From a narrative-critical standpoint, one can say that 4.2 refers to a prior event beyond the story-time of the narrative,[9] but another explanation lies ready at hand in the only other reference to Jonah in the Old Testament. Arguments put forth above in Chapter 2 show that the book of Jonah begins in such a way as to presuppose earlier reference to the figure of Jonah. The only other reference to him is the short episode of 2 Kings 14, and when that text is read in relationship to Jonah's remark of 4.2, a key correspondence is evident. In 4.2 Jonah says, in light of God's pardon of the Ninevites, that such an outcome 'was my word while I was yet in my own land'. Turning to 2 Kgs 14.25-27 one reads that Jonah, while in his homeland, prophesies the expansion of Israel's borders under Jeroboam II in spite of that king's wickedness. This divine blessing is explicitly due to Yahweh's sorrow at the thought of the complete destruction of Israel. Thus, in Jon. 4.2 reference is made to a word concerning divine forgiveness made while Jonah was still in Israel, and in 2 Kgs 14.23-25, the only extant text in which Jonah speaks on his own homeland, there is an oracle which highlights Yahweh's temporary forgiveness of a wicked Israelite king. This exact correspondence cannot easily be attributed to coincidence, but rather is an indication that the book of Jonah both draws upon and makes reference to the story of Jonah found in 2 Kings.

God's response to Jonah's lengthy speech is a three-word question.[10] While certainly elegant in English, the KJV's translation 'Doest thou well to be angry?' and the tradition upon which it rests is not an accurate rendering of the Hebrew.[11] *Hiphil* infinitive absolutes, such as

8.   So Sasson's translation and JPSV.

9.   For example, this is how some narrative critics understand Jesus' remarks in the Gospels concerning the parousia.

10.   Kenneth M. Craig notes that in Jonah 1–3 Yahweh speaks only in the imperative, while in ch. 4 he speaks only in questions (*Poetics*, pp. 67-68).

11.   This reading is found in Symmachus, Theodoret, the Vg, Wycliffe, KJV, RSV and NAB. Among recent commentators Douglas Stuart continues this line of interpretation with his 'What right do you have to be angry?' (*Hosea–Jonah*, pp. 498-99).

the form of יטב in Jon. 4.4, function adverbially.[12] Thus, rather than a questioning of the validity of Jonah's feelings, God's inquiry attempts to ascertain the extent of Jonah's distress: 'Are you deeply grieved?'[13]

Jonah does not respond to Yahweh's question, but rather exits the city and builds a hut from which he will observe what (if anything) is to transpire. Verse 5 puzzles commentators in its violation of narrative logic: Why would Jonah need a plant to shade him if he has built a hut? What happens to the hut in that it obviously is no longer available to shade him after the plant's demise? What can Jonah possibly be waiting to see, since he already knows that God has spared the city?[14] This has led some to classify 4.5 as a gloss added to clarify Jonah's actions during the 40-day warning period he announced to the Ninevites in 3.4.[15] Taking a different approach, Hugo Winckler resolves the temporal tension by moving 4.5 to a position immediately after 3.4. Thus, Jonah announces his message in Nineveh, exits the city to watch the outcome and thus is made aware of the Ninevites' repentance and reprieve.[16] Writing against Winckler's position, Norbert Lohfink argues for leaving 4.5 where it is on the grounds that it exhibits two characteristics common to Jonah: a wordless reply to a question or command (1.3, 5), and the presence of a pluperfect sense in perfect verbs which indicate flashbacks in the story (1.10, 2.1).[17]

12.   GKC, 113k, Joüon, *Grammar*, 123r and BDB, p. 406. BDB lists Deut. 9.21, 13.15, 17.4, 19.18, 27.8, 2 Kgs 11.8, and combines the two interpretations discussed to translate Jon. 4.4 as: 'Art thou rightly angry?'

13.   So *Tg. Ps.-J.*, the LXX, Tyndale, and JPSV. Commentators who argue for this reading are Ehrlich, *Ezechiel*, p. 270; C. Brekelmans, 'Some Translation Problems: Judges v 29, Psalm cxx 7, Jona iv 4,9', *OTS* 15 (1969), pp. 170-76 (175-76); Cohen, 'Tragedy of Jonah', p. 171; and Sasson, *Jonah*, pp. 286-87. Rabbinic tradition within the last century derives an infinitive sense from the placement of the disjunctive accent after the first word of God's question, which thus casts it as: 'So to do good grieves you?' (Zlotowitz, *Yonah*, p. 135). Herbert Chanan Brichto's interpretation of God's question as a scornful remark, dripping with sarcasm and equivalent to 'I couldn't care less', is unfounded and serves more as an eisegetical support for his literary reading (*Grammar*, p. 77).

14.   *Tg. Ps.-J.* answers this question by remarking that Jonah sat outside the city to see what would happen to it 'in the end' (בסוף). In doing so it thus makes reference to Nineveh's eventual destruction (Levine, *Aramaic Version of Jonah*, pp. 93-94).

15.   Bewer, *Jonah*, pp. 58-59. Peter Weimar understands 4.5 to be a gloss which is part of a larger, comprehensive redaction of Jonah ('Jon. 4.5', p. 89).

16.   Winckler, 'Zum Buch Jona', p. 264.

17.   'Jona ging', pp. 185-203. The notion of the flashback in Jonah has led

While Lohfink's position has become dominant,[18] there are those who still argue for a transposition of 4.5 to a place after 3.4.[19] As with other issues in this book, no conclusive case for either approach can be made. Those who hold that 4.5 belongs where it is have difficulty explaining its purpose.[20] Those who move it back to 3.4 have as daunting a task in trying to support this transposition without any MSS support, or explanations as to how the verse becomes misplaced. As stated before in this study, this type of exegesis is based upon the ultimate priority of criteria of strict narrative logic. The unfounded assumption in this method is that the same degree of rigidity and importance is accorded to these criteria by the biblical authors; this has not been shown to be the case. The author of Jonah may have had other reasons for writing the story as it is which were deemed to be more important than any kind of chronological integrity. The task of exegetes is to determine what these reasons were, rather than to correct a long-dead writer for not holding the same priorities as they.[21]

At this point God raises the plant over Jonah's head. The *piel* of מנה is used four times in Jonah (2.1, 4.6, 7, 8).[22] Each time God appoints

---

both Brichto, *Grammar*, p. 269 n. 22, and Stuart, *Hosea–Jonah*, p. 501, to understand Yahweh's debate with Jonah over the plant as an elaborate flashback which occurs prior to Jonah's complaint in 4.1-3.

18.   For example, Wolff, *Obadiah and Jonah*, p. 163; Magonet, *Form and Meaning*, pp. 59-60; and Almbladh, *Studies*, p. 37.

19.   Trible, 'Studies', pp. 92-102, 198, more cautiously in *idem*, *Rhetorical Criticism*, p. 119; and Day, 'Problems', pp. 42-43.

20.   Some commentators attempt to read a covenantal/cultic purpose in Jonah's construction of a סכה; so Eubanks, 'Cathartic Effects', p. 136 and Lacocque and Lacocque, *Jonah*, pp. 153-55. James Ackerman compares the juxtaposition of the booth and Jonah's joy (שמח) in 4.6 with the relationship between joy and the feast of booths recounted in Deuteronomy 16 and Nehemiah 8 ('Satire and Symbolism', p. 241). A similar relationship remains in Jewish liturgical practice, in that the last day of the feast of Sukkoth (סכות) is known as Simchat ha-Torah (שמחת התורה). Ackerman's case for this relationship in Jonah is weakened by the fact that Jonah specifically does not rejoice over his booth, but over the plant which has grown and replaces the need for his constructed shelter.

21.   It must be stressed that, to say that the author has reasons for constructing a narrative as he/she has does not mean that there is *a priori* some hidden genius at work that needs to be teased out of a text. See the remarks above in Chapter 1 concerning narrative poetics and the apotheosis of the author.

22.   A thorough analysis of this word's use in the Old Testament is that of R.D.

a non-human agent (fish, plant, worm, wind). Each occurrence is used with a different divine epithet,[23] and each agent appointed is either part of or closely related to a paronomastic construction.[24] Although meant to be a comfort to Jonah, God's botanical feat has been the source of consternation among exegetes for centuries. The vigorous debate between Jerome and Augustine over the term is examined above in Chapter 1. The Hebrew קִיקָיוֹן is a hapax legomenon in the Old Testament.[25] Bernard P. Robinson has clearly and comprehensively set forth the different translations of the term as found both in the versions and commentators.[26] They fall into the following categories:

1) *Transliteration: Tg. Ps.-J.*, Aquila and Theodotion (κικεῶνα).[27]

2) *'Gourd'*: The LXX (κολοκύνθη), Augustine, and the OL (*cucurbitæ*).

3) *'Vine'/'Ivy'* Symmachus (κισσός) and the Vg (*hedera*).

4) *Ricinus Plant*: Commonly known as the castor oil plant, this equation has long been attributed to both Jerome and the Talmud. But as Robinson has shown, the assumed support of Jerome for this interpretation is in fact due to a printing error made in a 1579 edition of Jerome's works.[28] While the Babylonian Talmud equates Jonah's plant with the ricinus (designated by the term קִיק, *b. Šab.* 21a) the Jerusalem Talmud, commenting on the same passage, understands קִיק to be an ivy.[29] The exact relationship between קִיק and קִיקָיוֹן is

Wilson, 'מנה "To Appoint", in the Old Testament', *Princeton Theological Review* 16 (1918), pp. 645-54.

23.   Magonet, *Form and Meaning*, p. 35. The names are: יהוה (2.1), יהוה אלהים (4.6), האלהים (4.7) and אלהים (4.8). Sasson points out that in the two instances where the Tetragrammaton is used, the results are beneficial to Jonah, while the opposite case obtains in the remaining two occurrences (*Jonah*, p. 291).

24.   דג with גדול, צל with להציל, תולעת with בעלת and רוח with חרשת; Sasson, *Jonah*, p. 148.

25.   Assyrian botanical texts mention a plant known as the *kukanitu*, but the species of the plant, and any relationship with the *qîqayôn* of Jon. 4 is uncertain.

26.   Robinson, 'Jonah's Qiqayon Plant', *ZAW* 97 (1985), pp. 390-403; especially helpful is Robinson's chart on p. 403.

27.   The Greek transliteration of Aquila and Theodotion is very close to the term κυκεῶνα, which denotes a mixed beverage of meal, grated cheese and wine (LSJ, p. 1006). Lacocque and Lacocque understand Jonah's plant to be a reference to this beverage and its use in Eleusinian mysteries (*Jonah*, pp. 156-57).

28.   Robinson, 'Jonah's Qiqayon Plant', pp. 394-95.

29.   Robinson, 'Jonah's Qiqayon Plant', p. 399. Robinson points out that the first Jewish commentator to explicitly designate Jonah's plant as a ricinus is the

uncertain. The former term is thought to be from the Egyptian *kiki*, which designates the ricinus and comes directly into Greek as κίκι.[30]

Working from an entirely different viewpoint are those modern commentators who understand the term in Jonah as a neologism and therefore seek to uncover its role in the context of the biblical account. Baruch Halpern and Richard E. Friedman offer a possible solution to the problem in the observation that the name of Jonah's plant 'resembles nothing so much as the sound of the words "the vomiting of Jonah."'[31] Thus, the term can be understood as having been coined by the biblical author in order to make a subtle reference to Jonah's undignified exit from the fish in 2.11 (ויקא). The relationship between Jonah's plant and the Hebrew verb 'to vomit' allows a reconsideration of the ricinus as the plant in question for, as botanists (and generations of schoolchildren) will attest, the ricinus plant and its oil are nauseous to the taste.[32] The author of Jonah found in the ricinus plant a handy term which suits the purpose of functioning as a shade for Jonah and calls to mind Yahweh's prior beneficial display of power.

The purpose of the plant is twofold: to be a shade over Jonah's head and to be a deliverance from his distress. The text in v. 6 links these two purposes by means of a play on sound between the term for shade (צל) and the verb 'to deliver' (להציל), which comes from the root להצל לו. Some have proposed emending the verb to להצל לו from צלל ('shade'), on the basis of the LXX reading, τοῦ σκιάζειν αὐτῷ ἀπὸ τῶν κακῶν αὐτοῦ.[33] Against this emendation it is important to note

---

thirteenth-century Samuel ben Hophni (p. 395).

30.   This term occurs in many Greek travelogues (LSJ, p. 951).

31.   Halpern and Friedman, 'Composition and Paronomasia', pp. 85-86. This is also the reading of Robert Coote, who translates the term as 'vomit-plant' (*Amos among the Prophets*, p. 133) and Cooper, 'In Praise of Divine Caprice', p. 153. Duane Christensen uses the later rabbinic method of cryptic encoding known as *athbash*, which consists of determining a letter's distance from the beginning of the alphabet and replacing it with the letter equally distant from the end of the alphabet. Thus, for example, in English, A=Z, B=Y, C=X, etc. Through this esoteric method, in addition to the transposition of a letter, Christensen extracts the phrase דם נקיא (found in Jon. 1.14) from קיקיון ('Andrzej Panufnik', p. 138).

32.   Pliny remarks on this as well, noting that the oil of the *kiki* plant is 'disgusting' (*foedus*) and not to be ingested (*Nat. Hist.* 15.7.25-26). Herodotus states that the plant has an unpleasant smell (2.94).

33.   For example, Snaith, *Hebrew Text of Jonah*, p. 38. The emendation requires only the removal of the yodh from the verb. *Tg. Ps.-J.* also supports an emended

that the MT makes good sense as it stands. The modifying prepositional construction, מרעתו, not only refers back to Jonah's distress in 4.1, but reads more coherently with the MT's verb: 'to deliver him [Jonah] from his distress'. The emendation creates an awkward redundancy in the final two infinitive clauses:

> But Yahweh God appointed a *qiqayon* plant to grow up over Jonah, *to be a shade over his head, to shade him from his distress.*[34]

Moreover, while the author of Jonah shows a predilection for the cognate accusative construction (1.10, 16 [3 times], 4.1, 6) the emended reading does not follow the standard pattern found in the book, a verb followed by its cognate noun as direct object. Rather, in the emendation the noun precedes the verbal form and occurs in a different clause. The reading of the MT, creating as it does a *double entendre* between two similar sounding terms, is a technique (already examined above in Chapter 4) used in the king's command of 3.7-8 that the animals not eat and the people turn away from evil. In this instance, as in 4.6, a verb is played off against a similarly spelled noun and a double meaning is apparent. While the text-critical preference for the more difficult reading can be applied here in arguing for the priority of the MT, it is clear from the translations of Jerome, the LXX and *Tg. Ps.-J.*, that an alternative reading came into the Hebrew very early in the transmission history.[35]

---

reading with its לאגנא ליה (Levine, *Aramaic Version of Jonah*, p. 94). Levine wrongly argues that the Targum is an accurate rendering of the MT by appeal to a Hebrew verb הצל, which he translates 'to save'. No such verb is listed in the dictionaries, but rather there is a noun, הצלה, which occurs only in Est. 4.14 and is derived from נצל (BDB, p. 246). The verb in *Tg. Ps.-J.* is from the root גנן which means 'protect' and is used in the Talmud in contrast to the notion of deliverance (Jastrow [ed.], *Dictionary*, p. 260). Isa. 4.6 speaks of a booth (סכה) which will act as a shade.

34.   Author's translation of an emended Hebrew text. The LXX reads: 'But the Lord God commanded a gourd and it grew up over Jonah's head, to be a shade over his head so that it would shelter him from his evil'. The Vg follows the sense of the LXX with 'et protegeret eum'. It also adds the remark that Jonah was distressed ('laboraverat enim'). This addition is not found in any other versions and may be a gloss, especially since the Vg transforms Jonah's distress to anger elsewhere in ch. 4.

35.   Mur 88 supports the MT, while Jerome translates his Hebrew *Vorlage* exactly as the LXX. One can speculate that the *yodh* drops out of the Hebrew either through a deliberate excision in an attempt to clarify the text or through orthographic error, and that this tradition was the one used by the versions. This hypothesis is, of course, difficult to demonstrate and an argument can also be made that the change is

Jonah's intense but shortlived joy is eradicated by the destructive forces of the worm and the wind.[36] The east wind is described by the term חרישׁית, which occurs only here in the Old Testament but is also found in 1QH 7.4. The exact meaning of this term is uncertain, and many proposals have been offered.[37] Whatever the exact purpose[38] of the wind may be, its effects are quickly felt by Jonah. The reiteration in v. 8 of Yahweh's question in 4.4 takes on added meaning given Jonah's roasting by sun and hot wind. Through the use of חרה coupled with the adverbial sense of יטב (discussed above) God's query can be rendered, 'Are you thoroughly burned about the *qiqayon*?'[39] Whether one chooses to translate Jonah's response literally, and so make him upset enough to die, or rather to read the phrase with a superlative sense,[40] matters little in that the two options do not differ significantly

introduced, either deliberately or by accident, in one of the versions and then makes it way back into the Hebrew. Or one can argue for the independence of the variant's origins among the various witnesses.

36.   Some see in the worm's destruction of the plant a reference either to the Garden story in Genesis 2–3 (Elata-Alster and Salmon, 'Deconstruction', p. 55) or to the larger ancient Near Eastern folk motif of the serpent stealing the fruit of the tree of life from humankind (Lacocque and Lacocque, *Jonah*, p. 153; Orth, 'Genre in Jonah', p. 77). Kenneth Craig points out that Jon. 4.7 is the only instance in the Latter Prophets where the verb שׁמה is used of a prophet ('Poetics', pp. 168-69).

37.   Thus Wolff understands the term to mean 'cutting' from חרשׁ, 'plow, cut, stab' (*Obadiah and Jonah*, p. 161). Rashi reads the term from the root denoting silence and holds that it is used in Jonah to describe how this wind silences all others. David Kimchi appeals to the root for deafness and translates the term as 'deafening'; rabbinic citations in Zlotowitz (*Yonah*, p. 138). Wolff's interpretation is already found in *b. Git.* 31b. Summaries of the differing etymological interpretations are in Snaith, p. 39; Price and Nida, *Translator's Handbook*, p. 76 and Sasson, *Jonah*, pp. 302-303. The LXX uses the hendiadys καύσωνος συγκαίοντι to emphasize the wind's burning heat; so also the Vg 'ventum calido et urenti'; *Tg. Ps.- J.* reads שׁתיקקא ('silent, sultry').

38.   Sasson revives the rabbinic opinion that the wind is sent to blow down Jonah's hut in order to leave him completely unprotected from the sun (*Jonah*, p. 303).

39.   Sasson also notes a connection (*Jonah*, p. 307).

40.   Thomas, 'Superlative in Hebrew', pp. 219-21; and Price and Nida, *Translator's Handbook*, p. 78. Both of these works cite as support a tenth-century CE letter from a Jewish writer in Spain who uses the exact same phrase as that of Jon. 4.9 (חרה לי עד מות). It is difficult to see how this letter functions as support of a superlative reading. It could very well be quoting Jonah, or simply may be understood hyperbolically.

in their meaning. The literal reading ought perhaps to be favored, given the fact that Jonah twice longs for death in ch. 4.[41]

Before investigating exactly how Yahweh's final argument to Jonah functions, his remark concerning Nineveh's population in v.11 merits attention. Much of the past debate over the historicity of Jonah revolves around this verse, which states that in Nineveh there are 120,000 people who do not know their right from their left. Commentators who wish to argue for either side of the historicity issue appeal to the archaeological record as proof that the historical Nineveh either could or could not have had a population of that size in the neo-Assyrian period.[42] In addition to this debate is the opinion that the description 'who do not know right from left', designates the 120,000 as children.[43] Thus, for those who hold to the historical veracity of Jonah and to this interpretation, a city with a population of 120,000 children is therefore supposed to have a total population two to three times that size. Apparent in this ongoing discussion is that appeal to archaeological evidence, coupled with the highly speculative nature of determining population figures in antiquity, serves as little more than a dead end.[44] It has already been shown above in Chapter 4 that the author of Jonah uses literary traditions in combination with hyperbolic and stylized language in 3.3 to stress that Nineveh is a

41. The translation of William Tyndale satisfies the criteria of Hebrew grammar (with the exception of his translation of חרה as 'anger') while offering a lively English: 'I am angry a-good, even unto the death' (Daniell [ed.], *Tyndale's Pentateuch*, p. 643).

42. This in turn leads to the so-called 'greater Nineveh' hypothesis discussed above in Chapters 1 and 4.

43. For example, Bewer, *Jonah*, pp. 63-64. This interpretation is opposed by Wolff, who holds that the entire population is portrayed as ignorant (*Obadiah and Jonah*, p. 175). While not explicitly stating that Yahweh refers only to children, Trible argues that the witless population is compared to Jonah's plant, which is described as 'a child of a night' (*Rhetorical Criticism*, p. 216). Donald Wiseman observes that the Akkadian phrase 'right and left' (*kittu u mi-sá-ri*, CAD 10/2, pp. 117-18) is used to denote truth and justice or law and order ('Jonah's Nineveh', p. 40). Martin Luther holds that the text is not referring to children, but that the expression 'left from right', refers to worldly and divine matters, respectively (Oswald [ed.], *Lectures*, pp. 96-97).

44. By way of example Bewer cites an authority who estimates Nineveh's largest population at 174,000 (*Jonah*, p. 64). Sasson, albeit in a more recent work, quotes a letter from the editor of the State Archives of Assyria project in which the population is roundly and conservatively placed at 300,000 (*Jonah*, pp. 311-12).

fantastically large and exotic city destroyed long ago. With this in mind the author's choice of the phrase 'more than twelve myriads' (הרבה משתים עשרה רבו) bears renewed investigation, specifically in the use of the number twelve. This figure is used most frequently in the Old Testament to refer to the twelve tribes/eponymous ancestors of those tribes, and consequently functions as a circumlocution for Israel. Thus when an Israelite author states that more than twelve myriads of human beings live in Nineveh the remark serves to emphasize how much larger that city is than anything Israelite readers can imagine. Nineveh is larger than Israel to the nth degree. This description of Nineveh as phenomenally huge accords well with the author's previous statements in 3.3 that the city is large to God and requires a long time to traverse.

Yahweh's final remark to Jonah is cast in a form of argument known in Hebrew as קל וחומר, and which is the first of the seven *Middoth*, or exegetical principles, attributed to Rabbi Hillel.[45] The structure of the argument is commonly known in the west by the Latin terms *a fortiori*, or *a minori ad maius*, and is characterized by the analogous application of an argument that obtains in one case to a second case seen to be more significant than the first.[46] The unstated assumption of the argument lies in the concomitant increase between the applicability of a line of reasoning and the gravity of situation. It can therefore be stated: 'If such reasoning applies in this case, then how much more so does it apply in this other case of greater importance.' Crucial to the force and validity of such an argument is the establishment of correspondence between the two examples under discussion.

In Jon. 4.10-11 the two examples which form the argument are Jonah's feeling concerning the demise of the plant and Yahweh's feeling toward Nineveh and its fate. Both Yahweh's and Jonah's feeling towards their respective objects are described by use of the verb חוס. This term is commonly rendered 'pity', and that translation here in Yahweh's argument is used to support the interpretation that Yahweh is teaching Jonah about the breadth of a divine compassion

45. H.L. Strack and G. Stemberger, *Introduction to the Talmud and Midrash* (Minneapolis: Fortress Press, 1992) pp. 21-24.

46. This type of reasoning is, naturally, universal and much older than the Old Testament. Sasson cites an example from a Mari letter (*Jonah*, p. 308 n. 11).

which is beyond Jonah's narrow and rigid concept of justice.[47] This type of reading is due to a theologically motivated semantic myopia that overlooks the fact that חום has a wider range of meaning. Siegfried Wagner's analysis of the verb, prefaced by the remark that 'the predominant usage of *chus* is theological', is a good example of this one-dimensional understanding.[48] Wagner's primary examples of this theological meaning are taken from Deuteronomy, but examination of them demonstrates a lack of reference to anything theological. All five occurrences in that book (Deut. 7.16, 13.8, 19.13, 21, 25.12) use חום with a negation in the context of legal prescriptions: concerning certain statutes, punishment is to be applied to transgressors without חום. The fact that Wagner derives theological significance from instances involving murderers (Deut. 19.13), those who give false testimony (Deut. 19.21), or a woman who seizes a man by his sexual organs (Deut. 25.11), shows a dependence of his interpretation upon the assumption that law and theology are closely related (if not interchangeable) in the Old Testament. The verb has a wider range of meaning than 'pity'. In rabbinic literature, it expresses concern for the loss of goods or property, even things of little value.[49] In these contexts suitable translations are 'to have concern for' or 'to be sorry to lose'. חום in the Old Testament takes this meaning in Gen. 45.20, where it is used in relationship to goods (כלים). Some maintain that the connotation 'sorry to lose', rather than 'pity', is the correct rendering of Jonah's reaction to the loss of the plant.[50]

47.   Among those who translate this way are Tyndale (but with 'compassion' rather than 'pity'), RSV, Ehrlich, *Ezechiel*, p. 271 and Trible, who goes so far as to discern a 'theology of pity' at work in Jonah 4 (*Rhetorical Criticism*, pp. 222-23). Trible's position is similar to that of David Noel Freedman, who holds that the book of Jonah introduces a new teaching about divine pity in Israelite thought ('Did God Play a Dirty Trick on Jonah at the End?', *BibRev* 6 [1990], pp. 26-31 [31]).

48.   'חום', *TDOT*, IV, pp. 271-77, 272.

49.   Jastrow (ed.), *Dictionary*, pp. 436-37; Alexander Rofé lists all of the references in the rabbinic writings of this usage of the term (*Prophetical Stories*, p. 164 n. 71). Similarly, KB, p. 282, lists as the primary meaning of חום 'be sorry'. See also the translation 'be troubled about' in W.L. Holladay (ed.), *A Concise Hebrew and Aramaic Lexicon of the Old Testament* (Leiden: Brill, 10th edn, 1989) p. 98. These definitions are in contrast to that of BDB, p. 299: 'have pity, look upon with compassion'.

50.   G.M. Butterworth, 'You Pity the Plant: A Misunderstanding', *Indian Journal of Theology* 27 (1978), pp. 32-34; Rofé, *Prophetical Stories*, p. 164;

In support of this translation is the fact that the term 'pity' does not make sense as a description of Jonah's reaction because the word presupposes the sovereignty of the one exhibiting pity to the object of that feeling. Terence E. Fretheim notes that חוס in the Old Testament is most often used in reference to a ruler, the emissary of a ruler, or the administration of justice.[51] In this light, Jonah has no right to pity the plant in its demise because, as Yahweh pointedly reminds him, he has no power over it.[52] This idea of חוס as a free act of sovereign mercy lies behind the LXX use of φείδομαι ('spare') to translate the Hebrew of Jon. 4.10-11.

Jack Sasson takes another approach based on the fact that חוס for inanimate objects connotes 'concern about' while in relation to animates it means 'pity'. Thus in Jon. 4.10-11 it should be translated by two separate terms.[53] However, as noted above, the key assumption in the validity of an argument *a minori ad maius* is in the correspondence of circumstances between the two cases cited. There is no doubt that any correspondence to be found in Yahweh's argument hinges on the word חוס: it is the word which designates the issue at stake, the reactions of Jonah and Yahweh, and is the only term common to both parts of the argument. To understand the pivotal concept of this type of argument in two different ways shatters the correspondence upon which this reasoning is founded and from which it derives its validity.[54]

In sum there are three approaches to understanding Yahweh's argument, each of which centers on the meaning of the term חוס: 1) Both Jonah and Yahweh pity the plant/Nineveh; 2) Both Jonah and

and Golka, p. 124; so also NAB and JPSV.

51.   Fretheim, 'Jonah and Theodicy', pp. 235-36; Fretheim cites Deut. 7.16, 13.9, 19.13, 25.12, 1 Sam. 24.11, Ps. 72.13, Isa. 13.18, Jer. 21.7.

52.   So Fretheim: 'Clearly implicit throughout the usage of this term is the right of the sovereign... to have pity or not have pity as he sees fit... Jonah had no right to exercise חוס regarding the plant (and certainly not Nineveh!) for he had no sovereignty relating thereto' ('Jonah and Theodicy', p. 236); and Wagner: '*chus* means total renunciation of what one is empowered to do, not a mitigation of a punishment' ('חוס', p. 277).

53.   *Jonah*, pp. 309-10. Sasson chooses 'fretting' and 'compassion'; in this approach he is following the Vg, which uses 'doleo' and 'parco'. This double translation is also the case in the versions of Wycliffe, the KJV and JB.

54.   Trible also argues for a necessity of correspondence in vv. 10-11 (*Rhetorical Criticism*, pp. 220-23).

Yahweh are sorry to lose the plant/Nineveh; 3) Jonah is sorry to lose the plant and Yahweh pities Nineveh. The first option is ruled out because the attribution of pity to Jonah makes no sense. The third option, while based on a valid grammatical observation, violates the foundational principle upon which the argument and structure of vv. 10-11 is based. The second option does not violate the sense of either part of the argument and maintains the crucial correspondence between the argument's two parts. This is evident in translation:

> Yahweh said, 'You were sorry to lose the *qiqayon*, which you did not work for, nor make grow... yet I will not be sorry to lose Nineveh, the great city, in which there are more than twelve myriads of human beings...?'

With this translation established, closer examination of the argument can be made. For clarification, the various components of vv. 11-12 are displayed in tabular form.

	Subject	
Jonah		Yahweh
	Verb	
sorry to lose		sorry to lose
	Object	
qiqayon		Nineveh
	Elaboration on Object	
Jonah did not tend or make grow		120,000 people who do not know right from left
lived and died in a night		many animals

As can be seen, any correspondence is hard to discern in the elaborative statements made about the plant and Nineveh. Most commentators maintain that implicit in Yahweh's remark about the growth and care of the *qiqayon* is the fact that he has created Nineveh and hence cares for it.[55] Against such a view is the fact that the two verbs used by Yahweh in his rebuke of Jonah, עמל and גדל, are nowhere used in the Old Testament to denote creation. Use of the *piel* of מנה to designate the appearance of the *qiqayon* also further distances the notion that it

---

55.   Fretheim describes this interpretation as 'an argument from creation to compassion' ('Jonah and Theodicy', p. 231).

is the result of a divine act of creation. In addition to these lexical shortcomings, this understanding overlooks the function of the remark concerning Nineveh's human and animal population, and requires taking the illustrative statement about the *qiqayon* from the first part of the argument and affirming its opposite in the second—in violation of the principle of correspondence. A simpler approach, which takes both illustrative statements into account without requiring the affirmation of their antitheses, is to see the mutual applicability of each statement in both parts of the argument. Thus, just as the *qiqayon's* incredibly short lifespan was completed without the care of Jonah, so too has Nineveh grown large apart from Yahweh's care—and so too are its days numbered. Conversely, just as the witless Ninevites exhibit a foolishness which puts them on equal footing with their beasts,[56] so too is the *qiqayon* a living object without sense.[57] Finally, as Yahweh destroyed the one, so too did he deal with the other.

In addition to these relationships a more fundamental one comes to the fore, based upon the fact that Yahweh is telling Jonah that his sorrow over the loss of the plant is inappropriate. Jonah has not contributed to its growth, and in the end it is merely a senseless object which only lives a short while. In this elaboration, Yahweh is not teaching Jonah that he has no *right* to care about the plant,[58] but that he *should not bother* to care about something in which he has invested nothing and whose existence is fleeting. Applying the principle of correspondence and intensification, which are the distinguishing features of the *a minori ad maius* argument, to the second half of Yahweh's final remark follows this same reasoning. Should Yahweh be sorry to lose a large city over which he has not labored and whose inhabitants are foolish? Yahweh's final question about Nineveh and its fate functions rhetorically, and its implied answer is a firm no.[59] In

56.   Cf. Qoh. 3.18-21.

57.   This denial of human intelligence which separates it from the remainder of animal and plant life is further justification for reading חוס in regards to Nineveh identically to its meaning in regards to the plant, *contra* the Vg and Sasson.

58.   This type of interpretation often arises from the mistranslation of Yawheh's question in 4.8 as 'Do you do well to be angry about the *qiqayon*?'

59.   Cooper argues for the same interpretation, Yahweh's lack of concern for Nineveh, by reading v. 11 as a statement rather than a question: 'As for me, I do not care about Nineveh' ('In Praise of Divine Caprice', p. 158). Wolff points out that, of the ten instances in the Old Testament where חוס is used in relation to Yawheh, seven speak of how Yahweh does not possess it; two beg him to exhibit it, and only one

support of this reading is the fact that, apart from Jon. 4.11, the phrase, אֲחוּס לֹא is present only in Jer. 13.14 and Ezek. 24.14. In all three instances, Yahweh uses the phrase in speaking about himself, and the texts from Jeremiah and Ezekiel are clear that Yahweh will not show sorrow in the execution of punishment upon Israel. To this it should be added that the author's choice of Nineveh, the city renowned for being large, foolish and destroyed,[60] shows that history also has answered Yahweh's question in the negative.

This use of the language denoting concern or sorrow in the context of demonstrating Yahweh's lack of it in regards to Nineveh is analogously present in Jonah's citation in 4.2 of the frequently attested biblical tradition of divine attributes. The use of this tradition in the Old Testament and its meaning in Jonah merits further investigation.

The Divine Attribute Tradition in the Hebrew Bible

Exodus 34

In the course of the regiving of the Law at Mount Sinai after the apostasy of the golden calf, Moses is allowed to see Yahweh pass before him. As he does so, God extols himself:

> The LORD, the LORD, a God merciful and gracious, slow to anger, and abounding in steadfast love and faithfulness, keeping steadfast love for thousands, forgiving iniquity and transgression and sin, but who will by no means clear the guilty, visiting the iniquity of the fathers upon the children and the children's children to the third and fourth generation (Exod. 34.6-7).

This is the fullest articulation of a tradition that appears throughout the Old Testament. Many exegetes consider the passage in Exodus to be the original formulation of this tradition, the other uses functioning as 'citations' of sorts in later biblical literature.[61] Such a traditio-historical opinion is difficult to prove, and in reality is more an exegetical assumption than a result. The choice of the Exodus example as the originating point of this tradition is no doubt due to its use in the origin tale of the giving of the Law, to the impact of the added

text (Ezek. 20.17) attributes it to him (*Obadiah and Jonah*, p. 174).

60. Cf. the discussion on Greek traditions about Nineveh above in Chapter 4.
61. Schmidt, *'De Deo'*, p. 91; Price and Nida, *Translator's Handbook*, p. 69 and M. Fishbane, *Biblical Interpretation in Ancient Israel* (Oxford: Clarendon Press, 1985), pp. 335-36.

weight given the Torah/Pentateuch within the biblical canon, and to the influence of the Documentary Hypothesis, which attributes the text to J.[62]

Concerning the place of Jon. 4.2 in this tradition history, some exegetes note that Jonah's citation mentions only Yahweh's forgiveness, breaking off before the passage concerning the punishment of children and grandchildren for the sins of their forebears. It is thus argued that Jonah's utterance is a partial citation of Exod. 34.6-7 and, in its omission of divine punishment, serves to further the point of the book, the extension of God's mercy and forgiveness to sinners.[63] Implicit in this approach is the notion that Exodus 34 is the earliest form of this tradition, and that all other manifestations of it in the Old Testament function as references utilized in the different theological contexts of the various biblical books in which these citations appear.[64]

This view of Jon. 4.2 as one of many commentaries on the Exodus text not only requires that a facile answer be given to difficult historical questions, but also overlooks the many different forms in which this tradition is found in the Old Testament.[65] Even a brief perusal of these texts will show that one is not so much faced with an Exodus *Urtext* and its subsequent history, but instead various examples of clustered motifs and language about God, of which

62. For example, M. Noth, *A History of Pentateuchal Traditions* (repr.; Englewood Cliffs, NJ: Prentice-Hall, 1972 [1948]), p. 31. Against this view, Robert C. Dentan argues that the formula is post-Deuteronomic and exhibits many lexical similarities with the wisdom tradition ('The Literary Affinities of Exodus xxiv 6f', *VT* 13 [1963], pp. 34-51 [48-51]). However, the notion of a distinct wisdom vocabulary or tradition has been substantially undermined by the analysis of R.N. Whybray, *The Intellectual Tradition in the Old Testament* (BZAW, 135; Berlin: de Gruyter, 1974), pp. 121-48, 155-56.

63. Tigay, 'Book of Jonah', *Conservative Judaism* 38 (1985–86), pp. 67-76 and Brichto, *Grammar*, p. 85. David Gunn and Danna Fewell see in the partial citation of Exodus 34 a caricature of God (*Narrative*, pp. 144-45). Trible's dissertation also argues that Jonah functions as a midrash on Exodus 34; cf. Chapter 1. A verbal link between Exodus 34 and Jonah exists in the phrases הצאן והבקר אל ירעו (Exod. 34.3) and הבקר והצאן...אל ירעו (Jon. 3.7).

64. Ward, *Thus Says the Lord*, p. 248 and Cooper, 'In Praise of Divine Caprice', pp. 160-62.

65. Good illustrative lists/charts are those of Fretheim, *Message*, p. 119; G. Vanoni, *Das Buch Jona* (ATAT, 7; St. Ottilien: Eos, 1978), p. 139; Sasson, *Jonah*, p. 280 and Clark, *Ḥesed*, p. 248.

Exodus 34 is but a single manifestation. As in the discussion in Chapter 3 of the so-called borrowing of the Psalter in the song of Jonah, the issue here has to do with variant usage of standard formulaic language, a patterned cluster of divine attributes, rather than with direct literary dependence.[66] These variant clusters form a larger unit of varying length in its use in the Old Testament which I call the divine attribute tradition. Each use merits individual examination, so that a picture can be gained of the different ways this formula is recast and used in the literary strata of the Old Testament. What follows is just such an examination. The texts are divided between those which mention both Yahweh's forgiveness and punishment of the wicked and those (including Jonah) which contain no reference to punishment.

The Tradition of Divine Forgiveness and Punishment
Exodus 34. The formula occurs in the re-establishment of the covenant with Moses and the giving of the second draft of the Law after the apostasy of the golden calf in Exodus 32. The entire cycle of stories in Exodus 32–34 shows the notions both of divine forgiveness and of divine punishment. Yahweh exacts a terrible vengeance for the Israelite apostasy (discussed above in Chapter 4), but does not entirely abandon the idea of entering into a covenant with the people.

Numbers 14. After the report of the spies, the people murmur against Moses. In anger, Yahweh proposes to strike the Israelites with yet another pestilence. Moses recites the full formula in an effort to appease the divine wrath and beg forgiveness. In this reminder of God's great mercy Moses refers to the damage to Yahweh's reputation that destroying the Israelites would cause (v. 15-16). God subsequently mitigates the punishment by dooming the Israelites to wander in the desert until the entire generation that complained is dead (vv. 22-23), by killing all the spies who brought back an unfavorable report (vv. 36-37) and by subjecting the Israelites to a crushing military defeat at the hands of the Amalekites and Canaanites (vv. 39-45).

Nahum 1. In the introduction to the taunt-song over Nineveh there

---

66.   In addition to these arguments Sasson points out that כִּי is never used to introduce direct speech or quotations and hence its use as the introductory particle of the formula in Jon. 4.2 rules out the notion that it is a quotation of another text (*Jonah*, pp. 75, 279). Stanislav Segert observes that the uncharacteristic length of the clauses in 4.2 designates the verse as formulaic language ('Syntax and Style', p. 125).

is a shorter variant of the formula which, nonetheless, clearly sets out both elements found in the longer versions: Yahweh is longsuffering and patient, but also powerful and relentless in the pursuit of the guilty (v. 3).

The Tradition of Divine Forgiveness

Nehemiah 9. In the course of a lengthy rehearsal of Israelite history, the text refers to a variant of the tale of Israelite murmuring found in Numbers 14.[67] Although omitting the part of the tradition concerning Yahweh's punishment of the guilty, this entire account of Nehemiah is clear in the fact that the Israelites have suffered much due to divine punishment for their offenses.

Psalm 86. In this personal lament, the psalmist reminds God of his merciful attributes in an effort to gain divine aid in the poet's struggle against evildoers (v. 15). Even though no reference is made in the formula to God's punishment of the wicked, it is clear in the psalm that those who are wicked and guilty (the psalmist's enemies) are to be punished (v. 17). It is clear in the limited reference to Yahweh's compassion that the psalmist is claiming this mercy for himself alone.

---

67. As the note in the RSV points out, Num. 14.4 states that the Israelites only suggested appointing a leader so that they might return to Egypt; Neh. 9.17 is clear in that they did appoint such a leader. This is one of several divergences between the résumé of Israelite history found in Nehemiah and that of Genesis–2 Kings. For example, in Neh. 9.16-18, the episode of the golden calf (Exodus 32) is placed after this particular instance of murmuring (Numbers 14). The account in Nehemiah, while summarizing Israelite history from Abraham to the Persian period, makes no mention of Jacob/Israel or Moses. The omission of Moses is most curious, because no less than fifteen of the total twenty-two verses are devoted to the Exodus–Sinai–wilderness themes. That such a divergent account (in regards to the Pentateuch and Former Prophets) of Israelite history exists in the Persian period gives good reason to question the long-held opinion in scholarship that the bulk of the Old Testament had come to be written in its present form and viewed as authoritative by the fifth–fourth centuries BCE. This issue is examined in T.M. Bolin, 'When the End Is the Beginning: The Persian Period and the Growth of the Biblical Tradition', *SJOT* 10 (1996), pp. 3-15. Recent studies and critiques of this assumption are G. Garbini, *History and Ideology in Ancient Israel* (London: SCM Press, 1988); T.L. Thompson, *Early History of the Israelite People: From the Written and Archaeological Sources* (Studies in the History of the Ancient Near East, 4; Leiden: Brill, 1992), pp. 401-24; P.R. Davies, *In Search of 'Ancient Israel'* (JSOTSup, 148; Sheffield: Sheffield Academic Press, 1992); and N.P. Lemche, 'The Old Testament: A Hellenistic Book?' *SJOT* 7 (1993), pp. 163-93.

Psalm 103. This song of divine praise uses the formula in the context of a lengthy enumeration of Yahweh's mercy (vv. 6-14). There is no hint of punishment of the wicked, although reference is made to the feeble and transient nature of human life (vv. 15-16).[68]

Psalm 145. As is the case with Psalm 103, this psalm uses the formula in the context of the praise of Yahweh's kindness. It also is similar to Psalm 86 in its insistence that the wicked will not escape their deserved punishment (v. 20).

Joel 2. The tradition occurs at the turning point of the book, wherein Yahweh averts his anger and relents from the military threat he has sent upon the people (v. 13). From this point until the end of the book are given utopian oracles of blessing for Judah and Jerusalem and prophecies of destruction for the nations.

In looking at these texts it can be seen that, with the exception of Psalm 103 and Joel 2, all of them in both categories speak of the continued certainty of divine punishment for the guilty. Where this punishment is explicitly mentioned in the formula, the context relates the exacting of a severe penalty by God. Where the formula does not have the punishment clauses, the surrounding text makes clear that Yahweh's goodwill is nevertheless not to be relied upon by the wicked, whoever they may be. With the background of this formula established, the assumption that the absence of the punishment motifs of the formula in Jon. 4.2 is due to the author's wanting to teach about the wonders of divine forgiveness appears unfounded, because in the majority of occurrences of this shorter formula in the Old Testament, their contexts are clear that punishment of the guilty is still to be expected. This observation is identical to the results of the investigations into divine repentance and the expression 'Who knows?' undertaken above in the previous chapter—the overwhelming majority of these cases refers only to the possibility of divine mercy and forgiveness, while being clear that Yahweh is a god who unfailingly punishes those with whom he has a quarrel.

Of the two exceptions cited above to this phenomenon, Joel 2.13-14 merits a separate and more detailed analysis because of its extensive similarities with Jonah.

---

68. This is similar to God's emphasis on the transience and fragility of the *qiqayon* in Jon. 4.10. This type of language, along with that which speaks of God's compassion and forgiveness of iniquity, also occurs in Ps. 78.38-39.

Jonah and Joel
Joel 2.13-14 reads:

> Return to the LORD, your God, for he is gracious and merciful, slow to
> anger and abounding in steadfast love, and repents of evil. Who knows
> whether he will not turn and repent, and leave a blessing behind him...?

The necessity of examining the literary relationship between Jonah
and Joel lies in that: 1) Jonah and Joel are the only two variants of the
divine attribute tradition that have the order 'gracious and compassionate' (חנון ורחום) and also contain the phrase 'and repents of
evil' (ונחם על הרעה); 2) of the four uses of the phrase 'Who knows?'
in the Old Testament in reference to God, Jonah and Joel are the only
two texts that deal with the possibility of divine repentance.[69]

The vast majority of commentators on Jonah hold to the priority of
Joel, and argue that the author of Jonah is dependent upon Joel,[70]
although a few argue for the opposite opinion.[71] These arguments are
supported by appeal either to the dates of the two books, established
on other criteria, or to notions of how one book would use another or
argue against another. For example, Jonah is seen as borrowing from
the liturgical language of Joel and recasting it in narrative form, or as
undermining Joel's exclusivistic outlook through the application of
divine mercy to the gentiles. Needless to say, given the defiance on the
part of the biblical material to be dated with any certainty, in addition
to the easy reversibility of such literary arguments,[72] the question
remains open.

Two observations can be introduced into the debate which, while
not conclusively resolving the issue, lend credence to the view which

69.   Discussed above in Chapter 4.
70.   Feuillet, 'Livre de Jonas', p. 356; Allen, *Jonah*, p. 177; Vanoni, *Jona*, p.
139; Fishbane, *Biblical Interpretation*, pp. 345-46; Wolff, *Obadiah and Jonah*, p. 77;
Rofé, *Prophetical Stories*, pp. 164-65; Golka, *Jonah*, p. 119 and Nogalski,
Redactional Processes, p. 273 n. 79. Schmidt will argue against any relationship
between Jonah and Joel, but dates Joel earlier (*'De Deo'*, pp. 100-101).
71.   G.H. Cohn, *Das Buch Jona im Licht der biblischen Erzählkunst* (Assen:
Van Gorcum, 1969), pp. 28, 99 n. 2; and Magonet, *Form and Meaning*, pp. 77-79.
Sasson deems fence-straddling to be the best alternative (*Jonah*, p. 283).
72.   This state of affairs is clearly illustrated by Thomas B. Dozeman, who lists
the similar criteria of Magonet and Fishbane concerning the question, although both
these latter writers argue for opposite conclusions ('Inner-Biblical Interpretations of
Yahweh's Gracious and Compassionate Character', *JBL* 108 [1989], pp. 207-23
[216 n. 23]).

holds for the priority of Jonah. The first has to do with an implicit methodological assumption. Most writers on Jonah argue that it is dependent on Joel, and this argument is usually made in the context of a larger analysis of how Jonah uses/depends upon/borrows from many other biblical books.[73] Thus, in the larger process of explicating a particular biblical book in the light of other books, and in the more narrow approach of demonstrating a book's use of other books, the innate tendency is to view the remainder of the canon as background, and for all intents and purposes, chronologically prior.[74] This unstated influence at work in exegesis thus results in an almost *a priori* assumption that, given a compelling similarity between the text under examination and another text, the latter will be seen as influencing the former. This of course yields the happy state of affairs in which one therefore has more background and, hence, more things to say about the main text being studied.

That this is what has happened in the secondary literature concerning the relationship between Jonah and Joel, specifically regarding the latter's priority, is nowhere better illustrated than in the unstated influence this exegetical conclusion exerts on the analysis of Thomas B. Dozeman. Although Dozeman appears to conclude, as does Ludwig Schmidt before him,[75] that Jonah and Joel are unrelated texts which take the tradition of Exodus 32–34 and go their separate ways, his work implicitly argues for the priority of Joel and the dependence of Jonah upon it. Dozeman claims that one can argue the Jonah–Joel issue either way, and that he intends to do so as an illustrative exercise to show how each book utilizes the tradition. In spite of his intention, one cannot help but observe that, after an ostensibly full analysis of Jonah as an interpretation of Joel, Dozeman prefaces his section arguing for the dependence of Joel upon Jonah with the remark that: 'A thorough reading of Joel as an inner-biblical interpretation of Jonah is beyond the scope of this study'.[76] Then, in the course of his

73.   See, for example, the discussions above concerning Jonah 1 and Ezekiel 27, Psalm 107, Jonah 2 and the Psalter, Jonah 3 and Jeremiah 18, and the remarks below on Jonah 4 and 1 Kings 19.

74.   Although he discusses Jonah's use of other literary traditions, Magonet does not fall into this category since he argues for Joel's dependence upon Jonah.

75.   Dozeman, 'Inner-Biblical Interpretation', p. 209.

76.   'Inner-Biblical Interpretation', p. 216. No such disclaimer for the section arguing for the priority of Joel is apparent.

reading of Joel as a text borrowing from Jonah, Dozeman reverts to the position that Jonah is using Joel. And so he writes:

> However, this much is clear at the end of the story [Jonah]: that the prophet Jonah is meant to represent Israel in the larger context of the nations and that, if he is to move beyond his present wish for imminent doom, perhaps the best text for him to study would be Joel 2.1-17, since it explores in detail the more exclusive focus of Yahweh's compassion in the life of the covenant community, which is only hinted at in the closing of the book of Jonah.[77]

Dozeman's argument, that Joel refutes Jonah by subtly suggesting that the angry prophet read Joel's remarks concerning divine compassion, is too farfetched to be seriously considered, and demonstrates how the long tradition of reading Jonah in the light of Joel has left its mark on scholarship.

The second observation has to do with Joel's use of traditions and motifs found elsewhere in the Old Testament. I pointed out above in Chapter 4 that Joel is the only text to use the expression 'Who knows?' in relation to divine repentance in such a way that Yahweh actually does repent from a proposed destruction. Similarly, Joel is one of only two texts which use the tradition of divine attributes wherein no reference is made, either in the formula or the surrounding context, to divine punishment of the guilty. Jonah, on the other hand is categorized with the majority of cases in the Old Testament concerning both of these traditions. Given this type of data, it is more likely that the text which diverges from the established meaning of a tradition (or, in this case, two traditions) is to be viewed as the later entry into the literary fold. To this innovative reading of tradition can also be added Joel's anomalous ordering of motifs in the stock utopian vision found in Isa. 2.2-4 and Mic. 4.3

> Proclaim this among the nations: Prepare war, stir up the mighty. Let all the warriors draw near, let them come up. Beat your plowshares into swords, and your pruning hooks into spears. Let the weak say, 'I am a warrior.' (Joel 4.9-10)[78]

77.   Dozeman, 'Inner-Biblical Interpretation', p. 217.

78.   That the sword and plowshare imagery neither originates in nor is exclusive to the Old Testament is evidenced by Virgil's line: 'the curving sickle is beaten into a sword that does not yield' (*Georgica* 1.505).

In addition to this feature is the reference to the Ionians in Joel 4.6. The standard Hebrew term for this people is יָוָן, but only in Joel is a particular genitival form found, written יְוָנִים.[79] This occurrence is curious, given that the standard term can function in a genitival construction (e.g., Dan. 8.21) and more importantly that the term found in Joel is consonantally identical to the plural of 'dove' (and, hence, the proper name 'Jonah'). While admittedly there are no contextual reasons to support substituting these other nouns, the fact that this hapax legomenon occurs in a book which has indisputable literary ties to the book of Jonah is hardly coincidental. Thus, by way of conclusion:

1) Joel contains two biblical traditions that are also found in Jonah and uses them in a way which is quite different from their standard interpretations in the Old Testament (including Jonah).

2) This irregular reading is not isolated in Joel to these two traditions, as is evidenced by Joel's anomalous variant of the utopian vision found in Isaiah and Micah.

3) Joel utilizes an otherwise unattested form of a noun when a well-attested form is readily available. This divergent form is spelled identically to the plural of the proper name 'Jonah'.

These observations, in addition to the methodological remarks, constitute a case for arguing that the text of Joel 2.13-14 is dependent upon Jonah 3.10–4.2.

Jonah's Wish for Death

Jonah's Double Request

Jonah twice wishes for death in ch. 4. In 4.3 he prays to Yahweh to take his life. Some scholars who argue for the integrity of Jonah's psalm in ch. 2 point to the similar vocabulary shared in the psalm and in Jonah's prayer for death.[80] A more substantial relationship is evident between Jonah's request for death and the sailors' request for life in 1.14: Both use the interjection אָנָּה with the Tetragrammaton. Both use different verbs which, nevertheless, denote the same sense ('do not give'/'take'). Reference is made to Jonah's life with the word

---

79. BDB, p. 402.
80. Landes, 'Kerygma', pp. 3-31 (13-17); Allen, *Jonah*, pp. 198-99 and Craig, *Poetics*, p. 95.

נפש ('this man's life'/'my life'). Both end with subordinate clauses introduced by כי.[81]

Jonah's second wish for death in 4.8 is addressed not to Yahweh but to his own spirit. Sasson notes that this draws upon a motif at least as old as the early-second millennium Egyptian text, 'The Debate Between a Man and his Ka', in which an individual engages in an internal debate with the soul specifically on the question of suicide.[82] Closer to Jonah is this motif's presence in the identical request made by Elijah to himself in 1 Kgs 19.4.[83] This is but one of many similarities between Jonah and the Elijah cycle of 1 Kings 17–19: Jonah sleeps in the ship and Elijah sleeps under a bush; Jonah seeks refuge in a booth and Elijah in a cave; both Jonah and Elijah are shaded by plants, and are asked a question twice by Yahweh; both stories utilize the 40-day time span. This list could, of course, be lengthened. Suffice to say that most commentators on Jonah hold that the book is using the Elijah cycle as both a source and a foil.[84] While many of these similarities could be dismissed as incidental, one crucial to the plot in Jonah 4 is the request for death. But this motif is not limited in its use to the Elijah cycle and, as has been the case for so many other features of Jonah, the wider biblical context merits examination.

The Wish for Death in the Old Testament
David Daube analyzes every instance of a wish for death or act of suicide/killing on request in the Old Testament. Of interest here is his

81. These similarities are also noted in Fretheim, *Message*, p. 90.

82. Sasson, *Jonah*, p. 306; translation of the Egyptian text in Simpson (ed.), *Literature of Ancient Egypt*, pp. 201-209.

83. The Peshitta makes this connection even more explicit by attributing to Jonah the rationale behind Elijah's death wish, 'for I am no better than my ancestors'.

84. A partial list includes Driver, *Introduction*, p. 323; Feuillet, 'Livre de Jonas', pp. 168-69; Witzenrath, *Jona*, p. 81; Lacocque and Lacocque, *Jonah*, pp. 141, 147; Gregory, 'Elijah's Story', pp. 209-11; Magonet, *Form and Meaning*, p. 102; Christensen, 'Song', pp. 230-31; Wolff, *Obadiah and Jonah*, pp. 80-81, 168; Stuart, *Hosea–Jonah*, p. 435 and Craig, 'Poetics', p. 103. It should be pointed out that the historical reading of Stuart attributes any similarities between Jonah and the remainder of the Old Testament not to literary dependence but rather 'to the univocal nature of divine revelation' (*Hosea–Jonah*, p. 433). Sasson maintains that, since the *qiqayon* serves as a sign of Yahweh's continued concern for Jonah, it should be equated with the theophany granted Elijah in 1 Kgs 19.12, rather than with the broom tree (*Jonah*, p. 298).

designation of the requests of Moses, Elijah, Jeremiah and Jonah as the tradition of 'the weary prophet'.[85] But Jeremiah's so-called request for death is in reality a wistful (and futile) yearning that he should never have been born (Jer. 20.14-18) and not a desire that his life come to an end. Consequently, it should be categorized with Job 3.2-7 as a curse of life rather than as a request for death. This leaves the requests of Moses, Elijah and Jonah in a group for consideration.[86]

Numbers 11. In the course of the constant complaining of the Israelites, Moses in exasperation prays for death. He places the responsibility for his frustration on the people but also upon Yahweh. Hence, it is after Moses hears the weeping of the people and the anger of Yahweh is kindled, that he becomes displeased (v. 10). Moses also makes clear that his predicament is due to Yahweh's having dealt poorly with him (v. 11) and that the continuance of his misery is in part due to Yahweh's actions (v. 15). Put this way, it is clear that Moses is not only brought to despair by the murmuring of the Israelites, he is equally frustrated at the anger and vengeance of Yahweh which is continually being unleashed upon the people (here in v. 1). Yahweh's response is to anoint seventy assistants to Moses to ease the burden of dealing with people.[87]

1 Kings 19. In flight from Jezebel, Elijah comes to Horeb and begs Yahweh to kill him. Elijah's motivation appears to be twofold: he is a failure as a prophet and he is the only true follower of Yahweh left. Not only does this overlook Obadiah and the hundred Yahwistic prophets still in hiding (1 Kgs 18.3-4), but God also remarks that

---

85.   D. Daube, 'Death as a Release in the Bible', *NovT* 5 (1962), pp. 82-104 (96-97). A traditional Jewish interpretation is found in D.K. Wohlgelernter, 'Death Wish in the Bible', *Tradition* 19 (1981), pp. 131-40.

86.   Sasson also deems Moses and Elijah to be the closest to Jonah (*Jonah*, pp. 284-85). To the literary links between Jonah and the Elijah cycles should also be added the observation of Terence Collins that Elijah is patterned as a prophet after the figure of Moses (*Mantle of Elijah*, pp. 133-35). Collins lists as similar elements the fear for life, flight into the desert, miraculous feeding, the forty-day journey to the mountain of God, complaint, divine punishment and anointing of a successor. To Collins's list could be added the similarities between Yahweh's burial of Moses in a secret place (Deut. 34.5-6) and Elijah's ascension in the fiery chariot (2 Kgs 2.16-17).

87.   The variant of this tale found in Exodus 18 does not contain a wish for death from Moses. There, Moses' father-in-law Jethro advises Moses to appoint assistants.

there are 7000 people left in Israel who have not worshipped Baal (1 Kgs 19.18). In response, Yahweh removes Elijah from office and commissions him to anoint Elisha as his successor.

When looking at this motif in these two texts what is apparent is the fact that an immediate divine response to a request for death is a diminishment in or revocation of God's power and authority from the individual. Moses has a portion of his divine authority divided among the seventy elders,[88] and Elijah's office as prophet is abruptly terminated and a successor named. Of course, the most significant shared feature is the fact that these entreaties for death are denied by God. In this manner, the request and subsequent divine denial function to place the individual in a most helpless and pathetic state before the divine power. Reduced to despair by circumstances often brought about by God, Moses and Elijah can do nothing but appeal to divine mercy in an effort to bring their suffering to an end. This appeal (and its subsequent denial) reinforces the absolute authority of Yahweh, in that neither individual makes a move to bring about the request himself and both come to suffer an eventual fall from divine favor. In this broader context of the use of this motif, Jonah's request for death in 4.3, 8 serves a manifold purpose. It heightens the abject misery he feels at the turn of events in Nineveh, at the demise of the *qiqayon*, and at the physical toll taken on him by the sun and wind. It hints at an imminent reduction in Jonah's authority and status vis à vis Yahweh. Finally, it serves to reinforce the key theme that has been shown to run throughout the book, namely the absolute power of Yahweh over creation and an equally unfettered freedom in the exercise of that power.

Conclusion

In the final chapter of Jonah there is an ending to the story of the divine messenger which reiterates the one major theme of the book while heightening the tension concerning this theme and its implications. As the chapter begins, Jonah is overcome by great anxiety and dejection. He is not incensed at the divine pardon of gentiles. The Hebrew does not allow for this interpretation, and the author has

---

88. While this demotion is mitigated by the divine endorsement of Moses' special status in Numbers 12, it should not be forgotten that, like Elijah, Moses is ousted from his office by Yahweh and is replaced by a successor.

given several indications that Nineveh is not spared. Jonah's upset stems from the fact that he has been excluded from Yahweh's thoughts concerning the city. Jonah is saddened because, in spite of his status as God's messenger, he is unclear as to the intention or meaning of God's message and purpose concerning Nineveh.[89]

Jonah and Yahweh debate in ch. 4, each being allotted an exactly equal amount of dialogue. From this debate no clear winner emerges, insofar as neither party concedes. In spite of this impasse, the following points make clear the author's opinion concerning the debate and its outcome. These views are here cast in the form of lessons Yahweh teaches Jonah.

Yahweh's first lesson is that created life is frail, brief and potentially meaningless.[90] The transience and weakness is emphasized by the statement that the *qiqayon* lived and died at Yahweh's hands 'a child of the night',[91] and by the relative ease with which Yahweh brings Jonah to the edge of death.[92] The element of senselessness revolves around the large but foolish city of Nineveh, the famous destroyed metropolis full of people and animals who are, in the end, worth no more than a plant created for a temporary shade and a worm's breakfast.

The second lesson has to do with the extent of one's affections. Here the lesson deals with what is an appropriate object of such concern. Yahweh's point to Jonah is that things over which one has invested nothing are not to be cared for. Their loss is not to be mourned. For Jonah this acts as a check on any feelings he has about the loss of the plant. For Yahweh this functions as further illustration concerning his destruction of Nineveh, regardless of any penance the city has undertaken.

To further illustrate these two lessons the author draws upon two biblical traditions in the creation of this scene. The popular tradition of divine attributes is used in its shortened form. As with almost all

89. Sasson, *Jonah*, pp. 294-98.

90. One is reminded of the famous remark of Thomas Hobbes that, human life in its natural state, is 'solitary, poor, nasty, brutish and short'.

91. This is a literal translation of the Hebrew בֶּן לַיְלָה (4.10). P.A. Vaccari, arguing for the historicity of Jonah, holds that this expression does not denote a literal length of time for the *qiqayon's* growth and demise, but rather is a colloqial expression much like 'in the blink of an eye' ('Libro di Giona', p. 252).

92. So Sasson, who cites illustrative examples from Psalms 90, 144 (*Jonah*, p. 318) and S. Goodhart, 'Prophecy', p. 54.

the other uses of this shorter form, lack of explicit mention of divine punishment does not mean that God will not punish those whom he deems wicked or guilty. So too with the Ninevites. This standard use of the divine attribute tradition is identical to those of the traditions of Yahweh's repentance and use of the phrase 'Who knows?' While they all admit that God may repent, draw back from a pronounced punishment, or show mercy to an evildoer, more often than not this is not the case. The second tradition, the motif of the wish for death, draws attention to the utter powerlessness of Jonah in the face of his omnipotent God in addition to his fall from divine favor. Chased across the sea and to the depths of the earth, compelled to carry out a mission doomed to futility from the start, reduced to the barest remnant of life, Jonah now is to forfeit the last thing which gives him dignity, his status as divine mediator.

And so, while on a formal level the debate between Jonah and Yahweh is unresolved,[93] the author indicates through a renewed emphasis on God's unlimited power over creation that to engage in a debate with God in the hope of victory or resolution is pointless. Although the irrelevance of receiving answers from God to questions concerning the rationale behind the exercise of his power is also the point of Job, that book differs from Jonah in that Job unequivocally admits defeat. In Jonah the argument is more subtle: Argue with God if you will; win if you can, but to what end is your victory? Divine power is larger than any human conceptions of justice or logic, and so engage Yahweh at your own peril, for he needs no reason to crush you.[94] Apart from this difference between Job and Jonah, the former's remark concerning his debate with Yahweh, used as an epigraph for this chapter, well illustrates the author's point in Jonah 4.

It is clear that any notions about an extension of divine mercy, or of a new, more profound teaching about Yahweh's love have been left far behind. Any exegesis which finds them here is the result of a petrification of older readings.[95] As mentioned above, unlike Job, the

93.   Group from Rennes, France, 'Book of Jonah', pp. 90-91.

94.   Keller's remarks concerning the inscrutability of Yahweh's actions in regards to Jonah are fitting here ('Jonas', p. 337). Against Keller's reading there is no indication in the text that Yahweh is mischievously or maliciously toying with Jonah; there is no hint of divine pleasure at work in Jon. 4.

95.   An example of this type of exegesis is Nowell's analysis of Jonah 4:

author of Jonah does not allow the angry messenger to formally concede, for concession is pointless.[96] Different tradents of the story, uncomfortable with Jonah's silence, supplied him with the proper expression of surrender. The Yom Kippur liturgy gives Jonah a final response, taken from the end of Micah (Mic. 7.18-20), which duly transforms the book into a lesson on repentance and the assurance of final divine pardon.[97] The *Yal. Shimoni* offers yet another ending, which serves to emphasize Jonah's abject submission:

> At that moment he [Jonah] fell upon his face and said, 'Conduct your world according to the principle of your mercy, as it is written, "to the Lord our God are mercy and forgiveness"'.[98]

But in spite of the best efforts of scholars ancient and modern, the hanging end of Jonah and the precarious nature of human existence which it metaphorically represents remain a haunting biblical witness to a theology that defies easy expression or analysis.

God, on the other hand, is merciful because God knows who Jonah is. Instead of punishing Jonah for his flight, for his half-hearted prophesying, for his lack of mercy, God works with Jonah as if he were a child who 'cannot distinguish his right hand from his left.' God teaches Jonah a lesson. Near his hut God provides a gourd plant that gives Jonah joy and shade. The next day God allows a worm to destroy the plant; this angers Jonah. Then God sends an east wind so hot that Jonah desires death. This is the heart of the chapter and the center of the palistrophe. Divine mercy knows no bounds. God is even merciful to the recalicitrant prophet (*Jonah*, p. 15).

96. This point is itself demonstrated by Job's concession.
97. Discussion in Fishbane, *Biblical Interpretation*, p. 349.
98. Quoted in Zlotowitz, *Yonah*, p. 144.

Chapter 6

CONCLUDING REMARKS

All Christian commentators on the Bible... have disputed and wrangled
and anathematized each other about the supposed meaning of particular
parts and passages therein; one has said and insisted that such a passage
meant such a thing; another that it meant directly the contrary, and a third
that it meant neither the one nor the other, but something different from
the both; and this they call *understanding* the Bible.

—Thomas Paine[1]

The above quotation serves to bring together many of the various
lines of thought that have been pursued in this study. It should come as
no surprise that it deals with issues of methodology since, as the
reader no doubt already knows, much of this work has dealt with the
application and validity of several common methodological assumptions as they pertain to the book of Jonah. Thus these final remarks,
rather than offering a summary of exegetical results, will explore
these conclusions by means of analysis of Jonah's place within the
broader categories of Israelite history, the biblical corpus, and the
theological nature of the Old Testament. In many respects, then, this
conclusion is more of an introduction to further issues in need of
study than a tying of loose ends.

Jonah in its Israelite Context

Jonah and the History of Israel
As has been mentioned on several occasions, the once standard scholarly view of Jonah holds it to be a post-exilic reaction to the exclusivist, xenophobic type of Judaism assumed to be typified by Ezra–
Nehemiah. The debt this opinion owes to the historical reconstruction

1.   Paine, *Age of Reason*, p. 59.

of Julius Wellhausen in his massive and influential *Prolegomena*[2] is
apparent. Wellhausen constructs a great synthesis wherein a struggle
results between two opposing forces. On the one hand is a religious
tradition characterized by individuality, variety and high ethical criteria
(early Israelite religion, the classical prophets), while on the other is a
rigid, legalistic, centripetal force which seeks a stifling homogeneity
(the Deuteronomic school, P and the post-exilic era). In the ongoing
struggle between these two forces, which stretches over several
centuries, it is those who espouse centralization and codification who
emerge victorious.[3] That Wellhausen's vision is heavily informed by a
nineteenth-century Romanticism which extols individuality and the
primitive is clear. As is the case with everyone, Wellhausen is a child
of his day.

Yet in his caricature of post-exilic Israelites (who for Wellhausen
are no longer Israelite, but Jewish) as legalistic can be seen an understanding of Judaism which owes more to the polemical views of Paul
and the gospels than to any critical historical observations of the
sixth–fourth centuries BCE. Fresh knowledge gained concerning this
period has not substantiated Wellhausen's model in any way.[4] Of
course the shortcomings of Wellhausen's approach are endemic to the
scholarly field of Old Testament studies/Israelite history in that a
tightly closed circle is formed by the analysis of texts in order to
furnish a history which is then used as background to explain the
texts.[5] While Wellhausen is certainly correct in his assertion that the

---

2.   J. Wellhausen, *Prolegomena to the History of Israel* (repr.; New York:
Meridian, 1957 [1878]). A broader overview of the development of this scholarly
view of Jonah, and the underlying presuppositions and biases which inform it, is in
Bickerman, 'Deux Erreurs', pp. 232-64; ET in *idem*, *Four Strange Books*, pp. 19-27.

3.   This model is the guiding structure for each of Wellhausen's chapters ana-
lyzing the various elements of ancient Israelite religion; see *Prolegomena*, pp. 17-
170, 402-408, 411-18.

4.   For example, the Jewish papyri from Elephantine, which span the greater
part of the fifth century BCE, show a Judaism for which biblical texts and traditions,
almost all religious festivals (with the possible exception of Passover) and monothe-
ism play no role.

5.   This method is typified in the remark of Otto Eissfeldt concerning the
prophetic literature:

> The literary questions must be settled first as such, and only after their solution can we
> form an historical reconstruction; not contrariwise, so that the literary points are elabo-
> rated only after shaping the historical picture—which in such circumstances, is one

biblical texts have more to tell about the historical circumstances of their authors than of any events they purport to relate, the knowledge of these historical circumstances must be gleaned independently of the texts it is meant to elucidate. If this is not done (as more often than not is the case) a confusion results wherein a literary question is given a historical answer and vice versa.

Thus the reading of Jonah which draws its support from this reconstruction has justifiably given way to newer approaches. But closer examination of these more recent offerings reveals a common trait whose origins lie in the old view. These newer readings hold that in Jonah are two contrasting viewpoints, represented by Jonah and Yahweh, that concern God, prophecy, repentance or theodicy. In this conflict, Jonah represents the more rigid, dogmatic and inferior opinion to be contrasted and corrected by that of Yahweh (and the author) which emphasizes inclusivity, mercy and forgiveness. Even those authors who read Jonah as dealing with the profound mystery of the divine nature see that discussion as limited to the extent of God's care and concern for humanity.[6] And so the antithetical relationship between factions or parties, so key a factor in Wellhausen's model and a ubiquitous element in literary and historical analyses in the field,[7] remains the governing assumption out of which Jonah is still read. Consequently, these more recent approaches are in actuality new

---

simply drawn out of the air ('The Prophetic Literature', in H.H. Rowley [ed.], *The Old Testament and Modern Study* [Oxford: Clarendon Press, 1951], pp. 115-61 [158]).

6. For example, Terence Fretheim understands Jonah's teaching to be that 'God has the right to do what pleases him... because he is Creator. Jonah cannot bring God into court on the question of justice or injustice, mercy or condemnation. He is creature' (*Message*, p. 128). Fretheim qualifies this divine inscrutability by subordinating it to the assumption that Yahweh's ultimate will for humankind is its salvation (p. 114). This is consonant with other commentators who limit the idea of divine freedom in Jonah in such a way that God is free only to forgive whomever he will. Thus, while Jack Sasson understands Jonah to be dealing with the inscrutability of God, this God is for Sasson inscrutably kind (*Jonah*, pp. 350-51). André and Pierre-Emmanuel Lacocque succinctly elucidate this one-sided view: 'When all arguments are exhausted in the theological debate, what ultimately remains is love' (*Jonah*, p. 163).

7. A good example of the extent of this assumption is its use in M. Smith, *Palestinian Parties and Politics that Shaped the Old Testament* (London: SCM Press, 1971), a work which seeks to question some standard historical conclusions.

versions of older Christian arguments with their explicitly offensive
nature removed.

Jonah and the Old Testament

It has been determined that, while Jonah exhibits affinities to a great
deal of material found in the Old Testament, these relationships are
due more to a common cultural and literary tradition than any direct
borrowing or dependence. Such a conclusion is in contrast to much
other exegesis of Jonah, which delineates a wide array of quotes,
partial citations, reminiscences and allusions throughout the book's 48
verses. Of interest in this approach is the corresponding opinion that
Jonah refers to these other texts in a way which either recasts them
ironically,[8] subverts or otherwise reinterprets their meaning,[9] or calls
them into question through their attribution to Jonah, the antagonist of
the text. This view is predicated upon a hermeneutical stance which
implicitly casts all other biblical texts as background to the particular
text under study. Coupled with this is an *a priori* assumption about the
author and the work founded upon a so-called 'aesthetics of negativity'
which presupposes that the work in question (and hence, its author)
offers a challenge, or a new and in some way disconcerting alternative
voice, to long-held and cherished societal traditions, practices, or
writings.[10] While such modes of reading are certainly possible in an
anonymous literary corpus of unknown date, they do little to elucidate
what a text is saying. Rather, they show how a text may be given a
reading that is specific and predictable. Given that Jonah uses several
biblical motifs (water imagery for distress, Yahweh's repentance, the
expression 'Who knows?' and the tradition of the divine attributes) in
a way entirely consonant with their use in the majority of their other
biblical occurrences, the evidence does not allow for reading the book
as a counter-cultural tract of its day.

Concerning the date of Jonah, all that can be offered is a speculation
which begs a tolerant hearing. That the book's portrayal of Nineveh
finds its nearest correspondence in Hellenistic traditions about that city
is evidence for a date sometime in that period. That Jonah contains
motifs and traditions found throughout the Old Testament is not an aid

8.   Good, *Irony*, p. 50; Magonet, *Form and Meaning*, p. 52.
9.   Allen, *Jonah*, p. 177.
10.   The use of an aesthetics of negativity is discussed in its specific relation to
newer literary approaches to Jonah above in Chapter 1.

to determining a date, for it is impossible to determine the direction of dependence/attestation in almost all of the cases. To demonstrate that Jonah refers to a tradition from 2 Kings, or that Joel is drawing upon Jonah, as this study has done, offers only a fleeting glimpse into that great expanse of darkness which is the chronology of the biblical books.[11] A case can be made that Jonah influences other biblical texts, as the limited nature of knowledge and evidence allows for both extremes of the issue to be argued.[12] The paucity of conclusions concerning literary dependence offered in this study emphasizes the methodological caution with which such issues should be approached.

The Theological Perspective of Jonah

While the foregoing remarks have for the most part focused on what has been said about Jonah, and why certain things may no longer be said about it, through this line of critique observations of a more constructive nature can be expressed.

The Book's Portrayal of God

It has been shown that in Jonah the fundamental issue is the affirmation of the absolute freedom, power and sovereignty of Yahweh over all creation. These divine attributes are beyond the bounds of any human notions of justice, mercy or logic. This issue is expressed in a distinct way in each of Jonah's four chapters. In Jonah 1, Yahweh is portrayed as the all-powerful creator from whom no one may escape, and toward whom the only proper demeanor is fearful worship. In the following chapter Jonah's psalm acknowledges that, in a world where both distress and salvation come only from God, praise of Yahweh is one's sole recourse (but no guarantee of safety) in times of trouble. Jonah 3—which combines the exaggerated repentance and sparing of a city known to have been destroyed with the use of the motif of divine repentance—pointedly stresses that God's actions concerning wrongdoing and its recompense work according to a reasoning impenetrable to human understanding. Finally, the remaining

11. Even the most superficial survey of the voluminous literature on this topic will demonstrate the lack of consensus gained after almost two centuries of investigation.

12. By way of example, a case could be made for the dependence of Isa. 60.8-10 and Zeph. 2.13–3.2 on Jonah. Sasson argues that Sir. 51.1-12 and portions of 1QH draw upon Jonah (*Jonah*, p. 213).

scene of the book serves to teach Jonah and the reader not that God's concern for creation is wider than once thought, but precisely that divine care does not extend to things in which Yahweh has not bothered himself. In this theological view lies an affirmation of a God who is not only free to love whom he will, Jew or Gentile, but also perfectly free to change his mind on such matters, even those which concern the fate of 120,000 people and their animals.[13] It is summed up perfectly in the sailors' desperate plea, 'You are Yahweh, you do what you want' (1.15) and in Jonah's cry of surrender to Yahweh from the belly of the fish (2.10).[14] This theology is patently clear in the author's use of biblical traditions which allow for the possibility that Yahweh may repent, be gracious and forgive, but are clear in their contexts that such actions on God's part are no reason for anyone to feel released from the execution of divine retribution. It is at work in the story of Yahweh's sparing of a city renowned for having been utterly destroyed, and in the harsh lesson plant, worm, wind and deity teach a broken man about the foolishness of excess affection. Writing about this kind of portrayal, Roland Murphy observes that it is

> an understanding of God that the modern reader may be loathe to share. Ancient Israel obviously did not have such qualms. There was a dark side, or underside, to God that was simply accepted... How can one penetrate the mystery of divine decision, or should one say divine caprice?[15]

Jonah and Wisdom

While Murphy's description is an apt one for Jonah, it occurs in the context of his analysis of Job. As has been pointed out, similarities between Jonah and Job have been noted by commentators.[16] In many

---

13.   So also Alan Cooper: 'The dark side...is that God's destructive wrath might be just as arbitrary and unconstrained... One hopes and prays for God's love, while recognizing that nothing is certain' ('In Praise of Divine Caprice', p. 162).

14.   Cf. T.L. Thompson, 'The Old Testament as a Theological Discipline. II. "He is Yahweh; He Does what is Right in his Own Eyes"' (forthcoming).

15.   R.E. Murphy, *The Tree of Life: An Exploration of Biblical Wisdom Literature* (ABRL; Garden City, NY: Doubleday, 1990), p. 36.

16.   Goitien, 'Some Observations', p. 74; Vawter, *Job and Jonah*; Roffey, 'God's Truth', pp. 13, 17; Sasson, *Jonah*, p. 351; and Ward, *Thus Says the Lord*, p. 250. Robert C. Dentan argues that Jonah should be categorized as wisdom literature as it is a critique of prophecy arising from the wisdom tradition ('Literary Affinities', p. 50 n. 5).

respects the reading of Jonah offered here accords well with the standard scholarly understanding of the two wisdom books of Job and Qoheleth. All three emphasize the pain of an existence under the rule of an omnipotent but inscrutable deity. All three emphasize the futility of the foundational religious and theological issues of prayer, sacrifice, repentance and right living.

Simply to place Jonah in the small sub-category of wisdom writings comprised of Job and Qoheleth risks perpetuating a misreading of the latter two books which neutralizes their challenging theses. Biblical scholarship (again, mainly Christian) in its particular way of reading the Old Testament as a religious corpus interprets this large and various collection through several different theological categories, for example: sin, grace, salvation, covenant. The bulk of the wisdom material, specifically because of its so-called 'secular' nature, does not easily yield texts which lend themselves to these categories. Thus the wisdom books have been placed in a ghetto of sorts, their authors segregated into a special class with a distinct vocabulary and outlook. Into this quarantine Job and Qoheleth occupy another distinct group, being seen as tortured expressions of revolt or intense questioning on the part of specific individuals. What results from this double wall placed around these two books is a containment of their radical challenges which then preserves the neat theological schemata devised for the remainder of the canon. The placement of Jonah with Job and Qoheleth should serve as a dissolution of the sub-category in which the latter books have dwelt, rather than the admittance of a third text into that class.

Jonah and Biblical Theology
Presently a vacuum exists in the area of biblical theology. The death of the Biblical Theology Movement and the failure of its child, canonical criticism,[17] combined with the undermining of the historical and literary assumptions upon which the great theologies of Gerhard Von Rad and Walter Eichrodt are constructed, have left a space into which few have entered. New approaches to a theology of the Old Testament are easily and studiously avoided by recourse to the newer literary methods which have proliferated. However, in the course of

17. Sustained critiques of this method are in J. Barr, *Holy Scripture: Canon, AuthorityCriticism* (Philadelphia: Westminster Press, 1983), pp. 130-71; and Barton, *Reading the Old Testament*, pp. 77-103, 208-11).

this study it has become apparent that, in the observation that Jonah exhibits affinities with Job and Qoheleth and also draws heavily upon traditions found in all parts of the canon, using them in fundamentally the same manner, an entry point is gained which warrants and compels a re-examination of the theology of the Old Testament. If texts from the Pentateuch, the Deuteronomistic History and the Major Prophets speak about the nature of divine forgiveness and punishment in the same way as Jonah, then a new theological understanding of the Old Testament can be undertaken, one that is free from the burden of historical speculation and that takes into account all of biblical corpus. This is where the discussion next leads.

In Melville's *Moby Dick*, Father Mapple finishes an impassioned sermon on Jonah with the modest disclaimer: 'Shipmates, I have read ye by what murky light may be mine the lesson that Jonah teaches to all.' Father Mapple's words seem the most fitting means by which to bring this particular analysis of Jonah to a close. Here I wish to make two final remarks. The first is that one of the unstated aims of biblical research is to offer something new and original to the scholarly discussion on a given topic. While this may be a laudable goal, I cannot claim that, in placing the book of Jonah within a speculative theological tradition which claims that 'there is nothing new under the sun', I have accomplished this task. Secondly, lest anyone think that I have burdened this book with too much theological weight, it deserves to be noted that until very recently Jonah played a part in the major liturgical holidays of three religious traditions.[18] In this confessional usage is the acknowledgment, given here also, that although small the book of Jonah offers an entry into much larger and more foundational issues. Perhaps also it is no wonder that Q's Jesus chooses the figure of Jonah as a foil in pointing his hearers to a deeper greatness.

18.   Until the Second Vatican Council, Jonah was read at the Holy Saturday liturgy of the Roman Catholic Church. It retains this place in the liturgical calendar of the Greek Orthodox Church. In Judaism, Jonah is the *Haftarah* for Yom Kippur.

BIBLIOGRAPHY

Aalders, G.C., *The Problem of the Book of Jonah* (London: Tyndale House, 1948).

Abel, F.-M., 'Le culte de Jonas en Paléstine', *JPOS* 2 (1922), pp. 175-83.

Aberbach, D., *Imperialism and Biblical Prophecy 750–500 BCE* (London: Routledge, 1993).

Abramson, G., 'The Book of Jonah as a Literary and Dramatic Work', *Semitics* 5 (1977), pp. 36-47

Ackerman, J.S., 'Satire and Symbolism in the Song of Jonah', in B. Halpern and J. Levenson (eds.), *Tradition and Transformation* (Winona Lake, IN: Eisenbrauns, 1981), pp. 213-46.

—'Jonah', in R. Alter and F. Kermode (eds.), *The Literary Guide to the Bible* (London: Collins, 1987), pp. 234-43.

Ahl, R., *Fragender Glaube: Jeremia-Koheleth-Jona* (Meitinger Kleinschriften, 30; Freising: Kyrios, 1973).

Ahlström, G., 'The Nora Inscription and Tarshish', *Marrar* 7 (1991), pp. 41-49.

Albright, W.F., 'New Light on the Early History of Phoenician Colonization', *BASOR* 83 (1941), pp. 17-22.

Alexander, T.D., 'Jonah and Genre', *TynBul* 36 (1985), pp. 35-59.

Alexander, T.D., D. Baker and B. Waltke, *Obadiah, Jonah, Micah* (TOTC; Leicester: Inter-Varsity Press, 1988).

Allegro, J., *The Sacred Mushroom and the Cross* (Garden City, NY: Doubleday, 1970).

Allen, L.C. *The Books of Joel, Obadiah, Jonah and Micah* (NICOT; Grand Rapids: Eerdmans, 1976).

Allenbach, J., 'La figure de Jonas dans les textes préconstantiniens ou l'histoire de l'exégese au secors de l'iconographie', in M. Aubineau (ed.), *La Bible et le Péres* (Paris: Université de France, 1971), pp. 97-112.

Alles, G.D., 'Wrath and Persuasion: The Iliad and its Contexts', *JR* 70 (1990), pp. 167-88.

Almbladh, K., *Studies in the Book of Jonah* (Studia Semitica Uppsaliensis, 7; Stockholm: Almqvist & Wiksell, 1986).

Alter, R., *The Art of Biblical Narrative* (New York: Basic Books, 1981).

Andersen, F.I., and A.D. Forbes, *A Linguistic Concordance of Ruth and Jonah: Hebrew Vocabulary and Idiom* (Computer Bible, 9; Wooster, OH: Biblical Research Associates, 1976).

Anderson, B., *Out of the Depths* (Philadelphia: Westminster Press, 1974).

Andrew, M.E., 'Gattung and Intention of the Book of Jonah', *Orita* 1 (1967), pp. 13-18, 78-85.

Auffret, P., 'Pivot pattern: Noveaux exemples', *VT* 28 (1978), pp. 103-10.

Babcock, W.S., 'Image and Culture: An Approach to the Christianization of the Roman Empire', *PSTJ* 41 (1988), pp. 1-10.

Bachmann, P., 'Skandalon des Propheten Yunus und eine neue Arabische Jona-Geschichte: Yunus Fi Batn Al-Hut, von Abd al-Gaffar Mikkawi', in J. Barral (ed.), *Orientalia Hispanica*, I (Leiden: Brill, 1974), pp. 54-76.

Bal, M., 'The Bible as Literature: A Critical Escape', *Diacritics* 16 (1986), pp. 71-79.

Band, A.J., 'Swallowing Jonah: The Eclipse of Parody', *Prooftexts* 10 (1990), pp. 177-95.

Banks, W.L., *Jonah: The Reluctant Prophet* (Chicago: Moody, 1966).

Barker, S.F., *The Elements of Logic* (New York: McGraw–Hill, 4th edn, 1985).

Barr, J., *Holy Scripture: Canon, Authority, Criticism* (Philadelphia: Westminster Press, 1983).

Barré, M., 'Jonah 2.9 and the Structure of Jonah's Prayer', *Bib* 72 (1991), pp. 237-48.

Barton, J., *Oracles of God* (New York: Oxford University Press, 1988).

—*Reading the Old Testament: Method in Biblical Study* (Philadelphia: Westminster Press, 1984).

Bass, G., *A History of Seafaring, Based on Underwater Archaeology* (New York: Walker, 1972).

Baumgarten, M., 'On the Sign of the Prophet Jonah', *Methodist Review* 27 (1845), pp. 382-91.

Baur, F.C., 'Der Prophet Jonas: Ein assyrisch-babylonischen Symbol', *ZHT* 1 (1837), pp. 88-114.

Bauer, J.B., 'Drei Tage', *Bib* 39 (1958), pp. 354-58.

Ben-Yosef, I.A., 'Jonah and the Fish as a Folk Motif', *Semitics* 7 (1980), pp. 102-17.

Benoit, P., J.T. Milik and R. De Vaux, (eds.), *Les Grottes de Murabba'at* (DJD, 2; Oxford: Clarendon Press, 1961).

Berlin, A., 'Rejoinder to John A. Miles, Jr with Some Observations on the Nature of Prophecy', *JQR* 66 (1976), pp. 227-35.

Bewer, J.A., *Jonah* (ICC; Edinburgh: T. & T. Clark, 1912).

Bickerman, E.J., 'Les deux erreurs du prophète Jonas', *RHPR* 45 (1965), pp. 232-64.

—*Four Strange Books of the Bible: Jonah, Daniel, Koheleth, Esther* (New York: Schocken Books, 1967).

Bigger, S. (ed.), *Creating the Old Testament: The Emergence of the Hebrew Bible* (Oxford: Basil Blackwell, 1991).

Blank, S.H., '"Doest Thou Well to be Angry?" A Study in Self-Pity', *HUCA* 26 (1955), pp. 29-41.

Blenkinsopp, J., *A History of Prophecy in Israel* (Philadelphia: Westminster Press, 1983).

Böhme, W., 'Die Composition des Buches Jona', *ZAW* 7 (1887), pp. 224-84.

Bojorge, H., 'Los significados posibles de *lehassil* en Jonas 4,6', *Stromata* 26 (1970), pp. 70-77.

Bolin, T.M., '"Should I Not Also Pity Nineveh?": Divine Freedom in the Book of Jonah', *JSOT* 67 (1995), pp. 109-20.

—'When the End Is the Beginning: The Persian Period and the Origins of the Biblical Tradition', *SJOT* 10 (1996), pp. 3-15.

Bonner, C., 'The Story of Jonah on a Magical Amulet', *HTR* 41 (1948), pp. 31-37.

Boros, L., *The Closeness of God* (New York: Seabury, 1978).

Bowden, J., 'The Enlarging Spiritual Horizon of Judaism as Seen in the Books of Ruth and Jonah', *Methodist Quarterly Review* 73 (1924), pp. 684-90.

Bowers, R.H., *The Legend of Jonah* (The Hague: Nijhoff, 1971).

Bowman, J., 'Jonah and Jesus', *AbrN* 25 (1987), pp. 1-12.

Brekelmans, C., 'Some Translation Problems: Judges v 29, Psalm cxx 7, Jonah iv 4,9', *OTS* 15 (1969), pp. 170-76.

Brenner, A., 'Jonah's Poem out of and within its Context', in P.R. Davies and D.J.A. Clines (eds.), *Among the Prophets: Language, Image and Structure in the Prophetic Writings* (JSOTSup, 144; Sheffield: JSOT Press, 1993), pp. 183-92.

—'The Language of Jonah as an Index of its Date (in Hebrew)', *Beth Mikra* 24 (1979), pp. 396-405.

Brichto, H.C., *Toward a Grammar of Biblical Poetics: Tales of the Prophets* (New York: Oxford University Press, 1992).

Brockington, L.H., 'Jonah', in M. Black and H.H. Rowley (eds.), *Peake's Commentary on the Bible* (Nashville: Nelson, 1962), pp. 627-29.

Brown, P., *The Making of Late Antiquity* (Cambridge, MA: Harvard University Press, 1978).

Budde, K., 'Jonah, Book of', *The Jewish Encyclopedia* (12 vols.; New York: Ktav, n.d.), VII, pp. 227-30.

—'Vermutungen zum "Midrasch des Buches der Könige"', *ZAW* 12 (1892), pp. 37-51.

Bull, G.T., *The City and the Sign: An Interpretation of the Book of Jonah* (Grand Rapids: Baker, 1972).

Bull, J.L., 'Rethinking Jonah: The Dynamics of Surrender', *Parabola* 15 (1990), pp. 79-84.

Bultmann, R., *History of the Synoptic Tradition* (1921; Oxford: Basil Blackwell, rev. edn, 1963).

Burridge, R.A., *What Are the Gospels? A Comparison with Graeco-Roman Biography* (SNTSMS, 70; Cambridge: Cambridge University Press, 1992).

Burrow, J.A., 'Jonah', *Methodist Quarterly Review* 78 (1929), pp. 274-80.

Burrows, M., 'The Literary Category of the Book of Jonah', in T.H. Frank and W.L. Reed (eds.), *Translating and Understanding the Old Testament* (Nashville: Abingdon Press, 1970), pp. 80-107.

Butterworth, G.M., 'You Pity the Plant: A Misunderstanding', *Indian Journal of Theology* 27 (1978), pp. 32-34.

Calvin, J., *Commentaries on the Twelve Minor Prophets* (Grand Rapids: Eerdmans, 1847).

Carr, S. (ed.), *Early Writings of John Hooper* (Cambridge: Cambridge University Press, 1843).

Casson, L., *Ships and Seamanship in the Ancient World* (Princeton, NJ: Princeton University Press, 1971).

Cassuto, U., 'The Book of Jonah', *Biblical and Oriental Studies* (Jerusalem: Magnes, 1973), I, pp. 299-306.

Cathcart, K.J., and R.P. Gordon, *The Targum of the Minor Prophets* (The Aramaic Bible, 14; Wilmington, DE: Michael Glazier, 1989).

Charles, J.D., 'Plundering the Lion's Den: A Portrait of Divine Fury (Nahum 2.3-11)', *Grace Theological Journal* 10 (1989), pp. 183-201.

Childs, B.S., 'The Canonical Shape of the Book of Jonah', in G.A. Tuttle (ed.), *Biblical and Near Eastern Studies* (Grand Rapids: Eerdmans, 1978), pp. 122-28.

—*Introduction to the Old Testament as Scripture* (Philadelphia: Fortress Press, 1979).

—'Jonah: A Study in Old Testament Hermeneutics', *SJT* 11 (1958), pp. 53-61.

Chotzmer, J., *Humour and Irony of the Hebrew Bible* (Harrow: Wilbee, 1883).

Christensen, D.L., 'Andrzej Panufnik and the Structure of the Book of Jonah: Icons, Music and Literary Art', *JETS* 28 (1985), pp. 133-140.

—'Anticipatory Paronomasia in Jonah 3.7-8 and Genesis 37.2', *RB* 90 (1983), pp. 261-63.

—'Jonah and the Sabbath Rest in the Pentateuch', in G. Bradlik (ed.), *Biblische Theologie und Gesellshaftlicher Wandel* (Freiburg: Herder, 1993), pp. 48-60.

—'Narrative Poetics and the Interpretation of the Book of Jonah', in E. Follis (ed.), *Directions in Biblical Hebrew Poetry* (JSOTSup, 40; Sheffield: JSOT Press, 1987), pp. 29-48.

—'The Song of Jonah: A Metrical Analysis (Jon 2.3-10)', *JBL* 104 (1985), pp. 217-31.

Clark, G.R., *The Word Ḥesed in the Hebrew Bible* (JSOTSup, 157; Sheffield: JSOT Press, 1993).

Clements, R.E., 'The Purpose of the Book of Jonah', in J.A. Emerton (ed.), *Congress Volume* (VTSup, 28; Leiden: Brill, 1975), pp. 16-28.

Codex Alexandrinus in Reduced Facsimile (5 vols.; London: British Museum, 1909–57).

Coffman, J.B., *The Minor Prophets: Joel, Amos and Jonah* (Abilene, TX: Abilene Christian University Press, 1986).

Cohen, A.D., 'The Tragedy of Jonah', *Judaism* 21 (1972), pp. 164-75.

Cohn, G.H. 'Book of Jonah', *EncJud*, X, pp. 169-73.

—*Das Buch Jona im Lichte der biblischen Erzählkunst* (SSN, 12; Assen: Van Gorcum, 1969).

Collins, T., *The Mantle of Elijah: The Redaction Criticism of the Prophetical Books* (Sheffield: JSOT Press, 1993).

Cooper, A., 'In Praise of Divine Caprice: The Significance of the Book of Jonah', in P.R. Davies and D.J.A. Clines (eds.), *Among the Prophets: Language, Image and Structure in the Prophetic Writings* (JSOTSup, 144; Sheffield: JSOT Press, 1993), pp. 144-63.

Coote, R., *Amos among the Prophets* (Philadelphia: Fortress Press, 1981).

Correns, D., 'Jona und Salomo', in W. Haubeck (ed.), *Wort in der Zeit* (Leiden: Brill, 1980), pp. 86-94.

Couffignal, R., 'Le psaume de Jonas (Jonas 2.2-10): Une catabase biblique, sa structure et sa fonction', *Bib* 71 (1990), pp. 542-52.

Coulter, C., 'The "Great Fish" in Ancient and Medieval Story', *Transactions of the American Philological Association* 57 (1921), pp. 32-50.

Craghan, J.F., *Esther, Judith, Tobit, Jonah, Ruth* (Wilmington, DE: Michael Glazier, 1982).

Craig, K.M., 'Jonah and the Reading Process', *JSOT* 47 (1990), pp. 103-14.

—*A Poetics of Jonah: Art in the Service of Ideology* (Columbia, SC: University of South Carolina Press, 1993).

—'The Poetics of the Book of Jonah: Toward an Understanding of Narrative Strategy', (Ph.D. diss., Southern Baptist Theological Seminary; Ann Arbor, MI: University Microfilms, 1989).

Crenshaw, J.L., 'The Expression *mi yodea'* in the Hebrew Bible', *VT* 36 (1986), pp. 274-88.

—*Prophetic Conflict: Its Effect upon Israelite Religion* (BZAW, 124; Berlin: de Gruyter, 1971).

Cross, F.M., 'Studies in the Structure of Hebrew Verse: The Prosody of the Psalm of Jonah', in H. Huffmon and F. Spina (eds.), *The Quest for the Kingdom of God:*

Studies in Honor of George E. Mendenhall (Winona Lake, IN: Eisenbrauns, 1983), pp. 159-67.

Crossan, J.D., *The Dark Interval* (Niles, IL: Argus, 1975).

—*The Historical Jesus: The Life of a Mediterranean Jewish Peasant* (San Francisco: HarperCollins, 1991).

Crouch, W.B., 'To Question an End, to End a Question: Opening the Closure of the Book of Jonah', *JSOT* 62 (1994), pp. 101-12.

Cummings, C., 'Jonah and Ninevites', *Bible Today* 21 (1983), pp. 369-75.

Daniell, D. (ed.), *Tyndale's Old Testament: Being the Pentateuch of 1530, Joshua to 2 Chronicles of 1537 and Jonah* (New Haven: Yale University Press, 1992).

Daube, D., 'Death as a Release in the Bible', *NovT* 5 (1962), pp. 82-104.

—'Jonah: A Reminiscence', *JJS* 35 (1984), pp. 36-43.

Davies, G.I., 'The Uses of *R''* Qal and the Meaning of Jonah IV 1', *VT* 27 (1977), pp. 105-110.

Davies, L., 'Jonah: Testimony of the Resurrection', in M. Nyman (ed.), *Isaiah and the Prophets: Inspired Voices from the Old Testament* (Religious Studies Monograph Series, 10; Provo, UT: Brigham Young Religious Studies Center, 1984), pp. 89-104.

Davies, P.R., *In Search of 'Ancient Israel'* (JSOTSup, 148; Sheffield: JSOT Press, 1992).

Davies, W.W., 'Is the Book of Jonah Historical?' *Methodist Review* 70 (1888), pp. 827-44.

Day, J., 'Problems in the Interpretation of the Book of Jonah', in A.S. van der Woude (ed.), *In Quest of the Past* (*OTS*, 26; Leiden: Brill, 1990), pp. 32-47.

Deeley, M.K., 'The Shaping of Jonah', *TTod* 34 (1977), pp. 305-310.

Deissler, A. *Zwölf Propheten II* (Die Neue Echter Bibel, 8; Würzburg: Echter Verlag, 1984).

Deist, F., 'The Prophets: Are we Heading for a Paradigm Switch?', in V. Fritz, K.-F. Pohlmann and H.-C. Schmitt (eds.), *Prophet und Prophetenbuch* (BZAW, 185; Berlin: De Gruyter, 1989), pp. 1-18.

Dentan, R.C., 'The Literary Affinities of Exodus xxxiv 6f', *VT* 13 (1963), pp. 34-51.

Döller, J., *Das Buch Jona* (Vienna: Fromme, 1912).

Dozeman, T.B., 'Inner-Biblical Interpretation of Yahweh's Gracious and Compassionate Character', *JBL* 108 (1989), pp. 207-23.

Doty, W.G., 'The Concept of Genre in Literary Analysis', in L.C. McGaughy (ed.), *SBLSP* (2 vols.; Atlanta, GA: Scholars Press, 1972), II, pp. 413-48.

Driver, S.R., *An Introduction to the Literature of the Old Testament* (repr.; Gloucester, MA: Smith, 1972, [1907]).

Dubrow, H., *Genre* (London: Methuen, 1982).

Duval, Y.-M. (ed.), *Jerome: Commentaire sur Jonas* (SC, 323; Paris: Cerf, 1985).

—*Le livre de Jonas dans la littérature chrétienne grecque et látine* (2 vols.; Paris: Etudes Augustiniennes, 1973).

Dyck, E., 'Canon and Interpretation: Recent Canonical Approaches and the Book of Jonah', (Ph.D. diss., McGill University; Ann Arbor, MI: University Microfilms, 1986).

—'Jonah Among the Prophets: A Study in Canonical Context', *JETS* 33 (1990), pp. 63-73.

Eagleton, T., 'J.L. Austin and the Book of Jonah', in R. Schwartz (ed.), *The Book and the Text: The Bible and Literary Theory* (Oxford: Basil Blackwell, 1990), pp. 231-36.

Ebach, J., *Kassandra und Jona gegen die Macht des Schicksals* (Frankfurt: Athenäum, 1987).

Edwards, R.A., *The Sign of Jonah in the Theology of the Evangelists and Q* (SBT, 18; Naperville, IL: Allenson, 1971).

Ehrlich, A.B., *Ezechiel und die Kleinen Propheten* (Randglossen zur Hebräischen Bibel, 5; Leipzig: Hinrich, 1912).

Eisenman, R., *Maccabees, Zadokites, Christians and Qumran* (Leiden: Brill, 1983).

Eisenman, R., and M. Wise, *The Dead Sea Scrolls Uncovered* (Shaftesbury: Element Books, 1992).

Eissfeldt, O., 'Amos und Jona in volkstümlicher Überlieferung', in *...und fragten nach Jesus* (Berlin: Evangelische Verlagsanstalt, 1964), pp. 9-13.

—*The Old Testament: An Introduction* (New York: Harper & Row, 1966).

—'The Prophetic Literature', in H.H. Rowley (ed.), *The Old Testament and Modern Study* (Oxford: Clarendon Press, 1951), pp. 115-61.

Elata-Alster, G., and R. Salmon, 'The Deconstruction of Genre in the Book of Jonah: Towards a Theological Discourse', *Literature and Theology* 3 (1989), pp. 40-60.

—'Eastward and Westward: The Movement of Prophecy and History in the Book of Jonah', *Dor le Dor* 13 (1984), pp. 16-27.

Ellison, H L., 'Jonah', *Expositor's Bible Commentary* (Grand Rapids: Zondervan, 1985), VII, pp. 361-91.

Ellul, J., *The Judgement of Jonah* (Grand Rapids: Eerdmans, 1971).

Emmerson, G.I., 'Another Look at the Book of Jonah', *ExpTim* 88 (1976), pp. 86-88.

Epstien, I. (ed.), *The Babylonian Talmud* (18 vols; Hindhead, Surrey: Soncino, 1948-52).

Eubanks, L.L., 'The Cathartic Effects of Irony in Jonah', (Ph.D. diss., Southern Baptist Theological Seminary; Ann Arbor, MI: University Microfilms, 1988).

Evans, E. (ed.), *Tertullian: Adversus Marcionem* (2 vols.; Oxford: Clarendon Press, 1972).

Exbrayat, I., *Témoinage et contestation: L'actualité du livre de Jonas* (Lausanne: Ligne pour la lecture de la Bible, 1977).

Eynikel, E., 'The Genre of the Book of Jonah', (paper presented at the annual meeting of the Society of Biblical Literature, Chicago, IL, November, 1994).

Fairbairn, P., *Jonah: His Life, Character and Mission* (Grand Rapids: Kregel, 1964).

Fáj, A., 'The Stoic Features of the Book of Jonah', *Instituto Orientale di Napoli Annali* 34 (1974), pp. 309-45.

Feuillet, A., 'Jonas (le livre de)', *DBSup*, IV, pp. 1104-31.

—*Le livre de Jonas* (Paris: Cerf, 1966).

—'Le sens du livre de Jonas', *RB* 54 (1947), pp. 340-61.

—'Les sources du livre de Jonas', *RB* 54 (1947), pp. 161-86.

Fingert, H.H., 'Psychoanalytic Study of the Minor Prophet, Jonah', *Psychoanalytic Review* 16 (1954), pp. 55-65.

Fishbane, M., *Biblical Interpretation in Ancient Israel* (Oxford: Clarendon Press, 1985).

Fisher, L.R., *Ras Shamra Parallels* (AnOr, 49; Rome: Pontifical Biblical Institute, 1972).

Floyd, M.H., 'Prophetic Complaints about the Fulfillment of Oracles in Habbakuk 2.1-17 and Jeremiah 15.10-18', *JBL* 110 (1991), pp. 397-418.

Fohrer, G., *Introduction to the Old Testament* (Nashville: Abingdon Press, 10th edn, 1968).

Fowler, A,. *Kinds of Literature: An Introduction to the Theory of Genres and Modes* (Oxford: Oxford University Press, 1982).

Fox, M.V., 'The Identification of Quotations in Biblical Literature', *ZAW* 92 (1980), pp. 416-31.

Fredman, N., 'Jonah and Nineveh: The Tragedy of Jonah', *Dor le Dor* 12 (1983), pp. 4-14.

Freedman, D.N., 'Did God Play a Dirty Trick on Jonah at the End?' *BibRev* 6 (1990), pp. 26-31.

—'Jonah 1.4b', *JBL* 77 (1958), pp. 161-62.

Freedman, H., and M. Simon (eds.), *Midrash Rabbah* (10 vols.; Hindhead, Surrey: Soncino, 3rd edn, 1961).

Fretheim, T.E., 'Jonah and Theodicy', *ZAW* 90 (1978), pp. 227-37.

—*The Message of Jonah: A Theological Commentary* (Minneapolis: Augsburg, 1977).

Friedlander, G. (ed.), *Pirke de Rabbi Eliezer* (New York: Hermon, 1965).

Fuller, R.E., 'The Minor Prophets Manuscripts from Qumran, Cave IV', (Ph.D. diss., Harvard University; Ann Arbor, MI: University Microfilms, 1988).

Gadamer, H.-G., *Truth and Method* (Maryknoll, NY: Orbis Books, 1987).

Garbini, G., *History and Ideology in Ancient Israel* (London: SCM Press, 1988).

Garcia-Cordero, M., 'El libro de Jonás: Una novela didáctica?' *CB* 16 (1959), pp. 214-20.

García Martinez, F., *The Dead Sea Scrolls Translated: The Qumran Texts in English* (trans. W.G.E. Watson; Leiden: Brill, 1994).

Gaster, T., *Myth, Legend and Custom in the Old Testament* (2 vols.; New York: Harper & Row, 1975).

Gerhart, M., 'Generic Studies: Their Renewed Importance in Religious and Literary Interpretation', *JAAR* 45 (1977), pp. 309-25.

Gese, H., 'Jona ben Amittai und das Jonabuch', repr. in *Alttestamentliche Studien* (Tübingen: Mohr [Paul Siebeck], 1993), pp. 122-38.

Gevaryahu, H., 'The Universalism of the Book of Jonah according to the Teaching of Yehezkel Kaufmann', *Dor le Dor* 10 (1981), pp. 20-27.

Ginsberg, D., 'Ploughboys versus Prelates: Tyndale and More and the Politics of Biblical Translation', *Sixteenth Century Journal* 19 (1988), pp. 45-61.

Ginsberg, H.L., *The Five Megilloth and Jonah* (Philadephia: Jewish Publication Society, 1969).

Ginzberg, L., *Legends of the Jews* (7 vols.; Philadelphia: Jewish Publication Society, 1909-1938).

Glaze, A., 'A Historical and Critical Exegesis of the Book of Jonah', (PhD diss., Southern Baptist Theological Seminary; Ann Arbor, MI: University Microfilms, 1961).

Glück, J.J., 'A Linguistic Criterion for the Book of Jonah', *Die Outestamentiese Werkgemeenskap in Suid-Afrika* 10 (1967), pp. 34-41.

Goeser, R.J., 'From Exegesis to Proclamation (Luther's Commentary on Jonah)', *Historical Magazine of the Protestant Episcopal Church* 53 (1984), pp. 209-20.

Goitein, S.D., 'Some Observations on Jonah', *JPOS* 17 (1937), pp. 63-77.

—'The Song of Songs: A Female Composition?' repr. in A. Brenner (ed.), *A Feminist Companion to the Song of Songs* (Sheffield: JSOT Press, 1993).

Freedom beyond Forgiveness

Goldman, M.D., 'Was the Book of Jonah Originally Written in Aramaic?' *Australian Biblical Review* 3 (1953), pp. 49-50.

Goldman, S., 'Jonah', in A. Cohen (ed.), *The Twelve Prophets* (Hindhead, Surrey: Soncino, 1948), pp. 137-50.

Golka, F., *The Song of Songs and Jonah,* (International Theological Commentaries; Grand Rapids: Eerdmans, 1988).

Gollancz, I. (ed.), *Patience: An Alliterative Version of Jonah by the Poet of Pearl* (Oxford: Oxford University Press, 1913).

Good, E.M., *Irony in the Old Testament* (Sheffield: Almond Press, 2nd edn, 1981).

Goodenough, E.R., *Jewish Symbols in the Greco-Roman Period* (13 vols.; New York: Pantheon, 1953-1968).

Goodhart, S., 'Prophecy, Sacrifice, and Repentance in the Story of Jonah', *Semeia* 33 (1985), pp. 43-63.

Gordon, C., '"This Time" (Genesis 2.23)', in M. Fishbane and E. Tov (eds.), *Sha'arei Talmon* (Winona Lake, IN: Eisenbrauns, 1992), pp. 47-51.

Goulder, M.D., 'Ruth: A Homily on Deut 22-25?' in D.J.A. Clines (ed.), *Of Prophets' Visions and the Wisdom of Sages* (JSOTSup, 163; Sheffield: JSOT Press, 1993), pp. 307-19.

Greenspahn, F., *Hapax Legomena in Biblical Hebrew* (SBLDS, 74; Chico, CA: Scholars Press, 1984).

Gregory, R.I., 'Elijah's Story under Scrutiny: A Literary-Critical Analysis of 1 Kings 17-19', (Ph.D. diss., Vanderbilt University; Ann Arbor, MI: University Microfilms, 1983).

Grimal, P., *Dictionary of Classical Mythology* (Oxford: Basil Blackwell, 1986).

Groupe de Bergerac, 'Lectures Critiques de la Bible', *Foi et Vie* 79 (1980), pp. 31-87.

Groupe de Rennes, France, 'An Approach to the Book of Jonah: Suggestions and Questions by a Group of Rennes, France', *Semeia* 15 (1979), pp. 85-96.

Guilman, S., 'Jona', *ETR* 61 (1986), pp. 189-93.

Gunkel, H., *Einleitung in die Psalmen: Die Gattungen der religiosen Lyrik Israels* (repr.; Göttingen: Vandenhoeck & Ruprecht, 1966, [1933]).

—*The Folktale in the Old Testament* (repr.; Sheffield: Almond Press, 1987, [1917]).

—'Jonabuch', *RGG²*, pp. 366-69.

—'Jonapsalm', *RGG²*, pp. 369-70.

—*The Legends of Genesis* (repr.; New York: Schocken Books, 1964, [1901]).

—*The Psalms* (repr.; Philadelphia: Fortress Press, 1967, 1930]).

Gunn, D., and D.N. Fewell, *Narrative in the Hebrew Bible* (Oxford: Oxford University Press, 1993).

Gutarman, N. (ed.), *The Anchor Book of Latin Quotations* (Garden City, NY: Doubleday, 1966).

Halleaux, A., 'A propos du sermon Éphrámien sur Jonas et la pènitence des Ninevites', in R. Schulz and M. Gòrg (eds.), *Lingua Restituta Orientalis (Agypten und Alten Testament*; Wiesbaden: Harrassowitz, 1990), pp. 155-60.

Haller, E., *Die Erzählung von dem Propheten Jona (Theologische Existenz Heute,* 65; Munich: Chr. Kaiser Verlag, 1958).

Halpern, B., and R.E. Friedman, 'Composition and Paronomasia in the Book of Jonah', *HAR* 4 (1980), pp. 79-92.

Handy, L.K., 'The Great Ruler of the World: Variations on a Stock Character in Old Testament Short Stories', (paper presented at the annual meeting of the Eastern

Great Lakes Midwest Society of Biblical Literature, Notre Dame, IN, February, 1992).

Hanhart, R. (ed.), *Tobit* (Septuaginta Gottingensis, 8.5; Göttingen: Vandenhoeck & Ruprecht, 1983).

Hann, M.R. de. *Jonah: Fact or Fiction?* (Grand Rapids: Zondervan, 1957).

Hart-Davies, D.E., 'The Book of Jonah in the Light of Assyrian Archaeology', *Journal for the Transactions of the Victoria Institute* 69 (1937), pp. 230-49.

Harviainen, T., 'Why Were the Sailors Not Afraid of the Lord before Verse Jonah 1.10?' in E. Grothe-Paulin (ed.), *Studia Orientalia* 64 (Helsinki: Societas Orientalis Fennica, 1988), pp. 77-81.

Haupt, P., 'Jonah's Whale', *Proceedings of the American Philosophical Society* 46 (1907), pp. 151-64.

Hauser, A. J., 'Jonah: In Pursuit of the Dove', *JBL* 104 (1985), pp. 21-37.

Hegedus, T.M., 'Jerome's Commentary on Jonah: Translation with Introduction and Critical Notes', (M.A. thesis, Wilfrid Laurier University; Ann Arbor, MI: University Microfilms, 1991).

Heinen, K., *Das Bucher Malachi, Joel und Jona* (Dusseldorf: Patmos, 1991).

Helberg, J.L., 'Is Jonah in his Failure a Representative of the Prophets?' *Die Outestamentiese Werkgemeenskap in Suid-Afrika* 10 (1967), pp. 41-51.

Henrich, K., *Parmenides und Jona: Vier Studien uber das Verhaltnis von Philosophie und Mythologie* (Frankfurt: Suhkramp, 1966).

Hesse, E. and I. Kikawada, 'Jonah and Genesis 1–11', *Annual of the Japanese Biblical Institute* 10 (1984), pp. 3-19.

Hesseling, D.C., 'Le livre de Jonas', *Byzantinische Zeitschrift* 10 (1901), pp. 208-17.

Hirsch, E.D., *Validity in Interpretation* (New Haven: Yale University Press, 1967).

Hirsch, E.G., 'Jonah', *Jewish Encyclopedia*, VII, pp. 225-27.

Hitzig, F., *Der Propheten Jonas Orakel über Moab* (Heidelberg: Mohr [Paul Siebeck], 1831).

Holbert, J.C., '"Deliverance Belongs to Yahweh!" Satire in the Book of Jonah', *JSOT* 21 (1981), pp. 59-81.

Holladay, W.L., (ed.), *A Concise Hebrew and Aramaic Lexicon of the Old Tesament* (Leiden: Brill, 10th edn, 1989).

Holstein, J.A., 'Melville's Inversion of Jonah in *Moby-Dick*', *Illif Review* 42 (1985), pp. 13-20.

Hoope, R. de, 'The Book of Jonah as Poetry: An Analysis of Jonah 1.1-16', in W. van der Meer and J. de Moor (eds.), *The Structural Analysis of Hebrew and Canaanite Poetry* (JSOTSup, 74; Sheffield: JSOT Press, 1988), pp. 156-71.

Hope, E.R., 'Pragmatics, Exegesis, and Translation', in P. Stine (ed.), *Issues in Bible Translation* (United Bible Societies Monograph Series, 3; London: United Bible Societies, 1988), pp. 113-28.

Horwitz, W.J., 'Another Interpretation of Jonah I 12', *VT* 23 (1973), pp. 370-72.

Hurvitz, A., 'The History of a Legal Formula *kol 'aser hapes 'asah*', *VT* 32 (1982), pp. 257-67.

Hüsing, G., 'Tarshish und die Jona-Legende', *Memnon* 1 (1907), pp. 70-79.

Irvin, D., *Mytharion: The Comparison of Tales from the Old Testament and the AncienNear East* (AOAT, 32; Neukirchen–Vluyn: Verlag Butzon & Bercker Kevelaer, 1978).

Jastrow, M. (ed.), *Dictionary of the Targumim, Talmud Babli, Yerushalmi and Midrashic Literature* (repr.; New York: Judaica, 1992, [1903]).

Jauss, H., 'Das Buch Jona—Ein Paradigma der "Hermeneutik der Fremde"', in H.F. Geisser (ed.), *Wahrheit der Schrift—Wahrheit der Auslegung* (Zurich: Theologischer Verlag, 1993), pp. 260-83.

—*Toward an Aesthetic of Reception* (Minneapolis: University of Minnesota Press, 1982).

Jemielty, T., *Satire and the Hebrew Prophets* (Louisville, KY: Westminster/Knox, 1992).

Jepsen, A., 'Anmerkungen zum Buche Jona: Beiträge zur Theologie des Alten Testaments', in H. Stoebe (ed.), *Wort–Gebot–Glaube: Theologie des Alten Testaments* (ATANT, 59; Zurich: Zwingli-Verlag, 1970), pp. 297-305.

Johnson, A.R., 'Jonah II.3-10: A Study in Cultic Phantasy', in H.H. Rowley (ed.), *Studies in Old Testament Prophecy* (Edinburgh: T. & T. Clark, 1950), pp. 82-102.

Joüon, P., *A Grammar of Biblical Hebrew* (Subsidia Biblica, 14; 2 vols.; repr.; Subsidia Biblica, 14; Rome: Pontifical Biblical Institute, 1991, [1923]).

Kahn, P., 'An Analysis of the *Book of Jonah*', *Judaism* 43 (1994), pp. 87-100.

Kaiser, O., 'Wirklichkeit, Möglichkeit und Vorurteil: Ein Beitrag zum Verständnis des Buches Jona', *EvT* 33 (1973), pp. 91-103.

Kearley, F., 'Difficult Texts from Amos, Obadiah and Jonah', in W. Winkler (ed.), *Difficult Texts of the Old Testament* (Hurst, TX: Winkler, n.d.), pp. 404-14.

Keil, K.F., and F. Delitzsch, *The Twelve Minor Prophets* (Edinburgh: T. & T. Clark, 1900).

Keller, C.A., *Jonas* (CAT, 21a; Geneva: Labor et Fides, 1982).

—'Jonas, le portrait d'un prophète', *TZ* 21 (1965), pp. 329-40.

Kennedy, J.H., *Studies in the Book of Jonah* (Nashville: Broadman, 1958).

Kidner, F.D., 'The Distribution of Divine Names in Jonah', *TynBul* 21 (1970), pp. 126-28.

Knight, G.A.F., and F. Golka, *The Song of Songs and Jonah* (International Theological Commentaries; Grand Rapids, MI: Eerdmans, 1988).

Koester, H., *Ancient Christian Gospels: Their History and Development* (Philadelphia: Trinity International, 1990).

—'From the Kerygma-Gospel to Written Gospels', *NTS* 36 (1989), pp. 361-81.

Kohler, K., 'The Original Form of the Book of Jonah', *Theological Reveiw* 16 (1879), pp. 139-44.

Komlós, O., 'Jonah Legends', in *Etudes orientales á la mémoire de Paul Hirschler* (Budapest: Allamosított Kertész-nymoda, 1950), pp. 41-61.

König, E., 'Jonah', *Dictionary of the Bible* (New York: Charles Scribner's Sons, 1906), II, pp. 744-53.

Kraeling, E.G.H., 'The Evolution of the Story of Jonah', in *Hommages à A. Dupont-Sommer* (Paris: Adrien-Maisonneuve, 1971), pp. 305-18.

Krüger, T., 'Literarisches Wachstum und theologische Diskussion im Jona-Buch', *Biblische Notizen* 59 (1991), pp. 57-88.

Kugel, J., *The Idea of Biblical Poetry: Parallelism and Its History* (New Haven: Yale University Press, 1981).

Lacocque, A., 'Jonah as Satire, the Bearing of Genre on Date', in *SBL/AAR Abstracts* (Atlanta, GA: Scholars Press, 1986), p. 187.

Lacocque, A., and P.-E. Lacocque, *Jonah: A Psycho-Religious Approach to the Prophet* (Columbia, SC: University of South Carolina Press, 1990).

Laga, C., 'Maximi Confessoris ad Thalassuim Quaestio 64: Essai de lecture', in C. Laga, J. Munitiz and L. Van Rompay (eds.), *After Chalcedon* (Orientalia Lovaniensia Analecta, 18; Leuven: Department Oriëntalistiek, 1985), pp. 203-15.

Landes, G.M., 'Jonah', *IDBSup* pp. 488-91.

—'Jonah: A *Mashal* ?' in J. Gammie (ed.), *Israelite Wisdom* (Missoula, MT: Scholars Press, 1978), pp. 137-58.

—'The Kerygma of the Book of Jonah', *Int* 21 (1967), pp. 3-31.

—'Linguistic Criteria and the Date of the Book of Jonah', *Eretz Israel* 16 (1982), pp. 147-70.

—'The "Three Days and Three Nights" Motif in Jonah 2.1', *JBL* 86 (1967), pp. 446-50.

Lawrence, M., 'Ships, Monsters and Jonah' *AJA* 66 (1962), pp. 289-96.

Lawrence, P.J.N., 'Assyrian Nobles and the Book of Jonah', *TynBul* 17 (1986), pp. 121-32.

Layard, A.H., *Nineveh and its Remains* (repr. and abr.; New York: Praeger, 1970, [1849]).

Leclercq, H., 'Jona', *DACL* XVII/2, pp. 2572-2631.

Lemanski, J., 'Jonah's Nineveh', *Concordia Journal* 18 (1992), pp. 40-49.

Lemche, N.P., 'The Old Testament: A Hellenistic Book?', *SJOT* 7 (1993), pp. 163-93.

Levine, E., *The Aramaic Version of Jonah* (New York: Hermon, 1978).

—'Jonah as a Philosophical Book', *ZAW* 96 (1984), pp. 235-45.

Lewis, C., 'Jonah: A Parable for Our Time', *Judaism* 21 (1972), pp. 159-63.

Liber Duodecim Prophetarum ex Interpretatione Sancti Hieronymi (Biblia Sacra Iuxta Latinam Vulgatam Versionem ad Codicum Fidem, 17; Rome: Libreria Editrice Vaticana, 1987).

Licht, J., *Storytelling in the Bible* (Jerusalem: Magnes, 1978).

Lillegard, D., 'Narrative and Paradox in Jonah', *Kerux* 8 (1993), pp. 19-30.

Limburg, J., *Jonah* (OTL; Louisville, KY: Westminster/Knox, 1993).

Lindblom, J., 'Lot-Casting in the OT', *VT* 12 (1962), pp. 164-78.

Lohfink, N., 'Jona ging zur Stadt hinaus (Jon 4,5)', *BZ* 5 (1961), pp. 185-203.

—'Zur Konzentrischen Struktur von Jona 1', *Bib* 47 (1966), pp. 577-81.

Loretz, O., *Gotteswort und menshcliche Erfahrung: Eine Auslegung der Bücher Jona, Rut, Hohelied und Qohelet* (Freiburg: Herder, 1963).

—'Herkunft und Sinn der Jona-Erzhählung', *BZ* 5 (1961), pp. 18-29.

Lubeck, R.J., 'Prophetic Sabotage: A Look at Jonah 3.2-4', *Trinity Journal* 9 (1988), pp. 37-46.

Luckenbill, D.D., *Ancient Records of Assyria and Babylonia* (2 vols.; New York: Greenwood, 1968).

Lux, R., *Jona: Prophet Zwischen Vermeigerung und Gehorsam* (FRLANT, 162; Göttingen: Vandenhoeck & Ruprecht, 1994).

McCarter, P.K., 'The River Ordeal in Israelite Literature', *HTR* 66 (1973), pp. 403-12.

Mack, B.L., *The Lost Gospel: The Book of Q and Christian Origins* (San Francisco: HarperCollins, 1993).

Madhloum, T., 'Excavations at Nineveh: A Preliminary Report (1965–67)', *Sumer* 23 (1967), pp. 76-82.

Magonet, J.D., *Form and Meaning: Studies in Literary Techniques in the Book of Jonah* (Bible and Literature, 8; Sheffield: Almond Press, 2nd rev. edn, 1983).

—'Jonah, Book of', *ABD*, III, pp. 936-42.

Maillot, A., *Jonas, ou les farces de Dieu; Sophonie, ou l'erreur de Dieu* (Paris: Delachaux et Niestlé, 1977).

Mandelkern, S., *Veteris Testamenti Concordiantiæ Hebraicæ et Chaldaicæ* (2 vols.; Graz: Akademische Druck & Verlagsanstalt, 1955).

Marcus, D., *From Balaam to Jonah: Anti-Prophetic Satire in the Hebrew Bible* (BJS, 301; Atlanta, GA: Scholars Press, 1995).

Marti, K., *Das Dodekapropheton* (Tübingen: Mohr [Paul Siebeck], 1904).

Martin, W.W., 'A Study of the Book of Jonah', *Methodist Quarterly Review* 27 (1888), pp. 26-32.

Mather, J., 'The Comic Art of the Book of Jonah', *Soundings* 65 (1982), pp. 280-91.

May, H.G., 'Aspects of the Imagery of World Dominion and World State in the Old Testament', in J.L. Crenshaw (ed.), *Essays in Old Testament Ethics* (New York: Ktav, 1974), pp. 57-76.

Melville, H., *Moby Dick* (repr.; New York: Modern Library, 1926, [1851]).

Merrill, E.H., 'The Sign of Jonah', *JETS* 23 (1980), pp. 23-30.

Meschonnic, H., *Jona et le signifiant errant* (Paris: Gallimard, 1981).

—'Translating Biblical Rhythm', in L. Hirsch and N. Ashkenasy (eds.), *Biblical Patterns in Modern Literature* (BJS, 77; Chico, CA: Scholars Press, 1984), pp. 227-40.

Michaels, L., 'Jonah', in D. Rosenberg (ed.), *Congregation* (San Diego, CA: Harcourt Brace Jovanovich, 1987), pp. 232-37.

Miles, J.A., Jr, 'Laughing at the Bible: Jonah as Parody', *JQR* 65 (1974–75), pp. 168-81.

Moore, C., 'Scholarly Issues in the Book of Tobit before Qumran and after: An Assessment', *JSP* 5 (1989), pp. 65-81.

More, J., 'The Prophet Jonah: The Story of an Intrapsychic Process', *American Imago* 27 (1970), pp. 3-11.

Mowinckel, S., *The Psalms in Israel's Worship* (repr.; Nashville: Abingdon Press, 1962 [1951]).

Mozley, F.W., 'Proof of the Historical Truth of the Book of Jonah', *BSac* 81 (1924), pp. 170-200.

Müller, J.G.A., 'Jona: Eine moralische Erzählung', in *Memorabilien* (Leipzig: Cruisius, 1794), VI.

Murphy, R.E., *The Tree of Life: An Exploration of Biblical Wisdom Literature* (ABRL; Garden City, NY: Doubleday, 1990).

Murray, H.G., 'The Historicity of the Whale', *Methodist Review* 102 (1919), pp. 429-31.

Nachtigal, J.C.K., 'Über das Buch des Alten Testaments mit der Aufschrift: Jonas', in J. Eichorn (ed.), *Allgemeine Bibliothek der biblischen Literatur* (Leipzig: Weidmannschen Buchhandlung, 1799), IX, pp. 221-73.

Neil, W., 'Jonah, Book of', *IDB*, II, pp. 964-67.

Newsom, C., 'A Maker of Metaphors: Ezekiel's Oracles against Tyre', in J.L. Mays and P. Achtemeier (eds.), *Interpreting the Prophets* (Philadelphia: Fortress Press, 1987), pp. 188-99.

Nielsen, E., 'Le message primitif du livre de Jonas', *RHPR* 59 (1979), pp. 499-507.

Nogalski, J., *Redactional Processes in the Book of the Twelve* (BZAW, 218; Berlin: De Gruyter, 1993).

Noth, M., *A History of Pentateuchal Traditions* (repr.; Englewood Cliffs, NJ: Prentice Hall, 1972, [1948]).

—*Die Israelitischen Personennamen im Rahmen der gemeinsemitischen Namengebung* (BWANT, 3.10; Stuttgart: Kohlhammer, 1928).

Nowell, I., *Jonah, Tobit, Judith* (Collegeville Bible Commentaries, 25. Collegeville, MN: Liturgical Press, 1986).

O'Connor, M., *Hebrew Verse Structure* (Winona Lake, IN: Eisenbrauns, 1980).

Ogden, G.S., 'Time and the Verb היה in Old Testament Prose', *VT* 21 (1971), pp. 451-69.

Orlinsky, H., 'Nationalism–Universalism and Internationalism in Ancient Israel', in H.T. Frank and W.L. Reed (eds.), *Translating and Understanding the Old Testament* (Nashville: Abingdon Press, 1970), pp. 206-36.

Orth, M., 'Genre in Jonah: The Effects of Parody in the Book of Jonah', in W. Hallo (ed.), *The Bible in the Light of Cuneiform Literature* (Ancient Near Eastern Texts and Studies, 8; Lewiston, NY: Edwin Mellen, 1990), pp. 257-81.

Oswald, H.C., (ed.), *Luther's Works.* XIX. *Lectures on the Minor Prophets: Jonah and Habakkuk* (55 vols.; St. Louis, MO: Concordia, 1974).

Ovadiah, R., 'Jonah in a Mosaic Pavement at Beth Guvrin', *IEJ* 24 (1974), pp. 214-15.

Paine, T., *The Age of Reason* (repr.; Exton, PA: Wet Water, 1992, [1974]).

Parmentier, R., 'Les mesaventures du Pasteur Jonas', *ETR* 53 (1978), pp. 244-51.

Parrot, A., *Nineveh and the Old Testament* (London: SCM Press, 1955).

Parsons, W. (trans.), *St. Augustine: Letters* (Fathers of the Church, 9; 90 Vols.; Washington, DC: Catholic University of America Press, 1953).

Payne, D.F., 'Jonah from the Perspective of its Audience', *JSOT* 13 (1979), pp. 3-12.

Payne, R., 'The Prophet Jonah: Reluctant Messenger and Intercessor', *ExpTim* 100 (1989), pp. 131-34.

Peckham, B., *History and Prophecy: The Development of Late Judean Literary Traditions* (ABRL; Garden City, NY: Doubleday, 1993).

Pellegrino, M., T. Alimonti and L. Carrozzi (eds.), *Le Lettere di Sant'Agostino* (Opere di Sant'Agostino, 21; Rome: Città Nuova, 1969).

Peli, M., 'Jonah as an Artistic Story [in Hebrew]', *Beth Mikra* 39 (1994), pp. 210-23.

Penna, A., 'Andrea di S. Vittore: Il suo commento a Giona', *Bib* 36 (1955), pp. 305-31.

Perkins, L., 'The Septuagint of Jonah: Aspects of Literary Analysis Applied to Biblical Translation', *BIOSCS* 20 (1987), pp. 43-53.

Perowne, T.T., *Obadiah and Jonah* (Cambridge: Cambridge University Press, 1905).

Pesch, R., 'Zur konzentrischen Struktur von Jona 1', *Bib* 47 (1966), pp. 577-81.

Petersen, D.L., and K.H. Richards, *Interpreting Hebrew Poetry* (Guides to Biblical Scholarship; Minneapolis: Fortress Press, 1992).

Pinker, A., 'The Number 40 in the Bible', *JBQ* 22 (1994), pp. 163-72.

Porten, B., 'Baalshamem and the Date of the Book of Jonah', in M. Carrez, J. Doré and P. Grelot (eds.), *De la Tôrah au Messie* (Paris: Desclée, 1981), pp. 237-44.

Potgeiter, J.H., 'Jonah—A Semio-Structuralist Reading of a Narrative', *Old Testament Essays* 3 (1990), pp. 61-69.

—'A Narratological Approach to the Book of Jonah [in Afrikaans]', (DD diss., University of Pretoria; Ann Arbor, MI: University Microfilms, 1989).

—''n Narratologiese Ondersoek van die Boek Jona', *Hervormde Teologiese Studies Supp* 3 (1991), pp. 1-131.

Powers, J., 'Jonah the Dove', *Bible Today* 23 (1985), pp. 253-58.

Price, B.F., and E.A Nida, *A Translator's Handbook on the Book of Jonah* (New York: United Bible Societies, 1978).

Qimron, E., 'The Language of Jonah as an Index of the Date of its Composition (in Hebrew)', *Beth Mikra* 25 (1980), pp. 181-82.

Rad, G. von, *Die Botschaft der Propheten* (Munich: Chr. Kaiser Verlag, 1967).

—'The Prophet Jonah', in *God at Work in Israel* (repr.; Nashville: Abingdon Press, 1980, [1950]), pp. 58-70.

—*Theology of the Old Testament* (2 vols.; San Francisco, CA: HarperCollins, 1962).

Radermacher, L., 'Walfischmythen', *ARW* 9 (1906), pp. 248-52.

Rahlfs, A., *Septuaginta* (2 vols.; Stuttgart: Württembergische Bibelanstalt, 1935).

Ratner, R ,'Jonah, the Runaway Servant', *Marrar* 5–6 (1990), pp. 281-305.

Rauber, D.F., 'Jonah: The Prophet as Schlemiel', *Bible Today* 49 (1970), pp. 29-38.

Redfield, R., *Peasant Society and Culture* (Chicago: University of Chicago Press, 1956).

Reitzenstein, R., *Hellenistiche Wundererzählungen* (Stuttgart: Teubner, 2nd edn, 1963).

Relihan, J.C., *Ancient Menippean Satire* (Baltimore: The Johns Hopkins University Press, 1993).

Roaf, M., *Cultural Atlas of Mesopotamia and the Ancient Near East* (New York: Facts on File, 1990).

Roberts, A. and J. Donaldson (eds.), *Tertullian* (Ante-Nicene Christian Library, 18; Edinburgh: T. & T. Clark, 1870).

Robinson, B.P., 'Jonah's Qiqayon Plant', *ZAW* 97 (1985), pp. 390-403.

Rofé, A., 'Classes in the Prophetical Stories: Didactic Legend and Parable', in J.A. Emerton (ed.), *Congress Volume* (VTSup, 26; Leiden: Brill, (1974), pp. 143-64.

—*The Prophetical Stories: The Narratives about the Prophets in the Hebrew Bible* (Jerusalem: Magnes, 1988).

Roffey, J.W., 'God's Truth, Jonah's Fish: Structure and Existence in the Book of Jonah', *Australian Biblical Review* 36 (1988), pp. 1-18.

Ronner, P.M., *Das Buch Jona* (Zurich: Zwingli-Verlag, 1947).

Rosen, N., 'Jonah', in D. Rosenberg (ed.), *Congregation* (San Diego, CA: Harcourt Brace Jovanovich, 1987), pp. 222-31.

Rosenau, H., 'The Jonah Sarcophagus in the British Museum', *Journal of the British Archaeological Association* 24 (1961), pp. 60-66.

Rosenberg, J., 'Jonah and the Nakedness of Deeds', *Tikkun* 2 (1987), pp. 36-38.

—'Jonah and the Prophetic Vocation', *Response* 22 (1974), pp. 23-26.

Rudolph, W., *Joel–Amos–Obadja–Jona* (KAT, 13.2; Gütersloh: Gerd Mohn, 1971).

—'Jona', in A. Kuschke (ed.), *Archäologie und Altes Testament* (Tübingen: Mohr [Paul Siebeck], 1970), pp. 233-39.

Ryan, P.J., 'Jonah and the Ninevites: The Salvation of Non-Christians according to Some Twentieth-Century Theologians', *Ghana Bulletin of Theology* 4 (1975), pp. 21-29.

Sasson, J., *Jonah* (AB, 24B; Garden City, NY: Doubleday, 1990).

—'On Jonah's Two Missions', *Henoch* 6 (1984), pp. 23-30.

Savran, G., *Telling and Retelling: Quotation in Biblical Narrative* (Bloomington, IN: University of Indiana Press, 1988).

Sawyer, J.F.A., *Prophecy and the Biblical Prophets* (Oxford Bible Series; New York: Oxford University Press, rev. edn, 1993).

Saydon, P.P., 'Some Mistranslations in the Codex of Sinaiticus of the Book of Tobit', *Bib* 33 (1952), pp. 363-65.

Schaumberger, J.B., 'Das Bussedikt des Königs von Ninive bei Jona 3,7.8 in Keilschriftlicher Beleuchtung', *Miscellanea Biblica* 2 (1934), pp. 123-34.

Schierse, F.J., 'Jona und die Bekehrung Nineves—Die Frage nach der Historizität der Gestalt Jonas', *BK* 27 (1972), pp. 71-72.

Schildenberger, J.B., 'Der Sinn des Buches Jonas', *Erbe und Auftrag* 38 (1962), pp. 93-102.

Schmid, J., (ed.), *Ss. Eusebii Hieronymi et Aurelii Augustini: Epistulae Mutuae* (Florilegium Patristicum, 22; Bonn: Hanstein, 1930).

Schmidt, H., *Jona: Eine Untersuchung zur vergleichenden Religionsgeschichte* (FRLANT, 9; Göttingen: Vandenhoeck & Ruprecht, 1907).

—'Die Komposition des Buches Jona', *ZAW* 25 (1905), pp. 285-310.

Schmidt, L., *'De Deo': Studien zur Literakritik und Theologie des Buches Jona, des Gёspraches zwischen Abraham und Jahwe in Gen 18.22ff. und von Hi 1* (BZAW, 143. Berlin: De Gruyter, 1976).

Schmitt, G., 'Das Zeichen des Jona', *Zeitschrift für die Neutestamentliche Wissenschaft und die Kunde der Alteren Kirche* 69 (1978), pp. 123-29.

Schneider, D.A., 'The Unity of the Book of the Twelve', (Ph.D. diss., Yale University; Ann Arbor, MI: University Microfilms, 1979).

Schrekenberg, H., and K. Schubert, *Jewish Historiography and Iconography in Early and Medieval Christianity* (Minneapolis: Fortress Press, 1992).

Schreiner, S., 'Das Buch Jona: Ein Kritisches Resümee der Geschichte Israels', *Theologische Versuche* 9 (eds. J. Rogge and G. Schille; Berlin: Evangelische Verlag, 1977), pp. 37-45.

Schumann, S., 'Jona und die Weisheit: Das prophetische Wort in einer zweideutigen Wirklichkeit', *TZ* 45 (1989), pp. 73-80.

Schützinger, H., 'Das Buch Jona in der Älteren Islamichen Uberlieferung', in P. Scholz and R. Stempel (eds.), *Nubia et Oriens Christianus* (Bibliotheca Nubica, 1; Cologne: Dinter, 1987), pp. 47-58.

Scott, R.B.Y., 'The Sign of Jonah', *Int* 19 (1965), pp. 16-25.

Segert, S., 'Syntax and Style in the Book of Jonah: Six Simple Approaches to their Analysis', in J.A. Emerton (ed.), *Prophecy: Essays Presented to Georg Fohrer* (BZAW, 150; Berlin: de Gruyter, 1980), pp. 121-30.

Sellin E., *Das Zwölfprophetenbuch* (KAT, 12; Leipzig: Scholl, 1922).

Siegert, F., *Drei hellenistichen-judische Predigten: Ps.-Philon 'Uber Jona', 'Uber Samson', und 'Uber die Gottesbezeichnung "wohltatig verzehrendes Feuer."'* (WUNT, 20; Tübingen: Mohr [Paul Siebeck], 1980).

Simpson, W., *The Jonah Legend* (London: Richards, 1899).

Simpson, W.K. (ed.), *The Literature of Ancient Egypt* (New Haven: Yale University Press, 1972).

Smalley, B., *The Study of the Bible in the Middle Ages* (Notre Dame, IN: University of Notre Dame Press, 1964).

Smith, G.A., *The Book of the Twelve Prophets* (New York: Harper, 1928).

Smith, M., *Palestinian Parties and Politics That Shaped the Old Testament* (London: SCM Press, 1971).

Smith, N.H., 'Sendingperspektiewe in die Boek Jona', in D. Odendaal, B. Miler and H. Combrink *Die Ou Testamente Vandag* (Capetown: Kerk-Uitgemers, 1979), pp. 161-71.

Smitten, W.T. in der, 'Zu Jona 1.2', *ZAW* 84 (1972), p. 95.

Snaith, N.H., *Notes on the Hebrew Text of Jonah* (London: Epworth Press, 1945).

Snyder, G., *Ante Pacem: Archaeological Evidence of Church Life before Constantine* (Macon, GA: Mercer University Press, 1985).

Soggin, J.A., 'Il "segno di Giona" nel libro del Profeta Giona', *Lateranum* 48 (1982), pp. 70-74.

Sonda Metwole, J.B., *Le message du livre de Jonas á la lumie du genre littéraire* (Rome: Bernini, 1974).

Sperber, A., *The Latter Prophets according to Targum Jonathan* (The Bible in Aramiac, 3; Leiden: Brill, 1992).

Steffen, U., *Jona und der Fisch: Der Mythos von Tod und der Wiedergeburt* (Berlin: Kreuz, 1982).

Stek, J.H., 'The Message of the Book of Jonah', *Calvin Theological Journal* 4 (1969), pp. 23-50.

Stendahl, K., *The School of St. Matthew and its Use of the Old Testament* (Philadelphia: Fortress Press, 1st American edn, 1968 [1954]).

Stendenbach, F.J., 'Novelle oder Geschichte? Die literarische Gattung des Büchleins Jona', *BK* 27 (1972), pp. 66-67.

Stenzel, M., 'Zum Vulgatatext des Canticum Jonae: Prälat A. Allgeier zum 70 Geburtstag', *Bib* 33 (1952), pp. 356-62.

Strack, H.L., and G. Stemberger, *Introduction to the Talmud and Midrash* (Minneapolis: Fortress Press, 1992).

Strömberg-Krantz, E., *Des Schiffes Weg mitten im Meer* (ConBOT, 10; Lund: Liber, 1982).

Stronach, D., and S. Lumsden, 'UC Berkeley's Excavations as Nineveh', *BA* 55 (1992), pp. 227-33.

Stuart, D., *Hosea–Jonah* (WBC, 31; Waco, TX: Word Books, 1987).

Swetnam, J., 'Some Signs of Jonah', *Bib* 68 (1987), pp. 74-79.

Syrén, R., 'The Book of Jonah—A Reversed *Diasporanovella*?' *SEÅ* 58 (1993), pp. 7-14.

Szarmach, P.E., 'Three Versions of the Jonah Story: An Investigation of Narrative Technique in Old English Homilies', *Anglo Saxon England* 1 (ed. P. Clemoes; Cambridge: Cambridge University Press, 1972), pp. 183-92.

Thimmes, P.L., *Studies in the Biblical Sea-Storm Type-Scene: Convention and Invention* (San Francisco: Edwin Mellen, 1992).

Thoma, A., 'Die Entstehung des Büchleins Jona', *TSK* 84 (1911), pp. 479-502.

Thomas, D.W., 'A Consideration of Some Unusual Ways of Expressing the Superlative in Hebrew', *VT* 3 (1953), pp. 210-224.

Thompson, R.C., and R.W. Hutchinson, *A Century of Exploration at Nineveh* (London: Luzack, 1929).

Thompson, T.L., '4QTestimonia and the Composition of Texts: A Copenhagen Lego Hypothesis' (forthcoming).

—*Early History of the Israelite People: From the Written and Archaeological Sources* (Studies in the History of the Ancient Near East, 4; Leiden: Brill, 1992).

—'The Old Testament as a Theological Discipline II: "He is Yahweh; He Does What Is Right in His Own Eyes"' (forthcoming).

Thordarson, T., 'Notes on the Semiotic Context of the Verb *Niham* in the Book of Jonah', *SEÅ* 54 (1989), pp. 226-35.

Tigay, J.H., 'The Book of Jonah and the Days of Awe', *Conservative Judaism* 38 (1985-86), pp. 67-76.

Torrey, C.C., 'Nineveh in the Book of Tobit', *JBL* 41 (1922), pp. 237-45.

Tov, E. (ed.), *The Greek Minor Prophets Scroll from Nahal Hever* (DJD, 8; Oxford: Clarendon Press, 1990).

Trepanier, B., 'The Story of Jonas', *CBQ* 13 (1951), pp. 8-16.

Trible, P.L., *Rhetorical Criticism: Context, Method and the Book of Jonah* (Guides to Biblical Scholarship; Minneapolis: Fortress Press, 1994).

—'Studies in the Book of Jonah', (Ph.D. diss., Columbia University; Ann Arbor, MI: University Microfilms, 1963).

Tromp, N.J., *Primitive Conceptions of Death and the Netherworld in the Old Testament* BibOr, 21; Rome: Pontifical Biblical Institute, 1969).

Trudinger, P., 'Jonah: A Post-Exilic Verbal Cartoon?' *Downside Review* 107 (1989), pp. 142-43.

Trumbull, H.C., 'Jonah in Nineveh', *JBL* 11 (1892), pp. 53-60.

Vaccari, P.A., 'Il genere letterario del libro di Giona in recenti publicazione', *Divinitas* 6 (1962), pp. 231-52.

Van Heerden, W., 'Humour and the Interpretation of the Book of Jonah', *OTE* 5 (1992), pp. 389-401.

Van Seters, J., *Prologue to History: The Yahwist as Historian in Genesis* (Louisville, KY: Westminter/Knox, 1992).

Vanoni, G., *Das Buch Jona* (ATAT, 7; St. Ottilien: Eos, 1978).

Vawter, B., *Job and Jonah: Questioning the Hidden God* (New York: Paulist 1983).

Vischer, W., 'L'Evangile Selon Saint Jonas', *ETR* 50 (1975), pp. 161-73.

Wade, G.W., *The Books of the Prophets Micah, Obadiah, Joel and Jonah* (Westminster Commentaries; London: Methuen, 1925).

Wagner, S., 'חוס', *TDOT* IV, pp. 271-77.

Walls, J.L., 'Will God Change His Mind? Eternal Hell and the Ninevites', in W. Crockett (ed.), *Through No Fault of their Own?* (Grand Rapids: Baker, 1991), pp. 61-69.

Walsh, J.T., 'Jonah 2.3-10: A Rhetorical Critical Study', *Bib* 63 (1982), pp. 219-29.

Walton, J.H., 'The Object Lesson of Jonah 4.5-7 and the Purpose of the Book of Jonah', *Bulletin for Biblical Research* 2 (1992), pp. 47-57.

Walzer, M., 'Prophecy and Social Criticism', *Drew Gateway* 55 (1984-85), pp. 13-27.

Ward, J.M., *Thus Says the Lord: The Message of the Prophets* (Nashville: Abingdon Press, 1991).

Warshaw, T.S., 'The Book of Jonah', in L. Gros (ed.), *Literary Interpretations of Biblical Narratives* (Nashville: Abingdon Press, 1974), pp. 191-207.

Watson, W.G.E., *Classical Hebrew Poetry: A Guide to its Techniques* (JSOTSup, 26; Sheffield: JSOT Press, 1984).

Watts, J.D.W., *The Books of Joel, Obadiah, Jonah, Nahum, Habakkuk and Zephaniah* (Cambridge Bible Commentaries; Cambridge: Cambridge University Press, 1975).

—*Psalms and Story: Inset Hymns in Hebrew Narrative*. (JSOTSup, 139; Sheffield: JSOT, 1992).

—'"This Song": Conspicuous Poetry in Hebrew Prose', in J.C. de Moor and W.G.E. Watson (eds.), *Verse in Ancient Near Eastern Prose* (AOAT, 42; Neukirchen–Vluyn: Neukirchener Verlag, 1993), pp. 345-58.

Weimar, P., 'Jon 2.1-11: Jonapsalm und Jonaerzählung', *BZ* 28 (1984), pp. 43-68.

—'Jon 4.5: Beobachtungen zur Entstehung der Jonaerzählung', *Biblische Notizen* 18 (1982), pp. 86-109.

—'Literarische Kritik und Literarkritik: Unzeitgemäße Beobachtungen zu Jon 1,4-16', in L. Ruppert (ed.), *Künder des Wortes: Beiträge zur Theologie der Prophetten* (Würzburg: Echter Verlag, 1982), pp. 217-35.

Weinreb, F., *Das Buch Jonah: Der Sinn des Buches Jonah nach der ältesten jüdischen Überlieferung* (Zürich: Origo, 1970).

Weiser, A., *Die Propheten Josea, Joel, Amos Obadja, Jona, Micha* (Das Buch der Zwölf Propheten, 1; Göttingen: Vandenhoeck & Ruprecht, 1963).

Weitzman, S.P. '"Sing to the Lord a New Song": The Role of Songs within Biblical Narrative and their Resonance in Early Biblical Interpretation' (PhD diss., Harvard University; Ann Arbor: University Microfilms, 1994).

Wellhausen, J., *Prolegomena to the History of Israel* (repr.; New York: Meridian, 1957, 1878]).

West, M., 'Irony in the Book of Jonah: Audience Identification with the Hero', *Perspectives in Religious Studies* 11 (1984), pp. 233-42.

Wette, W. de, *Lehrbuch der historisch-kritischen Einleitung in kanonischen und apocryphischen Bücher des Alten Testament* (Berlin: Georg Reiner, 1817).

White, C. (ed.), *The Correspondence (394–419) between Jerome and Augustine of Hippo* (Studies in Bible and Early Christianity, 23; Lewiston, NY: Edwin Mellen, 1990).

White, M.C., 'Jonah', in C. Newsome and S.H. Ringe (eds.), *Women's Bible Commentary* (Philadelphia: Westminster Press, 1992), pp. 212-14.

Whybray, R.N., *The Intellectual Tradition in the Old Testament* (BZAW, 135; Berlin: De Gruyter, 1974).

Wiersbe, W.W., 'How Does your Version of Jonah End?' *Fundamentalist Journal* 4 (1985), pp. 18-20.

Wiesel, E., *Five Biblical Portraits* (Notre Dame, IN: University of Notre Dame Press, 1981).

Williams, W.C., 'Jonah, Book of', *ISBE*, II, pp. 1112-16.

Wilson, R.D., 'The Authenticity of Jonah', *Princeton Theological Review* 16 (1918), pp. 280-98, 430-56.

—'מנה "to Appoint", in the Old Testament', *Princeton Theological Review* 16 (1918), pp. 645-54.

Wilson, R.R., *Prophecy and Society in Ancient Israel* (Philadelphia: Fortress Press, 1980).

Wilt, T.L., 'Jonah: A Battle of Shifting Alliances', in P.R. Davies and D.J.A. Clines (eds.), *Among the Prophets: Language, Image and Structure in the Prophetic Writings* (JSOTSup, 144; Sheffield: JSOT Press, 1993), pp. 164-82.

Winckler, H., 'Zum Buch Jona', *Altorientalische Forschung* 2 (1900), pp. 260-65.

Wineman, A., 'The Zohar on Jonah: Radical Retelling or Tradition?' *Hebrew Studies* 31 (1990), pp. 57-69.

Wischmeyer, W., 'Das Beispiel Jonas: Kirchengeschichtlichen Bedeutung von denkmälern frühëchristlicher Grabeskunst zwischen Theologie und Frömmigkeit', *ZKG* 92 (1981), pp. 161-179.

Wiseman, D.J., 'Jonah's Nineveh', *TynBul* 30 (1979), pp. 29-51.

Witzenrath, H., *Das Buch Jona* (ATAT, 6; St. Ottilien: Eos, 1978).

Wohlgelernter, D.K., 'Death Wish in the Bible', *Tradition* 19 (1981), pp. 131-40.

Wolff, H.W., 'Jonah: A Drama in Five Acts', *CurTM* 3 (1976), pp. 4-19.

—'Jonah: The Messenger Who Grumbled', *CurTM* 3 (1976), pp. 141-50.

—'Jonah: The Messenger Who Obeyed', *CurTM* 3 (1976), pp. 86-97.

—*Obadiah and Jonah* (Minneapolis: Augsburg, 1986).

—*Studien zum Jonabuch* (Biblische Studien, 47; Neukirchen–Vluyn: Neukirchener Verlag, 1965).

Woodard, B.L., 'Death in Life: The Book of Jonah and Biblical Tragedy', *GJT* 11 (1991), pp. 3-16.

Woodhouse, J.W., 'Jesus and Jonah (Matt 12.39-40; Matt 16.4; Lk 11.20)', *Reformed Theological Review* 43 (1984), pp. 33-41.

Wright, C.H., 'The Book of Jonah', in *idem, Biblical Essays* (Edinburgh: T. & T. Clark, 1886), pp. 34-98.

Wright, G.A., 'The Literary Genre Midrash', *CBQ* 28 (1966), pp. 105-38, 417-57.

Wright, W., *The Book of Jonah in Four Oriental Versions, Namely Chaldee, Syriac, Aethiopic and Arabic with Glossaries* (London: Williams & Norgate, 1857).

Wright, W.W., 'The Message of the Book of Jonah', *Methodist Quarterly Review* 75 (1926), pp. 654-659.

Youtie, H.C., 'A Codex of Jonah: Berl. Sept 18—P.S.I. X, 1164', *HTR* 38 (1945), pp. 195-97.

Ziegler, J. (ed.), *Duodecimum Prophetae* (Septuaginta Gottingensis, 13; Göttingen: Vandenhoeck & Ruprecht, 3rd edn, 1984).

—'Studien zur Verwertung der LXX in Zwölfprophetenbuch', *ZAW* 60 (1944), pp. 107-31.

Zimmerman, F., 'Problems and Solutions in the Book of Jonah', *Judaism* 40 (1991), pp. 580-89.

Zlotowitz, M., *Yonah/Jonah: A New Translation with a Commentary Anthologized from Midrashic and Rabbinic Sources* (Brooklyn, NY: Mesorah, 1980).

Zmudi, J., 'Jonah's Qiqayon (in Hebrew)', *Beth Miqra* 92 (1982), pp. 44-48.

Zuckerman, B., 'The Nora Puzzle', *Marrar* 7 (1991), pp. 269-301.

Freedom beyond Forgiveness

INDEX OF AUTHORS

JOURNAL FOR THE STUDY OF THE OLD TESTAMENT
SUPPLEMENT SERIES